Urban Development
and
the Royal Fine Art Commissions

we shall come to an important decision; we shall come to consider as more important than the mechanism of the city, what we may call the soul of the city. The soul of the city is that part of it which is of no value from the practical side of existence: it is, quite simply, its poetry, a feeling which in itself is absolute, although it is so definitely a part of ourselves.

Le Corbusier

I believe in everything being beautiful, pleasant, and, if need be, useful.

Jessie Newbery

Urban Development
and
the Royal Fine Art Commissions

A. J. YOUNGSON

EDINBURGH UNIVERSITY PRESS

© A. J. Youngson 1990
Edinburgh University Press
22 George Square, Edinburgh
Set in Alphacomp Goudy by
Pioneer Associates, Perthshire, and
printed in Great Britain by
The Alden Press, Oxford
British Library Cataloguing
  in Publication Data
Youngson, A. J.
Urban development and the
  royal Fine Art Commissions.
1. Great Britain. Urban
  development, history
I. Title
307.140941
ISBN 0 7486 0114 7
      0 7486 0153 8 pbk

Contents

Acknowledgements

Thanks are due to *The New Yorker* for permission to reproduce Figure 15 from their March 1986 issue, to Reiach and Hall (Edinburgh) for Figure 19, to Ove Arup and Partners Scotland for Figure 20, and to Michael Laird and Partners (Edinburgh) for Figure 23.

Preface

This book deals equally with the nature of good architecture and the nature of good town planning—two subjects that are often kept well apart—and it deals also with the practical difficulties that lie in the way of building better cities. It is my contention that fewer mistakes would be made if there were a better public appreciation of architecture and town planning, and if stronger support were given and more attention paid to the work of the Royal Fine Art Commission for England and Wales and the Royal Fine Art Commission for Scotland. As Chairman of the latter Commission since 1983, I have seen something of the inside workings of urban development. But I emphasise that the opinions in this book are my own. No member of either Commission has read or in any way endorsed the least part of what I have written.

My debts to others are numerous. I am especially indebted to the Rockefeller Foundation, who appointed me as a Scholar in Residence at the Bellagio Center in Italy and thus gave an invaluable impetus to the beginning of my work. Without the help of the Rockefeller Foundation, this book would probably never have been written. I am also very much obliged to Mr J Carter Brown, Chairman of the Commission of Fine Arts in Washington, DC, for information about the work of the Commission in Washington—information which I could have obtained in no other way. Professor Allan Rodger and Mr George Tibbits of the Department of Architecture and Building, University of Melbourne, gave much kind assistance, and I was greatly helped by being allowed to use the Department's library. Use of the library of the Royal Incorporation of Architects in Scotland was also most valuable. Mr Charles Prosser, Secretary of the Scots Commission, has helped by finding documents and photographs. My obligations to Mrs Margaret Tierney, also of the Commission, are very numerous. Colonel James Bannatyne fortified my resolution on some points of history. And my friend Professor Arthur Knodel took pains to ensure that my translations of Diderot and Le Corbusier were up to his own high standards. I wish to express my sincere thanks to all who have helped.

CHAPTER ONE

Three Advisory Commissions

Analogies from mechanics come easily to the modern mind, and it would startle no one today to hear the city described as a machine for living in. This description was not put forward by Le Corbusier, the much admired architect/painter and planner/prophet of the previous age (or perhaps it was the age before that; over one hundred years have passed since he was born), but it could have been, for it is perfectly consistent with many of his pronouncements, in particular, with his well-known statements that 'une maison est une machine à habiter' and 'la ville qui dispose de la vitesse dispose du succès'. This emphasis on and adulation of speed and machinery is curiously characteristic of the 1920s, when aeroplanes were still a novelty and the land speed-record was raised, in 1924, to an exhilarating and breath-taking 146 miles an hour. In 1922 Le Corbusier's ideas became widely known when he exhibited his plan for a 'Ville Contemporaine' at the Salon d'Automne in Paris. His scheme was sensational, both in scale and style. The population of the city was set at three million. At the heart of the city there rose twenty-four widely spaced cruciform skyscrapers, all identical save that some were fifty storeys high and some were sixty storeys (Paris at this time prohibited buildings above approximately ten storeys, in London there was one tall building of fourteen storeys in Queen Anne's Gate which had led to an Act of 1894 imposing a height limit of eighty feet to the cornice or parapet). Around the skyscrapers there was to be widely spreading park land, with restaurants, theatres, shops and parking places; most of the population were to live in extensive dormitory suburbs, in large standardized apartment blocks[1] supplied with elevators and hanging gardens. The streets were arranged on three levels, below ground, ground level and elevated 'on immense reinforced concrete bridges', thus arranged to suit the needs of vehicles travelling at different speeds. Le Corbusier emphasized that his city was 'baignée de lumière et d'air' and rejoiced that each apartment 'donne sur des parcs'. He detested the irregularity and confusion of old cities, and here, certainly, was something different, a vision of the future to be realized in reinforced concrete, a very large and spread-out city of straight lines and repetitive forms, planned for fast-moving vehicles as much as for people. The whole conception astonished architects and public alike—Le Corbusier noted with satisfaction that 'Une stupeur l'accueillit; la surprise conduisit à la cholère ou à l'enthousiasme'—but the Ville Contemporaine turned out, in a number of important respects, to be no more than a foretaste of things to come, however surprising. This, in retrospect, is not in itself surprising, for speed and mechanization, mass production, 'megastructures' and industrialized building were, in the decades ahead, what the technology of the twentieth century was increasingly able to supply—or, as some may think, to impose.

Almost 160 years before Le Corbusier unveiled his contemporary city, another distinguished European sat down to define for the world and for posterity what a city was; or, more accurately, what a city should be. His ideas were not revolutionary but they were entirely up to date. Diderot was one of the great figures of the Enlightenment, one of that select band who had discovered that by abandoning the prejudices, superstitions, and worn-out conventions of mankind, and by trusting to reason, a new age of order and felicity would be brought in; and his *Encyclopédie* is one of the foundation stones of the modern world. If we look up *cité* in that many-volumed work, we learn that cities exist 'pour la sûreté, la tranquillité intérieure et extérieure, et tous les autres avantages de la vie'. But this is only a brief entry. Under *ville*, however, we find an entry of several hundred words, which begins with a straightforward definition: 'assemblage de plusieurs maisons déposées par rues . . . plusieurs quartiers, des rues, des places publiques, et d'autres edifices'. How very uncontroversial, we think. But wait! What are the very next words that Diderot writes? 'Pour qu'une ville soit belle . . .' What an amazing first step, we must think, to discussing the idea of a city! Diderot does not at once confront his reader with the importance of communications, or population, or segregation, or city government, or finance, paving, sanitation, or even the prospects of continuous development and expansion. He launches forth—and this occupies a very large part of the remainder of the entry—on a discussion of what makes a city beautiful.

It is true that Diderot's treatment of this subject, although up to date for 1765, is rather conventional, and he leans heavily on the ideas of spaciousness and regularity. This is what he says:

> For a city to be beautiful, the principal streets must lead to the city gates; these streets should be parallel or at right angles to one another, as far as possible, so that the corners of the houses are right angles; the principal streets should be sixteen metres wide, the secondary streets eight metres. It is also requisite that the distance between parallel streets should be such as to leave room for two town houses, of which one faces one street and one the other. Each of these houses should be about ten or twelve

metres in width, and fourteen or sixteen metres deep, with an inner court of corresponding size, which makes the distance from one street to the other to be sixty four or sixty six metres.[2] In the pattern of streets there should be squares, of which the grandest is at the junction of the main streets, and these squares are made handsome by maintaining uniformity in the façades of the buildings which surround them, and by means of statues and fountains.

A few cities, or parts of cities, had already been built along these lines, and more were to follow. Richelieu, built for the Cardinal in the 1630s, not far from Saumur, is an early example, small but exact. Edinburgh's New Town, contemporary with the Encyclopédie, is similarly planned. Symmetry and order were what the later seventeenth and the eighteenth century wanted. (Although sometimes they got too much of it: Madame de Maintenon once complained that in Louis XIV's France 'Il faut périr en symetrie'.) Turin, which demonstrated precisely the required qualities, was widely regarded in the eighteenth century as a model of what a city should be. Rousseau spoke with wonder of its architecture, 'la beauté des rues, la symétrie et l'alignement des maisons'. He expected Paris to be even better, but its 'narrow little streets, filthy and stinking', disgusted him. Eighteenth-century thinkers, especially in France, were not enamoured of irregular and overcrowded old cities, and Paris before Haussmann drove his boulevards through it in the 1850s and 1860s was an outstanding example. Many of its houses were six or seven storeys high, and most of its streets were winding, malodorous and congested. Rouen was similar. According to Pierre Patte, 'Rouen offre les spectacles les plus désagreables. Des rues étroites et mal percées, quantité de maisons de bois placées au hasard semblent rappeler la barbarie gothique . . .' Le Corbusier would have agreed with him.

But the fact that Diderot's ideas about order and regularity were no more than the latest received wisdom of the time and were not startlingly new is a great deal less noteworthy than his giving pride of place to the beauty of the city: its dignity, spaciousness and embellishment. Nothing else, for him, is nearly as important. His city is not a machine for doing something; it is a place to be admired and enjoyed.

It may be that the great encyclopaedist's enthusiasm for beauty embarrasses us. Certainly references to the beauty of the city, realized or proposed, are few and far between in modern publications on planning. We have other concerns, of course, and other priorities, and it is necessary that it should be so. The world has changed very much since the eighteenth century. In Diderot's lifetime (he died in 1783) the population of only some half-dozen European cities exceeded 100 000, and their economic structure, by comparison with that of most cities today, was fairly simple. Apart from a few great capital cities such as London and Paris (the population of both of these already exceeded half a million in 1750), important towns existed solely in order that goods made locally by hand could be exchanged against other goods made (mostly locally) by hand, or against the produce of the countryside; and, in the case of coastal towns, in order to carry on coastal or foreign trade; in order to facilitate the business of government in the surrounding region; and as places where enough people and money were brought together to enable the setting up of schools, universities, theatres, assembly halls, and other devices for the pursuit of culture and entertainment. Now all that is changed. The mere size of the modern town transforms the scene. Where once there were hundreds of people, now there are tens of thousands; to be housed, fed and as far as possible employed. And how are they employed? Not in handicraft industry, certainly. They work in factories, or with electrical or electronic machines in offices, or they are engaged in transporting goods, in every stage of manufacture, that may have come from or may be going to the other side of the world. They are also engaged in transporting themselves or one another, in complicated vehicles, and this process is so swift and yet so difficult that fatalities frequently result. Streets—or rather, traffic arteries—sixteen metres wide as recommended by Diderot would never do. And below the streets, where the thought of the eighteenth century never so much as penetrated, we find the foundations of the modern city, the basis of everything; a vast complex of cables, pipes and sewers.

Nor are the extent and the physical complexity of it all the only sources of the modern town-planner's troubles, for his objectives have multiplied almost as fast as the urban population. Let us make a heroic simplification and suppose that the twentieth century and all its urban problems began in 1898, the publication date of Ebenezer Howard's *Tomorrow: A Peaceful Path to Real Reform*. How does our century first envisage the lines along which progress should be made? What are the desiderata of Howard's 'higher and better form [he means built form] of industrial life'? They can be reduced to five: towns should be small, with a population not exceeding 32 000; they should have ample fresh air; they should provide easy access to the countryside; they should enable people to live close to their work; allied to the countryside round about them, they should enjoy a large measure of what could in no modern circumstances be remotely attainable, namely self-sufficiency. The whole vast problem of transporting raw materials and intermediate goods to factories, and finished products to consumers, and workers to and from their place of work is thus reduced to vanishing point; and it plays no further part in Howard's argument. Clustered round an existing large town, his new towns were to be rural in character; 'how to restore the people to the land . . . is indeed a Master Key'.[3] Howard's towns in fact resemble a throw-back, with qualifications, to the Middle Ages. Whereas Le Corbusier conceived of something new by looking forward, Howard conceived of something new by looking back. As a way to provide better low-cost housing, his suggestions were admirable. But far from being a solution to the general urban problem, what Howard proposed is really a recipe for doing away with towns as far as possible. Such a plan is patently absurd. It represents what the French call 'la pensée désurbaniste . . . strictement anglo-saxone!'.[4] The garden-city movement was in many respects distinctly naïve, a kind of cottage socialism. Yet Howard's work was extremely influential and his ideas had much influence on the development of the suburbs, although the changes that they helped to bring about were in every sense peripheral and not central to the urban problem. Two of his aims still stand. The present-day planner will certainly provide for fresh air (although he is left to hope that pollution controls will be imposed by others); and access to the countryside is to some extent taken care of by the motor car, a form of transport of which Howard had probably never seen even a solitary example. This, indeed, is perhaps the greatest single change between Howard's day and ours. Howard, like Diderot before him, thought of the town as inhabited by people, but the town of the modern planner is inhabited by people and vehicles, sometimes in almost equal proportions, and, in the consequent competition, priority seems often to be given to the vehicles.

As for the recognized objectives of urban planning, they have become a great deal more complicated than they used to be. The eighteenth century provided streets, squares and houses for the well-to-do, and left the rest of the population to live inconspicuously in older and neglected parts of the town, or, as servants, in garrets, cellars, and cupboards under the stairs in respectable dwellings. This concentration on the wants of the wealthy of course enormously simplified the problem. But now planners are expected to provide for everyone, and they are acutely conscious that society contains many 'social groupings' or 'income groups' or 'classes', and that the tastes and interests and purchasing power of all of these differ enormously. They therefore must decide how far to cater for these differences as they find them and how far to treat everyone as already equal, or at least potentially equal; for equality, whatever precisely it may mean, is one of the sacred cows of the century. In the absence of 'equality'—which of course does not exist—questions arise about expenditure on parks, schools, car parks, pedestrian precincts, bus shelters, facilities for disabled persons, and all sorts of other items not equally used by different groups. Also, the segregation of different social groups, not to be confused with the tricky questions of separating housing from manufacturing and vehicles from pedestrians, becomes another important issue. Planners, in principle and as a general rule, wish to avoid social segregation, and pursue the laudable aim of making all localities equally attractive to live in; but at the same time they are prone to seek a 'rich variety' in the life of the city and it is not altogether easy to achieve both these objectives at the same time. Next, provision has to be made for the future, that is to say, for economic growth. Howard's idea was that if the city had to grow, a satellite city would be established nearby. But this seems a rather expensive way of doing things, and besides, growth is apt to require renewal almost as much as extension. Modern planners have to think about new buildings within the town, about new routes for traffic and about changing social requirements. And in order to facilitate business and encourage new enterprise they invariably wish to provide good facilities within the city for education and possibly for research, attractive sites for offices and industry, and, not least, a swift, extensive and economical system of transportation, with good links to the rest of the world. Also, they must bear in mind the need for social services, a housing advisory service, and a civic centre. On top of all this, if there is time to think about it, there is the general appearance and impact of the whole thing. It is universally agreed that appearances count for something, and therefore no plan is complete without some optimistic references to 'visual impact', 'colour and character', 'strong local character', 'interesting buildings', 'bright and lively places' or some other such vaguely expressed hopes.[5] And finally, to complete the catalogue and complicate matters still further, there is the oft-expressed wish, genuine or otherwise, for public participation in planning.

It may well be asked whether, in any such terms as the above, town planning is possible. On the merely physical level it seems to call for the reconciling of irreconcilables, or near-irreconcilables: variety with uniformity; peace and quiet with rapid transportation everywhere; friendly neighbourhoods of low density; secluded parks which are readily accessible to everyone. And on the social level the objectives are bewildering in number and many of them are of doubtful validity. To take a particularly vexatious question, if the economic system provides some families with larger incomes than others, how can the town planner—or should he—try to reduce the real differences? Should he help those who are poorer and inconvenience those who are richer by, for example, earmarking suitable housing sites in the middle of the town for low-cost housing even if this means that there are no sites left to be used as city-centre car-parks for those with access to a car? Or, looking to the longer term, should he plan to have different qualities of housing distributed uniformly throughout all areas of the city in the hope that this will 'integrate' the community, or should he concede the point that one of the major advantages of a larger income is the ability to choose the kind of neighbourhood one lives in? It seems that planning has become so comprehensive—at least on paper—as to cover everything: that no aspects of the citizen's life are to be left untouched by it, from the siting, scale and accessibility of the maternity hospital to those of the crematorium; that the luckless planner is required to find the solution—or at any rate a solution—to every social problem of the twentieth century.

Faced with so many herculean tasks, it is not surprising that urban planners show signs of discouragement and that planning itself has fallen into a certain amount of disfavour; Lord Clark felt so strongly on the subject that he included planning among 'those forces that threaten to impair our humanity: lies, tanks, tear gas, ideologies, opinion polls, mechanisation, planners, computers'.[6] In a recent excellent critique of British planning, Alison Ravetz seems at last to lose hope, and to take refuge in the idea that social and economic development will soon take an entirely new turn, in favour of 'alternative life styles', 'intermediate technological societies' and 'small systems'.[7] Likewise abandoning the traditional city but for different reasons, several American authors have suggested—especially with reference to southern California—that the majority of people no longer wish to live in cities. They 'vote with their wheels', that is, they drive out of Los Angeles and establish their homes almost anywhere else within a radius of one hundred miles or more. To try to re-plan and revive the run-down areas of a large modern city, it has been argued, would be a waste of time, because an up to date factory brought into the city could not hope to compete with a similar factory located 'on the crossroads of a couple of super-highways' somewhere out of town. This sort of argument supported the American Inter-State Expressway planning of the late 1950s and early 1960s. It has also been claimed that people want to live in houses with plenty of space around them, so they move to ideal settlements, like Westlake:

> Westlake has no old people, no modern architecture, and no Negroes. Besides, it has no poor, no advertisement hoardings, no overhead wires, no television aerials, no works of art, no bars, no poolrooms, no weeds, no city centre, no annoyances . . . no vulgarity, no visible sex . . . no flashy night-time scene.[8]

Indeed, Westlake seems to have a peace that passeth all understanding, and some of us may conclude that it would very rapidly drive us out of our minds; unless, of course, we could find an interesting traditional city, not too far away, that we could visit.

But we cannot escape from our dilemmas. There is no reason to suppose that a flight to ideal suburbs—'communities of limited liability' they have been called—or to novel life-styles is going to change the path of progress, at any rate in the forseeable future. The existing interests and the impetus of society are too great. The mass of people show no sign that they wish to give up the comforts and conveniences of industrial life, dependent as it is on a vast accumulation of capital, on an extremely complex technology and on the division of labour. Few people are content with things as they are, and almost everyone hopes for improvement; but it must be emphasized that abandoning present arrangements for an altogether new style of living is not a popular idea. It is high levels of consumption that are popular. And it has to be added that those who do 'opt out' very often remain dependent, and sometimes heavily dependent, on the present system. Few who 'reject' modern society fail to draw whatever social security benefits it offers, or, if they become seriously ill, decline to enter one of its hospitals. Another remedy that is sometimes proposed is radical reconstruction of city centres. In its less extreme forms this may make good sense. But it is quite unhelpful to suggest, as Le Corbusier did,

> that the centres of our great cities must be razed to the ground and rebuilt, and that the wretched belts of surrounding suburbs must be demolished and taken further out.[9]

This is the kind of wild talk that alienated Le Corbusier from the French authorities and helped to bring urban planning into disrepute. Unfortunately, his followers were not good at distinguishing the practicable from the absurd, and the idea of total rebuilding persisted. But it was never a starter. A modern city is a network of expensive capital installations. Over a period of time these could be dispersed; that is to say, replacement factories, replacement office buildings, replacement roads, replacement sewage disposal plants and all the rest could be built elsewhere. Because the maintenance and renewal of capital has constantly to be carried out, the entire cost of dispersion would not be a net addition to national expenditure, but the net addition would nevertheless be enormous. We simply could not afford, even over the course of the next fifty years or more, to abandon a large number of the dwellings that have been built in large cities in Britain, nor could we afford to replace until seriously obsolescent many other items of urban capital equipment; the British economy is by no means overendowed with capital as compared with many of its competitors. Furthermore, some businesses relocated in new small centres would find their communications more difficult and therefore their costs higher. Thus, from a purely economic point of view, proposals to rebuild existing cities elsewhere are equivalent, in present circumstances, to proposals for a fairly drastic reduction in the country's standard of living; that is to say, for a new life-style that not 1 per cent of the population would vote for. Building new towns, on the other hand, is a realistic idea, and it has been put into practice with good results. But the limited dispersion of industry and population that can be brought about by building new towns is not going to cause the problems of life in big cities to disappear. We just have to face it: most of us are stuck with cities more or less as they are.

Nor does this seem to be an unmitigated misfortune, for there are signs in many places of an active wish to live in them.

So urban planning, in some form, must go on; we cannot afford to despair. The think-of-everything-at-once approach to planning, fuelled by a variety of moral imperatives supplied by so-called social science, has not been a success. But because planning has not achieved everything, it does not follow that it should attempt nothing; that we should content ourselves with laying the whole business to rest under a few volumes of speculation, dreams, prayers, nightmares and wild regrets.

The planning, or more often the alteration, extension and partial replanning of towns is, after all, an activity with a very long history. This chapter began with Le Corbusier and Howard, the latter, partly by sleight of hand, squeezed into the twentieth century. But over many previous centuries the planning of towns has taken place. Planning is, of course, in the abstract, a singularly inexact idea. No one can 'believe in planning' unless he has decided what the word means. Nothing that is built is unplanned, or it would stand up only by accident, and any collection of buildings, even of mud huts, is planned in the minimal sense that each additional dwelling has to be placed deliberately in some relation to the others. The question about planning is not whether it should happen or not, but what should be its scope in space and time, and how extensive should be its social implications.

It is the business of the planner to plan, in some degree, a building or a group of buildings, a street, a neighbourhood or a whole town; and it is equally his business to alter and re-plan any of these. The smaller the physical plan the sooner it can be completed; but the building of a new town from start to finish—if there ever is a finish— can occupy several decades and hence require much foresight. So we may think of a spectrum of planning, with big planning at one end of the spectrum and little planning at the other. Big planning seldom happens. It is not often that opportunities occur for designing a whole new town, or even a substantial part of a town. So most plans are little plans concerned with alteration, replacement, or modest extension. The basic structure of the city does not alter, but nevertheless the atmosphere and details alter. Cities grow outward and lose cohesion. Skylines change. Traffic grows heavier. Some good buildings disappear, and perhaps some new good buildings take their place. The majority of towns as we have them now have been built by a process of replacement and accretion going on for several centuries, and as a result they consist in general of a consortium of little plans, or of the replanned fragments of little plans; and what we notice in them is not so much the overall plan, because it has been so much altered and overlaid, as pieces of planning, and occasionally the architecture. Now no sensible person is going to deny that the architecture of the town is important, and that each individual building can be well or badly designed. But if good buildings are not given a good site and setting—if they have no space around them, if they achieve no harmonious relation to other buildings or to the landscape nearby or within sight—then their value and the agreeableness of the whole place are substantially reduced.

It follows that little planning can be very important. New buildings have to fit in and harmonize with whatever is on the ground already (unless, of course, the surroundings are so dreadful that they had better be ignored as far as possible). Success depends on siting, which is largely up to the planner; on scale, which is also partly the planner's responsibility; on style, which is the business of the architect. Proposals to alter or demolish existing buildings have of course to seek the planner's approval, and such proposals may be every bit as important as plans for new building.

It seems sometimes to be thought that these things were better managed in olden times, and that cities which on the whole we admire today grew up 'naturally' and without conflict. But a good deal of evidence points the other way. Major planning interventions have often taken place in the course of a city's development, and they have not been without cost. Medieval Rome, for example, incorporated within its ancient walls a maze of muddy dark alleys where most of the population lived, and much of the remaining space was given over to villas, vineyards, deerparks, hostels for pilgrims, churches and large areas of waste ground. A comprehensive reconstruction of Rome was begun by Pope Nicholas V in the fifteenth century. Plans were drawn up for new or improved streets, piazzas, loggias and bridges; most of these plans required extensive demolitions. Houses began to be razed in order to improve communications and to open up new vistas; whole streets, lanes and alleys disappeared, and people had to find new homes; and as the existing open spaces were progressively built over, peasants no longer came down from Lombardy to work in the vineyards in spring and autumn. The shape and life of Rome were decisively altered, for some people quite abruptly. Meanwhile, the project for a new St Peter's had been conceived, and Julius II 'defied the Sacred College, the commune of Rome and public opinion throughout Christendom when he ordered that the old church be pulled down to make way for a more fitting building'.[10] The old basilica was declared unsafe. Perhaps it really was unsafe. In any case, Julius got the new building started, 'encouraging Bramante on that career of destruction which earned him the soubriquet "il Maestro Ruinante"'.[11] Paris is a much more notorious case. Napoleon III had sufficient power, and was able to borrow sufficient money, to enable Haussmann to drive his new roads and boulevards through the densely populated city more or less as he pleased. Compulsory purchase, alongside eviction without compensation, were, on a horrendous scale, the order of the day. The result may be admired, but the process was far from painless for a very large number of people. As for civic conflict and outrage on a small scale, these have always been commonplace. In Como, to take an early example, the façade of the Romanesque basilica of San Fedele, the church of the Annunciation, completed early in the twelfth century, occupies part of one side of a small piazza. The façade is elegant, but it is obstructed by a house which abuts the church and projects, at an odd angle, into the square, destroying its symmetry and repose. This house was built in the sixteenth century, no doubt amid protests that history does not record. New developments have always been taking place. We cannot expect to live without them. It is the successful supervision of these intrusions that is the planner's principal task, especially difficult when the new impinges upon what is old and worth keeping.

When modern (that is to say twentieth-century) British town planning was in a formative stage, it did not see its problems in this way. Howard and his close followers, as has already been remarked, observing the state of the towns and cities around them, turned their backs upon what existed. They made no suggestions for adaptation or improvement, but fled to the countryside. They were idealists — which is no bad thing — with far-reaching aims. They thought to improve matters by building quite new cities amid the fields and in the fresh air beyond the old industrial towns. These would be garden cities with tree-lined roads, curving streets and village greens, where each family would realize the dream of 'a cottage all of our own, with its little garden, its healthy air, its clean kitchen, parlour and bedrooms'. So, at any rate, the future was seen by Raymond Unwin, quoting Ruskin; and Raymond Unwin was recognized as the most practical and level-headed, the least given to dreaming, of the early planners. This is important, because the garden-city movement, which Howard began, was not only about building new towns. It was also a romantic revolt against mass production, the labour market and Victorian over-crowding. These early planners wanted, as some planners still do, to re-order society on socialistic lines, and re-ordering the environment was part of their programme. Howard and his disciples were the heirs of William Morris. They were also the heirs of Robert Owen, and others, who during the nineteenth century devised ideal communities, run on communistic lines, as an escape from the evils of pre-Victorian and Victorian capitalism. Owen's 'villages of co-operation' were to combine agriculture with manufacturing and thus achieve self-sufficiency, and in each of them 3 000 inhabitants were to live harmoniously in four large buildings arranged in a rectangle. Parallelograms of paupers, Cobbett called them, and none was built. Such schemes have always failed. Howard's ideas were far less crude, and far more practical. Moreover, beauty and nature were a prominent part of his dream, and these gave it originality and life.

His *Tomorrow: A Peaceful Path to Real Reform* has been a very influential book. It is not as path-breaking as has often been claimed, because new ideas about low-cost housing had already found expression at Port Sunlight, begun in 1888, and at Bournville, begun in 1895. These paternalistic developments broke with the standard nineteenth-century arrangement of tight and regular rows of small houses built along a straight narrow street, and instead provided cottages, semi-detached or in units of five or six, along curving streets bordered by trees and gardens. Both schemes were highly innovative, with excellent visual lay-out; but they were uneconomic; and perhaps it was for this reason that Howard devoted a good deal of space in his book to explaining, in considerable detail, the economic bases of his proposals. He seemed to prove that 'garden cities for all' was a viable idea. He also presented the garden city as a module in a scheme of national planning, with emphasis on low-density housing, green belts and land zoning. These were ideas that Howard put into circulation, although he did not invent them. And garden cities were actually built: Letchworth, completed in 1906, and Welwyn, begun in 1920. (Hampstead Garden Suburb was also built, under the influence of Howard's ideas, between 1905 and 1914.) But the overall picture did not change very much, because alongside these new developments (which were too expensive to be of much use to those most in need of housing) the old towns continued to exist and to grow very much as before. Straight treeless streets of small houses, many of them four-roomed with a yard (or yards) at the back, continued to be built with seemingly endless monotony by speculative builders.[12] Beyond the town limits the city fathers had no authority, and were left 'looking on helplessly', as Unwin put it, while properties 'all around their towns have been covered with buildings without any provision having been made for open spaces, school sites, or any other public needs'.[13]

The first town planning Act was passed in 1909. Its 'general object' was stated to be 'securing proper sanitary conditions, amenity and convenience in connection with the laying out and use of land'. This Act was of no great significance, except as a first step in a new direction. A show of official concern about amenity and convenience in housing was entirely novel, and supporters of the Act hoped that it would encourage development along garden-city—or more accurately garden-suburb—lines. There was not much in the Act itself to justify this idea, but at the time when the Bill was passed town planning was associated in many minds with ideas about garden cities and garden suburbs, and therefore more 'suburbs salubrious' were expected to ensue. In the event, not a great deal changed. There was no compulsion on local authorities to plan or to build. A handful of residential estates were developed along garden-city lines, but this would have occurred in any case. In spite of some vaguely expressed aspirations, the Act was essentially a consolidation of previous housing legislation, and it reduced Howard's ideas to little more than the encouragement of suburban growth at low densities. It ignored the urban areas already in existence, and had very little to do with either civic art or nature.

So much for the world before 1914; after the war, almost everything was different. Ideas had changed, physical circumstances had changed, and information about what was wrong and what steps should be taken to improve the situation was far more available than before. The task of building a country fit for heroes to live in was now expected to begin, both in new social arrangements and in bricks and mortar. A fresh start was possible, and it was recognized, as never before, that the government would have to play a conspicuous part.

The war had made government action familiar in almost every sphere of life. This was a remarkable — indeed a dramatic — change, because it had been the accepted view for over half a century that governments should act as little as possible, and that private enterprise, self-reliance and competition would get things right. But by 1918 there were Ministries of Labour, Transport, Information, National Service, Blockade, Reconstruction, Munitions, Food and Shipping: all war-time creations. And although most of these were abolished before the end of 1921, the old presumption that government action was undesirable did not revive. The war, as Keynes put it, had been 'an unprecedented divergence [from laissez-faire] into centralised social action on a great scale'; and this great war-time experiment had, on the whole, worked successfully, leaving 'some near observers optimistically anxious to repeat it in peace conditions'.[14] So centralized social action stayed acceptable; and it stayed acceptable nowhere more definitely than in the provision of housing, which from the earliest post-war years came to be recognized as a national social service.

Housing was the concern of the newly created Ministry of Health. During the war almost no new houses had been built, and repairs to those that existed had been carried out on a quite inadequate scale. As a result, it was determined in 1919 that there was a deficiency of half a million houses of all kinds to be made good, in addition to a forecast annual requirement for about 100 000 new houses for lower-income families. This opened up the prospect of house-building on a previously unheard-of scale. But besides housing there was a general need for building, rebuilding and reconstruction. During the war factories had been poorly maintained and now many of them were out of date; the transport system was run down and the motor car was beginning to make quite new and extensive demands for roads and bridges; population growth, continuing urbanization and the business of laying the foundations for what turned out to be the future welfare state (health insurance, unemployment insurance, old age pensions) meant a need for more shops, more hospitals, more schools, more electricity and therefore more generating stations, more government offices, more public buildings of every kind. And — surprisingly enough — it was recognized that quality mattered, in some spheres at any rate. In 1915 a memorandum was presented to Sir Hubert Llewellyn-Smith, Permanent Secretary to the Board of Trade, pointing out that German export successes before the war had been partly due to the 'untiring efforts which the Germans had made to improve the quality of their work'. The Design in Industry Association ('A Body with New Aims') was founded in 1915; in 1919 the Ministry of Reconstruction published a pamphlet entitled *Art and Industry*, and soon afterwards a bureau of information concerned with the problems of art and industry was set up. The results, it is true, were meagre. But that the government should take an interest in design (for anything except battleships and such like) was altogether unprecedented.

The public housing programmes of the 1920s, the like of which had never been seen in Britain before, were governed, directly or indirectly, by the Housing and Town Planning Act of 1919. Can it be said that this Act was a genuine attempt to encourage good design, or was it concerned almost solely with accommodation and sanitation? Primarily, it made town planning, within narrow limits, a statutory duty for local authorities; and it provided financial assistance for local authorities to build their own houses. But above and beyond this, the Act explained in considerable detail the standards, and provided design guide-lines, for the housing estates which were to be built, and these standards and guide-lines were taken from the Tudor Walters Report of 1918, which was to a substantial extent the work of Raymond Unwin. Unwin had helped to design both Letchworth and Hampstead, and the housing estates that the 1919 Act pre-figured were clearly intended to be built along the same lines. Thus garden-city ideas entered legislation, in the form of statutory house types, norms of lay-out, and a recommended density of twelve houses to the acre. Up to this point, therefore, the Government had done well. The 1919 Act was not only a stimulus to house building, it was also a praise-worthy attempt to promote the building of well-planned picturesque suburbs that would have some resemblance to the traditional English village. But in this secondary aim the Act failed. Designs and layouts require to be interpreted, and after local interpretation — usually by borough engineers, who did much of the work between the wars — little of the original conception was left save

the measurements. Most local councillors and officials had a totally
inadequate understanding of what might be done and how to do it,
and gross mistakes were repeatedly made. Unwin, now acting as
chief government architect for housing and town planning (those
were still the days when one person did both jobs), strove to make
the new council estates resemble garden suburbs; but it is only too
well known that he had very little success. Many estates were built
without schools, playgrounds or reasonable access to public transport,
and lay-outs soon became a caricature of garden-city ideas. And
when the government subsidies were reduced after only a few years
'the graceful style of the earliest council houses, which clearly showed
their garden-city origins, gave way to crudely utilitarian designs'.[15]
Thus the housing estates of the 1920s were a much-needed addition
to the nation's stock of houses, but they did virtually nothing to
improve architectural quality, or to provide for the amenities of
space and nature. On the contrary, the great majority of them were
ugly and soul-less. The drive to implement new ideas had not been
strong enough to overcome local ignorance and lack of imagination.
As far as most people were concerned, a move towards better civic
design might as well never have been made, nor *A Peaceful Path to
Real Reform* ever have been written. The garden-city vision had
faded before it had ever reached them.

To be fair to the local councils and the borough engineers, it has to
be added that the architects did very little to help. The 1920s were
rather a dreary time in British architecture. Voysey had been the
greatest 'traditional' architect of the late Victorian and Edwardian
era, just as Charles Rennie Mackintosh had been the greatest
innovative architect.[16] But Voysey, although he lived until 1941,
was responsible for very few houses after 1900; and Mackintosh built
little after the completion of his masterpiece, the Glasgow School of
Art, in 1909. He died in 1928, when the *Architectural Journal*
described him in a brief obituary notice as 'a master of general form',
but added that the form itself was apt to be unpleasant and that his
work was in any case 'marred to a great extent' by the use of motifs
and decorations belonging to Art Nouveau. Voysey and Mackintosh
had few admirers in the post-war years, and they had no successors
of equal stature. The outstanding British architect of the 1920s was
Lutyens, best known as a country-house architect in the grander
manner beloved of *Homes and Gardens*. His work was at first
derived from William Morris and the Arts-and-Crafts style, then it
became, more or less successively, neo-classical, neo-Georgian, neo-
Palladian, and even, it has been suggested, neo-Wren. He built some
ponderously 'classical' commercial buildings in London, and some
flats. But he was no innovator, and his post-war pre-eminence helped
to fix British architecture in a backward-looking stance. The study of
architectural history became firmly established after 1920 as the

principal subject-matter in architectural education, and not much else than 'period design' was produced or found acceptable. Large-scale housing schemes were never thought of as an opportunity for architects.

In America, on the other hand, there was innovative and distinguished work by Frank Lloyd Wright, as well as ever loftier skyscrapers—an American art form, it has been said—which were now being built in every big city from New York to Los Angeles. On the Continent both Walter Gropius and Mies van der Rohe were designing flats for very large housing programmes. This was part of the Modern Movement, an exciting response, its admirers felt, to a new and exciting age, an age in which 'the marvellous applications of electricity were startling the world and scientific inventions were abolishing space and time'.[17] But the British did not wish to be startled, nor did they seem to relish the impending abolition of space and time. They did not admire the Modern Movement, which had been brought in by Le Corbusier and his worship of machines: 'les autos, les avions, les paquebots'. Architecture, according to Le Corbusier, was to be like engineering, stripped of all decoration, plain and purposeful. But the British distrusted the new approach, and some of their criticisms were not without force. One writer, in 1927, wanted to know why a house should be like an aeroplane, or a ship, or a motor car. Why should it not just be like a house? Another complained that modern Dutch architects 'have been ready to throw aside all tradition, all logic, and everything except the desire to do something new'.[18]

It is certainly true that Le Corbusier, in his unfailing efforts to *épater les bourgeois*, talked and wrote a great deal of nonsense ('The curve is ruinous . . . it is a paralysing thing'; 'Culture is an orthogonal state of mind'; 'Louis XIV made do with picks and shovels. Even wheel-barrows had just been invented by Pascal';) [19] and that many of his followers did the same ('the problem of housing and the organisation of space is entirely [sic] one of economics and social welfare').[20] New ideas were pushed too far, as often happens, and it had to be admitted a few years later that the curve was due for re-instatement, and that the aesthetics of architecture were not dead after all. The British were right to be sceptical about all this Gallic fervour and German exactitude. But their scepticism was of a deadening kind, and the fact that few good original buildings were built in Britain in the 1920s is therefore not surprising. Lutyenesque classic was the standard fare for public buildings. London County Hall, large dignified and uninspired, is one of the better examples, the result of a competition decided in 1908. Described by the *Architectural Journal* in 1924 as 'forcible and artistic', it was opened in the same year as the Stockholm Town Hall. Liverpool Cathedral was going up in a form of Gothic, the Scottish National War Memorial, completed in 1927, seems to belong to some unidentified period of the Middle Ages, while steeply pitched roofs and Jacobean chimneys were *de rigeur* for private houses with any pretensions. Except for Elizabeth Scott's admirable Shakespeare Memorial Theatre in Stratford-on-Avon, accepted as the winning design in a competition judged in 1928, when the architect was still not thirty, and a house in Northampton designed by Peter Behrens, living in Vienna, very little that is still interesting in Britain can be traced back to the 1920s. These were the dog-days of British architecture, when not even cinemas, garages or airport terminals were memorable (they improved in the 1930s), and not even vulgarity was triumphant.

It can thus be argued that the British architects of the day failed to come forward with new ideas or even to inspire much interest in their own work. Certainly they contributed nothing worth mentioning in the field of low-cost housing; and twenty-five years were to elapse before real architecture and large re-housing schemes were successfully brought together in Britain. So the good intentions of the newly-created Ministry of Health were frustrated. The indifference of the architects, local incompetence, and the Treasury's familiar concern to save money without understanding the cost prevented progress.

Within already built-up areas, however, where the 1919 Act had almost no effect, a quite different move towards better design was made. These areas experienced considerable post-war pressures for development. The volume of new building and the increase of vehicles constantly intensified the difficulties of finding suitable sites for civic, domestic or industrial use, and satisfactory solutions to everyday urban problems became harder and harder to find. In London there were special requirements, and one person who felt that he faced more difficulties than he could handle in the usual way was Sir Lionel Earle, Permanent Secretary to the Office of Works.

Earle was an exceptionally distinguished public servant, and a man of a distinctly independent turn of mind. Born in 1866, he received the kind of education that scarcely anyone today can hope for. He first went to Marlborough, where he found the education 'unenlightened', and then continued his studies at Göttingen, Paris and Oxford, without feeling obliged to acquire any kind of degree. He was well-off and well connected — he dined with Balfour and entertained the Duke and Duchess of Devonshire — and as a young man he travelled extensively on the Continent, taking a keen interest in architecture. (He considered Milan Cathedral to be superior to Bruges, Seville or Chartres, and indeed 'more magical than any other'.) His first government appointment was as Assistant Secretary to the Royal Commission at the Paris Exhibition 1898–1900, and in 1912, at the relatively early age of 46, he became Permanent Secretary of the Office of Works, a position which he retained for twenty-one years.[21]

During this period the work of the Department greatly expanded. After the passing of the Ancient Monuments Act in 1913, the preservation of historic buildings and ancient monuments became one of the Department's concerns, and Earle was responsible for, *inter alia*, the repair of the magnificent timber roof of Westminster Hall, built late in the fourteenth century, and for much-needed restorations at Hampton Court. New public buildings of all kinds, the re-furnishing of official houses, improvements to the Royal Parks — these also were all within Earle's sphere. He was urbane, energetic, artistic and not without a certain endearing optimism: 'the beauty of the trees and flowers in the parks', he once wrote (not quite grammatically), 'have a very humanizing influence on the citizens of London'.

It was after the war that the Office of Works became heavily involved in new building projects. Particularly numerous, and often very important, were plans for war memorials. Earle's own view was that the best possible national war memorial would have been created by continuing Portland Place through Regent's Park to the heights of Primrose Hill, or even better to Highgate, with a fine monumental triumphal arch at the crest of the hill: 'it would have made a highway far more impressive than the Champs Elysées'. But instead, bodies innumerable wanted war memorials of their own — the Guards, the Artillery, the Merchant Marine — and not one of these or any other memorial could be erected in a public place in London without the sanction of the Commissioner of Works. Earle found the task of selecting sites and approving designs extremely difficult, so he set up an unofficial advisory committee to assist him. This committee appears to have worked reasonably well, but it encountered the usual sort of trouble. It approved, for example, although 'with some reluctance and misgiving', the Hudson Memorial in Hyde Park by Epstein, 'Rima'. Cut in high relief, Rima is depicted as an elemental wood nymph — strong straight arms, big hands, pointed breasts, belly like an inverted pear; not what was expected by strollers in the Park who were accustomed to the sight of Prince Albert and Peter Pan. No sooner was the memorial in place than angry demands arose for its removal. Earle resisted. Ten or twenty years would have to pass, he believed, before a sound judgement could be made; 'in matters of art one must not act too hastily'.[22] Was it not the case, he writes in his autobiography, that Michaelangelo's David, 'which stood for some centuries in the Piazza at Florence and is enormously admired, had to be protected by the civil guards against the outraged feelings of the populace, chiefly I believe on account of the nude'?[23] On this particular point Sir Lionel seems to have been misinformed. But he was perfectly correct in saying that in 1908, when the Epstein sculptures on the School of Medicine in the Strand were unveiled, they 'caused a street riot, and one hundred and fifty police had to appear, to control the fury of the populace'.[24] It is at least good to know that the British have occasionally taken a serious interest in art.

The trouble about the Hudson Memorial was only one difficulty among many, and as early as 1923 Earle had become dissatisfied with the unofficial consultative committees which he had set up a few years before. He wanted something more independent of government and more authoritative. He therefore decided that the country should take a leaf out of the American book, and follow the example of Washington, DC.

It was once the case that new ideas were pioneered in England, or possibly in Scotland, and the rest of the world came to learn. A Swiss historian, Simonde de Sismondi, author of *Histoire des Républiques Italiennes* in sixteen volumes and *Histoire des Français* in twenty-nine volumes and now very seldom read, describes England in one of his essays as 'this astonishing country, which seems to be submitted to a great experiment for the instruction of the rest of the world'. He is not referring to statutory town planning. His words refer not to the 1920s but to the 1820s, when Nash was building Regent Street and when what caused amazement among visitors to Britain was the progress of the world's first industrial revolution. But within a few decades the role of stage-manager for experiments in modern living was taken over by the United States, uniquely well-equipped with her remarkably egalitarian constitution and her endlessly innovative economy. European travellers flocked to see this enormous, expanding, energetic, ever-wealthier country, to admire it, to criticize it, and to learn from it. Their impressions differed widely, but from the beginning to the end of the nineteenth century there was one point on which they agreed: Washington, the capital of the United States, was the most miserable capital city that any of them had ever set eyes on.

Not that Washington was without a plan; far from it. At a very early date the need for a plan had been agreed, and the task of producing one had been entrusted to a French engineer, Major Charles L'Enfant. In 1791 L'Enfant submitted his plan for the capital of the young republic, and it was accepted. Most people admired it, and most people still do. Writing in 1921, Raymond Unwin stated that

> L'Enfant's plan of Washington . . . affords an example of French methods, admirably adapted to the nature and undulations of the site, having very definite main and subsidiary centres of interest, and an ample provision for diagonal intercommunication. The whole is treated with great skill, and no small share of architectural imagination.[25]

Unwin thought the placing of the Capitol on the edge of the hill overlooking the Mall especially praiseworthy, and that the Washington Memorial at the end of the Mall 'provides a fitting terminal . . . and completes this conspicuous example of the co-ordination of a plan with its site, and their combination into one harmonious design, which perhaps marks the supreme achievement in city planning'.[26]

This undiluted praise seems a little surprising. After all, Unwin was an earnest socialist who had declared only a few years before that 'the city plan should express the ideals and provide for the needs of the citizens',[27] and the ideals which L'Enfant's plan expresses are those of the *ancien régime*, and the needs of the citizens for which it provides do not include much in the way of housing. L'Enfant's plan (which seems to owe a good deal to Pierre Patte's *Monumens érigés à la Gloire de Louis* XV, published in 1765) is grand and authoritarian in the baroque manner, designed to overawe rather than to accommodate the ordinary man. There are main and subsidiary focal points, the chief of these being the Capitol, the White House, and the Washington Monument (500 feet high). The principal avenues are 160 feet wide, 80 feet being given to the roadway, 10 feet to each pavement alongside the roadway and 30 feet to gravel walks 'planted with trees on each side' flanking the pavements. Louis XIV would have thought it not inadequate. Of the 60000 acres in the plan, fewer than 2000 were set aside for housing. In many respects L'Enfant's imagined city is an admirable conception. It provides diversity as well as regularity, is even subtle, but it is dedicated not to democracy but to the glorification of order and centralized power. Washington was to be, as L'Enfant himself said, 'a grand idea'. 'The mode of taking possession of, and improving, the whole district at first must leave to posterity a grand idea of the patriotic interest which promoted it.' This was altogether another matter from building a city to be lived in. And it is significant that people have preferred for a hundred years (save for a few decades around 1900) to make their homes not along the imposing monumental avenues of Washington but in the older, narrow streets of Georgetown, built alongside the capital city on a humbler and more human scale.

The lay-out of Washington is magnificent and, for a republic, madly inappropriate. In the nineteenth century the inappropriateness caused little comment, but the magnificence did, because it was so obviously hollow. For a hundred years L'Enfant's 'grand idea' was scarcely discoverable (except in the mind's eye), because the young republic could not live up to it; there was lots of space, but not enough population, not enough construction, and not enough money. So the inhabitants of the city had to struggle along with a plan that was several sizes too large for their needs. During most of the nineteenth century, buildings were few and the distances between them enormous; avenues were open spaces and open spaces were deserts; the wind and the dust blew along half-deserted highways. Charles Dickens visited Washington in 1842 and waxed eloquent about it, and the Americans have not yet forgiven him. It is little wonder. He expressed his views as follows:

> Take the worst parts of the City Road and Pentonville, or the straggling outskirts of Paris, where the houses are smallest, preserving all their oddities, but especially the small shops and dwellings, occupied in Pentonville (but not in Washington) by furniture brokers, keepers of poor eating-houses, and fanciers of birds. Burn the whole down; build it up again in wood and plaster; widen it a little; throw in part of St John's Wood; put green blinds outside all the private houses, with a red curtain and a white one in every window; plough up all the roads; plant a great deal of coarse turf in every place where it ought not to be; erect three handsome buildings in stone and marble anywhere, but the more entirely out of everybody's way the better; call one the Post Office, one the Patent Office, and one the Treasury; make it scorching hot in the morning and freezing cold in the afternoon, with an occasional tornado of wind and dust; leave a brick-field without the bricks in all central places where a street may naturally be expected; and that's Washington.
>
> It is sometimes called the City of Magnificent Distances, but it might with greater propriety be termed the City of Magnificent Intentions; for it is only on taking a bird's eye view of it from the top of the Capitol that one can at all comprehend the vast designs of its projector, an aspiring Frenchman.

This state of affairs, or something like it, continued until after the Civil War, when the citizens of Washington at last began to catch up with the plan.

This catching up was to a large extent the work of Alexander Robey Shepherd. His name is not much known to fame. Born in Washington in 1835, he was active in construction and land speculation before he was twenty and rich before he was twenty-five. In 1861 he became president of the City Council, and shortly after the war he was appointed Governor of the District of Columbia by the President, General Ulysses S. Grant. Shepherd—soon to be known as Boss Shepherd—was energetic and dictatorial, and a good deal of his official efforts were put into an extensive programme of public improvements. Streets were paved, sidewalks constructed and 3000 gas lamps put in place. In particular, Shepherd saw to it that the trees which, according to L'Enfant's plan should line the prodigally wide avenues, were at last planted. Washington began to grow together. And by the closing years of the century, when Boss Shepherd, officially cleared of charges of corruption, had long since left his native town to develop (very successfully) a silver mine in Mexico, the capital of the United States was beginning to resemble more than just a collection of public buildings and official residences

having only a distant connection with one another on the shores of
the Potomac.

It is true that Shepherd's Washington remained a far cry from
London or Paris; but the gap was closing. The United States as a
whole, indeed, was rapidly becoming not only richer but also more
cultivated and more urbane. From the point of view of architecture,
Chicago was at this time the focus of her development. Not even a
frontier town when L'Enfant planned Washington, Chicago by the
1890s was a city of over one and a half million people, an agricultural
and trading centre of enormous importance situated in the heart-
land of industrial America. It was here that the world's first large-
scale steel-frame skeleton buildings were erected, and here, as a
consequence, that the skyscraper was pioneered. Henry Richardson's
Marshall Field Store, completed in 1888, was an iron skeleton with a
stone exterior, resembling, in the words of John McKean, 'an
expanded Quattrocento Palazzo . . . spacious, simple, resolved and
grand'.[28] The Reliance Building, by Daniel Burnham and John Root,
completed seven years later, was a slender fifteen-storey block of
perfectly repetitive form, terracotta cladding on an iron frame. In
Buffalo, in New York State, Louis Sullivan built the Guaranty
Building, perhaps the finest of all the early skyscrapers. Thirteen
storeys high, with slender but emphatic vertical lines, its severity is
relieved by simple low relief decoration in terracotta, and two porticos
with relieving arches. Buildings like these were technically and
architecturally new, and they brought to the notice of the world what
contemporaries soon learned to call 'the Chicago style'. The accepted
conventions of architecture were breaking up. This process was
taking place in Europe as well as in America, and the search for a
new style caused dismay in many Old World circles. But in America,
where architectural innovation was both spontaneous and conspicuous, the most prominent result was a sharp rise of public
interest in cities and buildings.[29]

The 1893 World's Exposition in Chicago intensified this interest.
In particular, the arrangement and co-ordination of buildings in the
Exposition so as to create a harmonious 'classical' urban scene, and
the 'Venetian effects' in the White City along the shores of Lake
Michigan—basins, canals, arcades, a winding lagoon—enormously
impressed the American public. It is true that the architecture was
not up to much, most of it being a pastiche of French and Italian
styles; Louis Sullivan thought it so bad that he declared that 'the
damage done to this country by the Chicago World's Fair will last for
half a century'. But American architecture survived quite comfortably,
while the new ideas about urban design that the Fair had suggested
led to the 'City Beautiful' movement; and this in its turn led to the
foundation of the Public Art League in Washington in 1895. The
object of the League was to persuade the Federal Government to set

up an official body which would pronounce upon the merits or demerits of any work of art or architecture to be commissioned or purchased by the Government. A Bill to this end was presented in 1897. But Congress threw it out, very sensibly, because the politicians considered that such a body should have advisory powers only; they also disliked the proposal that three of the five members should be the president of the American Institute of Architects, the president of the National Academy of Design and the president of the National Sculpture Society. Well-known establishment figures, Congress thought, should not have the final say in what was and what was not to be built in the nation's capital.

Three years later, in 1900, Washington's Centennial was celebrated. Inevitably, much was spoken and written about the capital's splendour, its beauty, its defects and its future. The American Institute of Architects, which had been behind the creation of the Public Art League, held its convention in Washington during that year, and members of the Institute put forward a number of suggestions for improving the city. There followed the establishment of the Senate Park Commission in 1901, charged with the duty of developing plans for parks in the District of Columbia, and the siting of public buildings. The Park Commission, commonly known as the McMillan Commission, lasted for only a few years, but it had time to pay a quick visit to Europe, where the members were enormously impressed by Haussmann's straight and tree-lined boulevards, and then to submit to Congress its recommendations, which were of the greatest importance. In this 1901 Report, which was largely the work of Daniel Burnham, the Commission recommended an extensive park system for the District of Columbia, and it paid particular attention to the Mall (at that time largely occupied by the tracks of what had become the Pennsylvania Railroad) and to the proposal for a memorial to Lincoln on the site where the memorial now stands. Above all, the Commission emphasized the extreme desirability of adhering to L'Enfant's plan of 1791, which had been largely neglected for three-quarters of a century, and in several important respects had been contravened. These recommendations became known, from the time that they were made public, as the McMillan Plan of 1901.

In 1909, the American Institute of Architects again appealed for the creation of a public body which would help to guide the artistic development of Washington and help to prevent serious mistakes in architecture and town planning. On this occasion they addressed their appeal to President Theodore Roosevelt, who replied on the same day. He asked for the names of thirty people whom he could appoint to a Council of Fine Arts, to which his cabinet officers would be obliged to go for advice on all matters relating to architecture, the selection of sites, landscaping, sculpture, and painting. The Council was set up within a few days, in January 1909.

Two months later, the fledgling Council was abolished by Roosevelt's successor, President Taft. Taft was not opposed to the Council in principle, but he believed that such a body should be established by Act of Congress, and not by Executive Order. As a result, a bill was introduced almost at once by Senator Root, who gave the following account of its conception:

> Sometime about the early spring of 1910 some Senator had introduced in the Senate a resolution providing for the purchase by the Government of a number of paintings that nobody wanted to buy and under the rule that resolution was referred to the Committee on the Library. The responsibility for protecting the Government against a waste of money was thus thrown upon the Committee.
>
> A little discussion developed the fact that all the members of the committee had an uncomfortable feeling that the pictures were probably worthless and no such purchase ought to be made, but that no member of the committee felt any such confidence in his own knowledge and judgment about such things as to feel like making a report to the Senate based on his opinion and maintaining that opinion on the floor. We all felt that the committee ought to have some way of getting an expert opinion to guide it in making its report.
>
> In the discussion we recalled Theodore Roosevelt's appointment of a Fine Arts Council, which fell to the ground because it had no legal standing, and we recalled also the advantage received from the report on park development of the informal commission selected by the McMillan Commission, and we finally determined to ask Congress to provide for the appointment of a fine arts commission which would meet the need that our committee was then experiencing and a similar need which was liable to occur in a multitude of cases under which government officers had to pass on questions of art without being really competent to perform such a duty . . .
>
> I drafted a very brief statute . . . and a little informal explanation of the need which the committee felt for expert assistance in the performing of its duties carried the bill through.
>
> And so, without creation of any power of legal compulsion, there was brought to the service of the Government the authority of competent opinion upon questions of art arising in the course of administration, and widespread and habitual deference to such an opinion has saved the Government and the community from God knows how many atrocities.

The legislation which set up the Commission of Fine Arts was approved in May, 1910. It provided for a Commission of seven members, each appointed by the President for a term of four years. The remit of the Commission was 'to advise upon the location of statues, fountains and monuments in the public squares, streets and parks in the District of Columbia . . . and upon the selection of artists for the execution of the same'. The Commission was also required to 'advise generally upon questions of art when required to do so by the President, or by any committee of either House of Congress'. A few months later the Commission's responsibilities were widened when the President gave the Commission authority to advise on plans for almost any public buildings erected by the Government in the District of Columbia.

Whatever powers they are given, committees and commissions may do much or they may do little; a great deal depends upon the members themselves and upon the opportunities for action that arise. The Commission of Fine Arts had from the outset a skilled and influential membership. The first chairman was Daniel Burnham, who had been in charge of the Board of Design for the Chicago World's Fair of 1893. He was one of the best-known architects in America, besides being the chief author of the so-called McMillan plan for Washington. Other members included F. L. Olmsted Jr, the country's leading landscape architect; a painter; a sculptor; and the President of the American Institute of Architects. The Commission had not been in existence for twelve months when proposals were referred to it for the building of the Lincoln Memorial. The Lincoln Memorial is one of the most important and majestic constructions in Washington. The Commission was asked 'to make suggestions as to the location, plans and designs . . . and to advise as to the best method of selecting the artists, sculptors and architects . . . to execute them'. The type of monument and the site in Potomac Park had already been proposed in the Plan of 1901, but there were counter-suggestions. One of these, strongly supported in real estate and automobile quarters, was for the memorial to take the form of a new highway to Gettysburg; another was for the erection of an obelisk similar to the Washington Memorial. The Commission rejected both these ideas, observing of the latter that to have two columns instead of one 'would degrade both shafts from the function of individual memorials to the position of a pair of colossal ornaments in a badly conceived architectural scheme', and that the case for having two obelisks might lead before long to proposals for having a dozen. After deliberating for some months, the Commission unanimously recommended the Potomac site:

> The comparative isolation of the Potomac Park site in the midst of a large area of undeveloped vacant land constitutes a peculiar advantage. For a long distance in every direction the surroundings are absolutely free for such treatment as would best enhance the effect of the memorial . . . Congress has here created a great park area, raised well above the highest river floods, and this area now awaits development . . . In judging the site of a memorial to

endure throughout the ages we must regard not what the location was, nor what it is to-day, but what it can be made for all time to come . . . It is impossible to overestimate the importance of giving to a monument of the size and significance of the Lincoln Memorial complete and undisputed domination over a large area, together with a certain dignified isolation from competing structures, or even from minor features unrelated to it . . . While this site is sufficiently isolated to give it dignity, it is readily accessible, being situated in a park which even in its partially developed state has become a place of great popular resort, and which is destined to be the chief centre of outdoor reunion in Washington, for people on foot as well as those in vehicles.

The Commission next nominated an architect, and approved his design, and then a sculptor (who happened to be a member of the Commission) and a designer for the murals. During the next several years the Commission worked closely with these three, selecting the type of marble and of granite to be used, and advising on the general grading, layout and approaches. By 1919 the Commission was considering schemes for planting, and in 1922 the Memorial was dedicated.

Even if the Commission had done nothing else during these years, its consultations concerning the Lincoln Memorial would have established it as an important body. Anyone who took any interest in Washington knew about the Lincoln Memorial; and anyone who knew about the Lincoln Memorial had heard of the Fine Arts Commission. But the Commission was also concerned at this time with two other very important schemes, the Arlington Memorial Bridge and the development and landscaping of the Mall. A bridge connecting the Lincoln Memorial directly across the Potomac with the Arlington Cemetery had been included in the Plan of 1901, and in 1921 Congress appointed a Commission to oversee the planning and construction of this bridge. Argument immediately began about the desirability of siting the bridge further up the river, away from the Memorial, and the Commission of Fine Arts was asked for its opinion. Taking the view that the Lincoln Memorial had been designed and built on the premise that the bridge to Arlington would be sited as originally proposed and that facilitating the flow of traffic was a secondary consideration, the Commission strongly recommended the Lincoln Memorial site, underlining the importance of the aesthetic advantage which would be secured by maintaining 'the one grand sweep from the Capitol to the Mansion on the heights of Arlington'. Towards the end of 1922, after a joint meeting with the Commission of Fine Arts and a conference with President Harding, the Bridge Commission opted for the Lincoln Memorial site. And a few months later the architect for the bridge was chosen by the

Bridge Commission from among three names suggested by the Commission of Fine Arts.

The proper development of the Mall was no less important an undertaking. The line from the Lincoln Memorial to the Washington Monument—a distance of over half a mile—continues straight on to the Capitol, and this other section of the main axis of Washington contains the Mall. A mile long and a quarter of a mile wide, this extensive open space had come to be used for a variety of purposes. In 1872 Congress had given the Baltimore and Potomac Railroad rights of way across the Mall, and had allowed a train-shed to block almost half its width. It was also occupied by the old Botanical Gardens, and, during the war, by an assortment of temporary buildings. In 1921 the Commission presented a report in which it gave its recommendations for the future development of the Mall. Roads, crossroads, walks and public buildings had to be accommodated. 'The landscape work in the Mall', the report stated,

> has now reached a point which will require an increasing amount of time and attention on the part of the Commission. The gradual disappearance of the temporary war buildings will leave large spaces for drives and planting. The location of the roads was in part fixed when the temporary buildings were located. While the treatment of the Mall must be progressive, yet large portions of it will call for attention in the immediate future.

This attention was indeed given, both by the Commission of Fine Arts and by the National Capital Park and Planning Commission, and planning and discussions went on through the 1920s. Not until 1931 did the Commission of Fine Arts approve the plan for roads and planting.

The Commission of Fine Arts thus established its position before and after the 1914—18 war as an influential and important body in matters of civic design. Its writ ran only in the District of Columbia but its fame spread much wider. By the 1920s Washington had become one of the world's great capital cities, and many Europeans had begun to realize that there was a great deal that America might teach them, if they had the wit to learn.

Sir Lionel Earle had never visited Washington, but he knew about the work of the Commission of Fine Arts and had that body in mind when he suggested to his Minister, the 27th Earl of Crawford, Minister of Works, that some similar organization should be set up in Britain. Lord Crawford was, in Earle's own words, 'a man of wide culture in all the realms of art and with a profound sense of the beautiful'.[30] Born in 1871, he had entered Parliament in 1895 and on the outbreak of war in 1914 he joined the RAMC as a private. He was extracted from the army in 1915 to join Asquith's cabinet as President of the Board of Agriculture, and thereafter was successively Lord Privy

Seal, Chancellor of the Duchy of Lancaster and First Commissioner of Works. In spite of occupying these high offices, Crawford's more profound and lifelong interest was in art and artistic affairs. He published a study of Donatello in 1903 and *The Evolution of Italian Sculpture* in 1909. He became a trustee of the National Gallery and of the National Portrait Gallery, and chairman of the Council for the Preservation of Rural England. Although sometimes thought to be brusque and dictatorial he was always imaginative and open to new ideas, and after the war he was widely regarded as one of the leading proponents of artistic interests in the United Kingdom. It is not surprising that he and his Permanent Secretary seem always to have worked in the closest accord.

The proposal to set up some kind of architectural Commission charged with the duty of advising the Government on the artistic aspects of new developments was put to the Cabinet by Lord Crawford late in 1923, and the establishment of the Commission was announced towards the end of January, 1924. The geographical territory of the Commission that was then set up was England and Wales, and the Commissioners' remit was 'to enquire into and report upon such questions of public amenity or of artistic importance . . . as may be referred to them'; or, from 1953 onwards, to report on any developments which 'may appear to affect amenities of a national or public character'. It was a remarkable initiative. Town planning, both as a profession and as a bureaucratic process, was in its infancy in the 1920s. The first serious text-book on the subject had just been published.[31] Town design was not an activity which aroused a great deal of interest in Britain, where Le Corbusier's recent proposals were virtually unknown, and what was done in Washington attracted only occasional attention. Setting up the Commission was in fact a pragmatic move, intended principally but not exclusively to solve the war memorials problem. There had been very little prior public discussion. A few suggestions had been made for setting up, as had recently been done in France, a Ministry of the Fine Arts—after all there were or recently had been Ministries of almost everything else in Britain—but this idea attracted little support. When the idea of a Commission was put forward instead, influential people preferred it. They thought that a Commission would be less likely than a Ministry to degenerate into a means of conferring sinecure honours upon inconvenient political colleagues; everyone agreed that a Commission would be cheaper; and almost everyone agreed that in any case it was a good idea not to follow the example of the French.

The establishment of the first Commission was greeted with murmurs of august approval. *The Times* considered that it would

> soon win the confidence of those whom it is designed to help.
> There is little doubt that it will be frequently consulted. England's
> towns and villages are still busy putting themselves in order after

the war and expanding to meet the modern needs. The
Government itself and many a municipal or other public body
will be glad to turn to a sane standard of taste, a few simple
counsels founded upon consultation and experience. No one of
us but has had under his eye of recent years distressing examples
of opportunities wasted in the building or rebuilding of a London
street or the planning of a group of cottages, of downright
damage done to an ancient fabric—all through want of co-
ordination of design and the lack of a standard of reference. The
Fine Art Commission for England will give the needed advice
for nothing; and, if it works as it may be expected to do, those
who apply to it will find themselves not confronted with rigid
rules, but guided away from possible waste and error by collective
experience and taste. That, at any rate, is the effect in the
United States, where an excellent Fine Arts Commission has
been at work for 14 years. To study the illustrated reports which
that body submits to the President is to find instance after
instance in which waste, not only of opportunity but of money,
has been converted by wise counsels to simplicity and dignity
and by the practical experience garnered from the consideration
of hundreds of cases. In the same way, we may hope, the English
Fine Arts Commission . . . will gradually build up a store of
knowledge and a standard of taste from which the art of the
future may develop along sound lines. There is likely, indeed, to
be a steadily increasing scope for the Commission. Its authority,
devoid of compulsion, will make it a valuable rallying point for
such bodies as the Architecture Club, the London Society, and
the 'Scapa'. The miscellaneous control of our ancient churches,
which results in true preservation in one diocese and woeful
destruction in the next, might turn to it for some sort of unity.
And its advice will be the more readily taken because it has no
power to command . . . There were signs on all hands of a want
of standard and of order—not to mention good taste—in the arts
expressing public sentiment and public requirements, such as
the architecture of public buildings, statuary, town planning, the
laying out of parks . . . The knowledge that such a body exists
cannot fail to bring upon it very rapidly an increasing rush of
demands for its advice, in years when there is much building
and rebuilding, when towns are expanding and garden cities
and other means of relieving congestion are needed on all sides,
and big schemes are on foot for the housing of the artisan classes
and not all the war memorials are yet finished and in place.[32]

The Royal Institute of British Architects exuded even greater
confidence in the Commission's future and in its own superior
judgement. The Commission's influence, the *Journal of the* RIBA
declared,

will gradually tend to establish a higher standard of public taste. The mere fact of its creation shows that the public are willing to be guided further along the path of aesthetic perception upon which their feet are already, although perhaps as yet somewhat falteringly, placed.[33]

And the editor added that the establishment of the Commission 'fulfills the long-cherished desires of architects, and in particular those of the Royal Institute'.

These comments, even if they serve for nothing else, remind us how far away we are today from the world of the 1920s. There is nothing unfamiliar, certainly, in the concern shown about money. But we stand astonished at the touching faith of our ancestors in a 'store of knowledge and standard of taste' which will allow art to develop 'along sound lines'; in 'a few simple counsels' to which everyone will be glad to listen; in a 'standard of reference' which will prevent all distressing waste of architectural opportunities; in a 'collective experience and taste' which will leave no room for waste or error; in the idea of a public which gropes and stumbles along 'the path of aesthetic perception' but is willing to be guided by a newly established Royal Commission and the Royal Institute of British Architects. It all seems remarkably ingenuous and remarkably unreal. And it was unreal—except for the war memorials, which are mentioned more than once; they were real enough, the Cenotaph in the Mall, the Scottish National War Memorial under construction on the Castle rock and literally thousands more scattered through the length and breadth of the United Kingdom.

There is some evidence that the Commission was rather casually set up. Thus it is referred to in early correspondence as the Fine Arts Commission (presumably after the Washington example), but on 25 March, when it had been in existence for two months, Sir Lionel wrote to the head of the Treasury saying,

> In reply to your letter of the 20th instant—which I have just received on my return from the North—in reference to the Fine Arts Commission, if the Commission itself prefers 'Fine Art', I see no objection.

Thus the Commission seems to have been responsible for the extraordinary title under which it operates, and which obscures its nature and functions from everyone who is not 'in the know'. At the same time doubts were raised about the scope of the Commission's activities. Sir Lionel Earle had told Lord Crawford that Wales and Scotland were excluded: 'if Scotland at any rate had been included, the personnel of the Commission would have been varied'. Crawford agreed with this line of thinking: 'I do not think that Scotland would accept decisions from so predominatingly southern a personnel'.[34] Nevertheless, the first secretary to the Commission was sufficiently

unsure of the position to write to Earle asking what the views of the
Government were. Sir Lionel was in no doubt. 'There is no question',
he wrote back, 'that the Fine Arts Commission was limited to England
proper, and neither Scotland nor Wales are at the present moment
incorporated in the body'. He further explained, in a letter to Sir
Russell Scott, that

> if either Scotland or Wales like to join up with the English body,
> it was always contemplated that they would be welcome. At the
> same time, they might prefer to have Commissions of their own.
> We have always taken the line that we did not want to force
> Scotland and Wales to join up with the English body if they
> prefer to have their own Advisory Commission, and with this
> view the present Secretary for Scotland, I know, strongly agrees.
> To do otherwise than what we have done might create a
> grievance, and this must be avoided at all costs.

That left the coverage question almost as unsettled as ever, but in
the meantime a more pressing problem had to be dealt with, for it
was discovered that the new Commission was without any agreed
terms of reference. Lord Crawford had suggested the following:

> To enquire into such questions of public amenity or of artistic
> interest and importance as may be referred to them by H M
> Government, and to report thereon:
>
> Furthermore, to give advice on similar questions when so
> requested by public or semi-public bodies, where it appears to
> the Royal Commission that their intervention would be
> advantageous.

Sir Lionel was not too happy about this form of words. Is not 'public
amenity', he asked, 'a bit wide and dangerous? Would not that
include the placing of lavatories and such questions, which could
hardly, as a rule, come under the purview of this important body?'
He also disliked the word 'intervention' in connection with the
activities of public bodies; 'It might frighten them from referring
matters' to the Commission. Would not 'advice' be better? But Lord
Crawford did not give way. He argued that 'public amenity' was right
precisely because it was wide:

> No doubt it may be construed to cover various topics which it
> would not be worth our while to discuss, but you must read that
> ugly phrase in connection with the discretion retained by the
> Royal Commission to withhold their intervention, if we do not
> think action on our part would be advantageous.

And as for 'intervention', he agreed that it raised a serious problem:
'the last thing we desire is to alarm public authorities'. But the terms
of reference stated in so many words that 'we only give advice when
so requested', and therefore no public authority need be alarmed.
Later, however, Lord Crawford changed his mind, and 'intervention'

became 'assistance', 'our object being to minimise the danger of making public authorities fear executive action or interference on our part'.

When the setting up of the Commission was announced — many weeks before doubts arose about its scope and terms of reference — its membership was already decided. The Commission's first chairman was the Earl of Crawford, the Government of which he had been a member having just been defeated at the General Election in December 1923. He was supported by one other non-professional, Lord Curzon. Curzon had been Viceroy of India before the war and had recently served as Foreign Secretary under three Prime Ministers, resigning with Crawford and his other colleagues on the fall of Lloyd George's government. He was, according to *The Times*, 'notable for his munifence and skill in preserving ancient buildings'. There were four architects: Sir Aston Webb, President of the Royal Academy, who had designed several prominent public buildings in the 1890s, including the Victoria and Albert Museum; Sir Reginald Blomfield, chief architect to the Imperial War Graves Commission; A. J. Gotch, President of the RIBA; and Sir Edward Lutyens, famous for his country houses, his work in New Delhi and the Cenotaph. The other members were T. H. Mawson, President of the Town Planning Institute, and Sir D. Y. Cameron, a highly respected RA. It was certainly an establishment team, and the average age was over sixty. The RIBA approved the membership: 'its composition appears to be apt'. But Sir Lionel Earle was not so sure. In June, when the Commission had been in existence for only five months, an interesting conversation took place between Sir Lionel and H. C. Bradshaw, the first secretary to the Commission. The memorandum of this conversation reads as follows:

> Personnel, Sir Lionel said, is the crux. He is not altogether satisfied with the original personnel of the English Commission. Orthodoxy as represented by the Royal Academy is perhaps too numerously represented to the exclusion of modernists. But it was expedient to avoid offending the susceptibilities of the R.A. at the outset. Certain modifications in the personnel are about to be made. Sir Aston Webb and Mr Mawson are in bad health.

This sounded ominous for Sir Aston Webb and Mr Mawson, as indeed it was. Both were replaced on the Commission within the next twelve months, Sir Aston having already reached the age of seventy-six.

To study the work of the English Commission is not the purpose of this chapter. But it is worth noticing how the Commission performed in its first few years. According to the Secretary of the English Commission, the following matters were referred to it in 1924 and 1925:

The design and emplacement of public monuments.

The desirability of constructing a new bridge across the Thames and of preserving an old one.

The design of telephone kiosks and Post Office signs.

The architectural style, heights, projection and orientation of important additions to public buildings.

The design of a large new municipal building and of an Exhibition building in Paris.

The layout of a cemetery and questions arising in the development of a town planning scheme.

The decoration of the interiors of public buildings by mural painting or otherwise.

The desirability of granting Royal Charters to Art Societies.

This is certainly a mixed bag. There is everything from telephone kiosks to town planning, and monuments—i.e. war memorials nine times out of ten—appear yet again.

Some further information is to be gained from the Commission's early Reports. The work of the Commission first came to public notice when in 1924 it was asked by the Lord President of the Council to comment on the aesthetic aspects of the proposal to build a new bridge across the Thames just south of St Paul's Cathedral. In its reply, the Commission did not spend much time on the aesthetic aspects because it took the view that

all considerations of access, construction, town planning and vista are subordinate to the central and all-important risk to the Cathedral itself. The piers supporting the dome are in a precarious condition; serious fears have been entertained as to the safety of the dome itself . . . Heavy motor traffic is increasing . . . Further shaking of the Cathedral fabric may lead to a catastrophe.

Had it not been for these considerations, the Commission stated, it would have recorded a 'sense of disappointment' that the bridge had not been planned to lead to the southern transept as its axial point; but the preservation of the Cathedral was an overriding necessity, and it was therefore unthinkable that the proposed new bridge and its approaches should be built. These observations formed the Commission's First Report, a document of not much more than five hundred words published in July, 1924. For a variety of reasons the bridge scheme was soon afterwards abandoned.

Two years later the Commission's Second Report appeared, more substantial and far more wide-ranging. Some matters, the Commission stated, had been referred to it in confidence, and the Commission thought it 'inopportune' to publish its replies in these cases. It seems clear, however, that monuments and statues figured largely in the confidential referrals, and the Commission was not averse to making its general views on these quite plain. Most people, according to the Commission, believed that 'the beauty of a town is necessarily enhanced by the erection of a monument'; but the truth was that 'monuments should be accepted only if, in addition to their purpose as memorials, they have definite artistic value'. The Commission had accordingly exercised 'a protective and restraining influence'. With statues it was the same. Statues were often proposed by 'powerful and influential committees', who usually wanted them in crowded thoroughfares or public parks. But many proposals had been refused. An offer had come from America to erect a monument to Sir William Blackstone beside the porch of the Law Courts, opening onto the Strand, but this had been disapproved; and, in general, it had been 'felt inadvisable to multiply statues in the London parks with the freedom exercised in Paris, Rome and Berlin'.

The Commission had also been consulted about extensions to public buildings. Advice had been given relating to the National Portrait Gallery, the Natural History Museum, and University College. In this last case, 'a skilful design for a colonnade' had been turned down because although it provided convenience it provided no new accommodation and would have obscured the fine central façade by William Wilkins, visible from Gower Street. This gives added meaning to the Commissioners' statement; 'Whenever possible we have advised in the interest of conservation'. But the Commissioners were not merely conservative in their approach. Thus they gave sound progressive advice on a perennial problem that is to this day discussed and often badly misunderstood. They did not hesitate to report, they said, that no architect was under any obligation to copy the style of a building for which he was designing an extension:

> To do so would entail a mechanical reproduction of material or method, while such addition might injure the unity and proportions of the original structure . . . The architect should be free to make the addition according to his own ideas and in conformity with the latest requirements of . . . design.

Two other points of interest emerge from this Second Report. The first is that the Government did not consult the Commissioners about the highly controversial proposal to demolish and replace Rennie's Waterloo Bridge across the Thames which had been completed in 1817. The Commissioners therefore asked that their views should be heard. The London County Council accordingly heard the Commission's representations against demolition, but the representations were made by Lord Crawford after, and not before, a decision to demolish the bridge had been announced. Lord Crawford informed the LCC that the bridge was 'a great achievement of the metropolis—the only monument in London of the nineteenth century which commands world-wide admiration', and that it combined with another great building of an earlier date, namely

Somerset House, to produce a scene of 'extraordinary distinction'. He also reminded the Council that they had decided on an earlier occasion to demolish the church of St Mary-le-Strand because it obstructed traffic, but had later reversed their decision with advantage to traffic-flow as well as to architecture. The Council hesitated and the row dragged on. At one point Lutyens, when consulted officially, went so far as to suggest that, as the existing bridge could not be widened without damaging its appearance, a new and more serviceable bridge should be built over the top of it. This suggestion was greeted with a good deal of derision. The matter was debated in the House of Commons, to no advantage, and in 1926 demolition was finally ordered. But as if to conciliate the opposition, the Commissioners were then invited by the LCC to promote a competition for the design of the new bridge; and in doing this the Commissioners advised that Assessors must take account of the visual relation of the new bridge not only to nearby buildings but also to some more distant such as Somerset House and St Paul's Cathedral; and they further suggested that the arches of the new bridge might incorporate the terminal arches of the existing bridge. The second point arising from the Report is the Commissioners' comment on the Disposal of Churches Bill, which was before Parliament in 1926; they were, they reported, 'opposed in principle to a Measure which provides for the destruction of some twenty national monuments of great historic and architectural value'. That this proposal, or something like it, continued to be made into the 1930s shows how far the conservation movement has progressed in the last sixty years.

The Commission's Third Report was published towards the end of 1928. This Report is interesting in that it is concerned almost entirely with bridges. Throughout the 1920s the construction of new bridges and the reconstruction of old bridges was being undertaken all over the country as a consequence of the remarkable growth of road traffic. What was built was seldom good. There was a tendency, the Commission observed, to think of bridges as merely utilitarian; but their visual impact upon the landscape was in fact profound, and the aesthetic qualities of their design should therefore be considered from the earliest stage. Engineers paid little if any attention to 'the choice of colour and material, the relevance of the bridge to the immediate neighbourhood, and its character in relation to the general surroundings'. It was therefore essential that architects should be employed alongside the bridge engineers. Previously, this had not been necessary. Men like Rennie had been 'guided by the fine traditions of eighteenth century design'. But it was evidently useless to rely on this support any longer.

Two bridges were singled out for special mention, both of them near London. At Marlow-on-Thames it had been decided to replace

the existing suspension bridge with one built of concrete. Strong
objections had been raised about the design, and the Commission, at
the request of the local authority, had made representations to the
Ministry of Transport. The Commission's fundamental criticism was
that

> the proposed bridge . . . does not appear to be designed in
> relation to the river and the town of Marlow. It is prepared in
> relation to the road rather than the township, doubtless for the
> convenience of through traffic. [It] will impose a new scale on
> the little township, which is notable for its domestic street
> architecture dating from the seventeenth and eighteenth
> centuries. Moreover it will injure a well known section of river
> scenery, which is in fact an exceptionally unspoilt reach of the
> Thames.

As for the use of concrete, that was not condemned out of hand,
although it was noted that concrete 'tends to shabbiness and
frequently to surface decay'. What the Commissioners objected to
was the attempt to use concrete in such a way as to imitate masonry.
There was to be a balustrade cast in concrete, and the suspension
rods carrying the roadway were designed to look like stone pillars.
'Concrete', the Commission remarked, 'should be treated honestly . . .
without the addition of irrelevant architectural detail'. In a rather
similar way the new bridge at Richmond was found to be unsuitable
in character for its site and its environment. It exhibited 'a dramatic
and fortified appearance' which conflicted with 'a peaceful landscape
. . . the slow moving stream and the widespread expanse of
meadowland studded with fine trees'. These Reports are brief and
they deal specifically with only a few cases. But it would not be easy
to find more serious faults to comment upon. Misuse of materials,
building out of scale, architectural assertiveness—these are fundamental and very serious faults, and they were destined soon to form all
too large a part of the national heritage.

It is thus clear that from the very beginning the English Commission
did what it could to stem the rising tide of bad design, and gave
much useful and reasonable advice. It was sympathetic to conservation, including the conservation of domestic architecture, at a time
when conservation was a great deal less supported than it is now; it
laid down some sound general principles; and, although it was
sometimes not consulted when it should have been, it was involved
in several major architectural and town planning decisions. In short,
it proved itself to be a worthwhile body, and both Sir Lionel Earle
and Lord Crawford must have been encouraged by its performance.
Nevertheless, one is bound to add that its circumstances were rather
special. It was not very visible beyond a radius of thirty miles from
the centre of London, where most of its cases were found. And much
of its success was due to the fact that more often than not it reported,

in effect, to Sir Lionel Earle, whose creation it was and who had set it up precisely because he wanted to receive advice about London problems. There was therefore reason to doubt whether a similar body working in different circumstances would do equally well. Nevertheless, the experiment looked as if it might be worth repeating elsewhere.

The idea that some similar provision should be made for Scotland had been in the minds of several people from the time that the English Commission was first discussed. It is therefore not surprising that the decision to set up the first Royal Fine Art Commission had scarcely been announced in 1924 when the Royal Incorporation of Architects in Scotland resolved to send a representation to the Secretary of State recommending the appointment of a Commission for Scotland. Soon afterwards the Town Council of Dundee wrote to the Scottish Office proposing either that there be a Scots Commission or, alternatively, that several Scots members should be co-opted to the existing Commission; 'With so many town planning schemes in Scotland at present . . . the advice of the Commission would be of great advantage to the Local Authorities'. At the end of the year Glasgow officially supported the co-option proposal.

Early in 1925 the Scottish Office wrote to the Office of Works asking 'how the English Commission is getting on, and how much it costs; also, whether the Office of Works think that a separate Commission for Scotland would be best, and/or cheapest'. The reply, as far as expense went, should have been reasonably reassuring; the English Commission was not costing more than £1 000 per annum. How it was 'getting on' was answered by sending a short list of the kinds of problems that it had so far commented upon. As for a separate Commission, the Office of Works (that is to say, Sir Lionel Earle) was opposed to the idea: 'it was preferable that Scottish members should be added to the English Commission'; but the English Commission was to be asked for its opinion.

The Commission considered the matter at its thirteenth meeting, in March 1925. Lord Crawford seems to have known what he wanted. He reminded the Commissioners that the balance in the numbers of 'laymen' and of 'artists' had been established after careful consideration when the Commission began, and he emphasized that this balance ought not to be disturbed. More frequent meetings in order to take care of Scots problems would be difficult, as so many Commissioners were busy professional men. Nor would it be easy for a sub-committee to visit Scotland. No doubt a single-commission system would in principle be best; but the burden of adding Scottish problems to the existing Commission's responsibilities might prove to be overwhelming. The Commissioners agreed. In spite of all this, the Secretary was instructed to write to the Office of Works saying that at the present juncture the Commissioners were reluctant to express a definite opinion, but as there seemed to be no hurry to reach a decision they hoped to discuss the matter with the Office of Works and with the Scottish Office. This temporizing may have been due to a feeling that insufficient experience of the working of the Commission had yet been gained, and there is more than a hint in the Minutes that some Commissioners were concerned that a purely Scottish body would be too parochial and too personal; but they may also have known that Sir Lionel thought that a separate Scottish commission would be too expensive.

After further discussions had taken place, the Secretary for Scotland (as he was then called) decided to call a conference to consider the alternatives, one of which was to do nothing 'pending further experience and consideration'. This conference took place in Edinburgh in April, 1926, and was chaired by the Secretary for Scotland. Those represented, besides the Royal Fine Art Commission, were the Town Councils of Aberdeen, Dundee, Edinburgh, Glasgow and Paisley, and the Convention of Royal Burghs. The towns spoke first. All felt the need for expert advice; town planning and war memorials were particularly mentioned; it was 'generally agreed that Scots cities contain some things which they would be better without'. Aberdeen wanted a separate body for Scotland. The others all voted for one Commission suitably enlarged, chiefly on the ground that greater weight would be attached to the advice 'of such outstanding men as those who served on the [existing] Commission'; Edinburgh improved on this by arguing that Scotland hardly needed a separate commission as it was already well represented by Lord Crawford and Sir D. Y. Cameron. The Convention of Royal Burghs thought that art was universal and that one commission would therefore be sufficient.

Lord Crawford was then invited to give the views of the Commission. He began by explaining how the Commission worked, without powers of intervention. The American Fine Art Commission, he said, had started in the same way, but had later been given statutory powers. No doubt the Royal Fine Art Commission would also, in due course, be given 'compulsory powers'. After referring to the new roads being laid down throughout the country, which were being lined with ugly buildings and were rapidly becoming 'canals of vulgarity', he told the conference that although in principle one national body was the right thing, it would in practice be unworkable. Sites often had to be visited more than once, and English members would find it as hard to visit sites in Scotland as Scots members would find it hard to attend meetings in London. He was reluctantly driven to the conclusion that a separate commission for Scotland was the only solution. He added, however, that there should be regular communication on matters of principle, and joint meetings on questions of national importance.

Sir D. Y. Cameron 'agreed with every word Lord Crawford had said', although he foresaw difficulties in 'manning' a Scottish commission. He was impressed by the extraordinary unanimity of the Scottish representatives in wanting advice on matters of art.

The discussion that followed was brief. However universal art might be, it had been made plain that if Scotland was to receive any advice on the subject it would have to be given by a Scots commission; so Scotland bowed to the inevitable. Only the details remained to be settled. A second conference was called in September, attended by members of 'representative artistic societies' such as the Royal Incorporation of Architects in Scotland and the Glasgow Institute of Fine Arts; Sir John Stirling Maxwell as chairman of the Council for Ancient Monuments and Buildings; Sir George Washington Browne; Lord Crawford and Sir D. Y. Cameron from the Commission; and a few other qualified persons. It was agreed that a commission very much on the lines of the English Commission should be set up. This advice was in due course accepted by the Government, and the Royal Fine Art Commission for Scotland came into existence eleven months later, on 22 August, 1927. There were nine Commissioners including the Chairman, who was Sir John Stirling Maxwell. Only two architects were included – Sir George Washington Browne and Sir Robert Lorimer – and one engineer. The Commission was thus much ·the same size as its London-based counter-part but less 'professional' in its composition – unless painters are included as professionals; the Scots Commission had two. What was almost certainly more important, the Commission was not given a full-time Secretary. Possibly this was regarded by the Treasury as a sensible economy, but it seems likely that it did more than anything else to render the new Commission largely ineffective for over thirty years.

Between the passing of the first genuine housing and town planning Act in 1919 and the establishment of the two Royal Commissions, there thus elapsed periods of five and then a further three years. The time-gap was not enormous; but the change of emphasis was. The Act was concerned with housing, the Commissions with beauty and amenity. Unfortunately, the Commissions were apparently not expected to affect the working of the 1919 Act, or of any subsequent housing legislation, in any way. The practicalities of town planning, which in the 1920s principally meant the practicalities of low-cost housing, were not seen as touching the business of the Commission. Housing was the pressing problem, as in a sense it always is. It required immediate action, and it deserved very careful and imaginative treatment. But the 1919 Act, in spite of some good provisions, was operated in a desperately limited and utilitarian way. The politicians of the day thought about housing, and it is to their credit that they also thought about beauty and amenity; but they thought about them in almost completely separated compartments

of life and legislation. Neither was planned to affect the other. This
was a very damaging mistake, for it nullified many good intentions.
In consequence housing and planning under Government auspices
very soon settled down on strictly utilitarian lines, and they have
tended to continue in that way, while the idea has been perpetuated
that beauty and public amenity are something to be touched in
afterwards, here and there. Furthermore, this 1920s attitude of mind,
which still persists, has downgraded architecture and town-planning
(which nowadays face quite enough difficulties of their own), and
has compelled the two Royal Commissions to appear largely
supernumerary and otiose, and to work all the time against the grain.
'Art', James Lethaby once wrote, 'is not a sauce applied to ordinary
cooking'.[35] But this seems to be pretty well what large numbers of
people think it is. This mistake has helped to condemn British
architecture and town planning, for many decades, to some very
ordinary cooking indeed.

NOTES AND REFERENCES TO CHAPTER 1

1. Le Corbusier was an enthusiast for standardization. Within a
   neighbourhood or town he favoured 'a consistent standard and
   complete uniformity of detail. In such conditions the mind is calm.'
   Urbanisme (Paris, 1980) p. 67 (1st edn. 1924).
2. Diderot's arithmetic is not entirely reliable.
3. E. Howard, Tomorrow: *A Peaceful Path to Real Reform* ed. F. J.
   Osborn (London, 1946) p. 44.
4. Michel Ragon, *Histoire Mondiale de l'Architecture et de L'Urbanisme
   Modernes* (Paris, 1972) vol. 2, p. 135.
5. For the phrases here I am indebted to the authors of *The Plan for
   Milton Keynes*.
6. K. Clark, *Civilisation* (London, 1969) p. 320.
7. *Remaking Cities* (London, 1980).
8. Michael Davie, 'In the Future now: A Report from California'
   quoted in, A. Blowers *et al.* (eds.), *The Future of Cities* (London,
   1974) p. 291ff.
9. Le Corbusier, *Urbanisme*, p. 88.
10. J. Hook, *The Sack of Rome, 1527* (London, 1972) p. 30.
11. D. Hay, *The Church in Italy in the 15th Century* (Cambridge,
    1977) p. 47.
12. Back-to-backs also continued to be built. Their building was made
    illegal in 1909, but the prohibition did not apply to developments
    which had already been approved. As a result, the number of such
    houses were still being added to in the 1930s. 'The chief character-
    istic of the back-to-back houses is that one has to go outside,
    through the public street, in order to get to the lavatory'. S. Muthesius,
    The English Terraced House (London, 1982) p. 140.

13. R. Unwin, *Town Planning in Practice* (London, 1909) p. 2.
14. J. M. Keynes, *The End of Laissez-Faire* (London, 1926) p. 35.
15. Ravetz, *Remaking Cities*, p. 29.
16. Yet Voysey's buildings, although seemingly traditional, were also *avant-garde*; and Mackintosh's originality never cut loose from the influence of Scottish castles, Scottish towers and lairds' houses.
17. *The Studio* (Apr. 1933).
18. *Journal of the RIBA*, vol. 31, p. 421.
19. Wheel-barrows were in use in the Middle Ages. There is a drawing of one in a French manuscript of 1470.
20. Leon Moussinac, in *The Studio* (Apr. 1932).
21. It is perhaps worth noting that Raymond Unwin was employed by the Office of Works from 1915 to 1919.
22. L. Earle, *Turn over the Page* (London, 1935) p. 177.
23. *Ibid.*, p. 171.
24. *Ibid.*, p. 171.
25. R. Unwin, in *Journal of the RIBA*, vol. 29, p. 77.
26. *Ibid.*
27. Reported in *Town Planning Review*, vol. 7 (1917) p. 105.
28. J. M. McKean, in, Michael Raeburn (ed.), *Architecture of the Western World* (London, 1980) p. 236.
29. In the following pages I have drawn upon an excellent study by Sue A. Kohler, *The Commission of Fine Arts: A Brief History, 1910–1976*.
30. Earle, *Turn over the Page*, p. 166.
31. S. D. Adshead, *Town Planning and Town Development* (London, 1923).
32. *The Times*, 24 Jan. 1924.
33. *Journal of the RIBA*, vol. 31, p. 198.
34. Crawford to Bradshaw, 21 Mar. 1924.
35. Quoted in, N. Pevsner, *Victoria and After* (London, 1982) p. 228.

CHAPTER TWO

Amenity and Architecture

The Royal Fine Art Commission for England and Wales and the Royal Fine Art Commission for Scotland were both active from the very beginning of their existence in dealing with submissions relating to new developments. It is perhaps for this reason that there is no record of their interpretation of their remit. That it had to be interpreted is clear, because the form of words that had been chosen for the remit left the Commissioners to decide, in several important respects, what their instructions really meant. In its first Report, which did not appear until 1960, the Scots Commission stated that in the early years there had been 'many deliberations to determine [the Commission's] precise scope and powers', and that 'frequent interchange of views with the Commission for England and Wales' had taken place. But the result of all these deliberations and mutual consultations is not recorded. Yet the problem of precisely what the Commissions were intended to encourage and protect—never mind how they were to do it—was at the heart of their existence. Set up quite independently of the passage of the first British Town Planning Act of any importance, and also of the first major housing Acts, they were clearly not expected to concern themselves with the provision of houses nor with the problems of industrial zoning and the like. They were to think about higher things. But what exactly were these higher things? The Commissioners faced two crucial questions, the answers to which, one would have thought, they had to agree about at least in a general way before they could do anything else. These questions were: 'What is to be understood by artistic importance?' and 'What is to be understood by public amenity?'

It is easy to see that both of these concepts must command respect. We must all approve whatever contributes to public amenity, and value whatever is of artistic importance. But unanimity of this kind is of no help. The difficulty—the very great difficulty—is to agree, in particular instances, especially when these instances are contemporaneous with ourselves, as to the artistic merit of a building, or a statue, or an open space, or whether or how much it contributes to amenity. There must, we suppose, be some principles, or at least some precedents, to guide us in reaching a decision. And indeed there are. Volumes—it might be said libraries—have been written on the history of architecture and on architectural aesthetics and architectural judgements. But there are no final, no inescapable conclusions. Professor Gombrich tells us that scepticism is still in order when authorities on aesthetics are heard 'pontificating about the Beautiful, the Sublime, or the Expressive'. As for amenity, it has been far less discussed, but the scope for disagreement is perhaps equally great. An amenity is something agreeable; a glass of wine, perhaps, or proximity to the shops, or the trees in a London square. But instances of this kind do not take us very far; the subject is vastly more complicated. Indeed, it is idle to hope either in the case of architecture or amenity for a set of final answers. Formula-hunting—so characteristic of our age—is a waste of time. What is not a waste of time is to ensure, as far as possible, that we understand the problem.

It is at least clear that public amenity and artistic importance are not the same. Artistic importance is an elevated idea, whereas public amenity is something easier, more relaxing and more extensive. Artistic importance in cities is provided basically by good architecture; what that consists of will be considered shortly. Public amenity, on the other hand, while it may be held to include the provision of buildings of high artistic quality, covers much more. Indeed, it easily covers too much. Sir Lionel Earle was quite right, as he so often was, in describing the notion of public amenity as 'a bit wide and dangerous'.[1] There is really no limit to what can be included under the heading of amenity. Whatever is wanted is agreeable to someone, and, we would then have to say, is an amenity to someone. A bus shelter, however ugly and conspicuous, is an amenity; a public lavatory is an amenity; there are those for whom a hot-dog stall set up in the middle of St Mark's Square in Venice would be an amenity. These things are or might be convenient and useful; and there is no end to the conveniences and utilities of modern life. But the Commissions were certainly not set up to advise on the location and design of public lavatories, although in an extreme case they might feel obliged to do so. We must therefore first of all distinguish between amenities that are useful and 'necessary', such as rubbish dumps, and those that are pleasant and agreeable. The word amenity is as commonly used in the second sense as in the first. Thus when a proposed urban development is turned down on the ground that it would be detrimental to the amenity of a neighbourhood or locality, it is evident that what is at stake is the agreeableness of the place, the scope that it provides for a varied and pleasant life rather than mere existence.

Many items contribute to this kind of amenity. An attractive and civilized city has well-dressed shop windows, a variety of restaurants and cafés, a theatre, an art gallery, places where people can walk or sit at leisure, perhaps an open-air market. Some of these, as well as being agreeable or even artistic in nature, can also be useful. This means that one kind of amenity shades into the other. An art gallery may contain a restaurant; a café can have a highly artistic interior (the Willow Tea Rooms in Glasgow were once an outstanding example); a modern shopping centre can provide a pleasant and even artistic location for people to meet and talk and relax, as well as to spend money. All of these are, or can be, agreeable amenities. None need be merely useful. Without such amenities a city would be dull and inelegant, and its life would be prosaic and restricted.

In interpreting their remit, however, the Commissioners have always paid more attention to public space and to the public appearance of things than to interior design and uses. It is true that each of these affects the other, and it would therefore be absurd to consider any one of them in isolation. In many cases the Commissions have commented upon the suitability or otherwise of a given location for a proposed use; thus they have frequently objected to multi-storey car parks being built on highly visible sites, and have encouraged housing rather than commercial developments in quiet inner-city areas, especially near parks or riverside walks. As a rule, however, the Commissions have concentrated their attention upon the visible urban scene rather than upon the inner life of the city; the latter would be altogether too large a problem. But even when public amenity is understood as visible public amenity, what is meant by the word 'amenity' has to be carefully considered. The original meaning of the word becomes important. If we look back to past times we find that the idea of amenity used to be inseparable from the idea of peaceful and beautiful natural surroundings. According to the *Oxford English Dictionary* the word was used with this association as early as 1611: 'For amenity of situation . . . it doth farre excel all other cities'. Sixty years later Evelyn observed of Norwich that 'the suburbs are large, the prospects sweete, with other amenities, not omitting the flower-gardens'. And in 1762 Horace Walpole wrote of England as 'a country profusely beautified with the amenities of nature'. Not until 1866 do we find a different use when a contributor to the Cornhill Magazine wrote about 'the amenities of home life'. So for a long time the idea of amenity was associated with ideas of whatever is pleasant or agreeable and is also provided by nature, fertile open country, trees, woods, rivers and far-away hills; such items as might remind us of the beautiful, remote, meticulously painted background in a picture by Bellini or Giorgione.

These variations of meaning do not provide absolute distinctions, nor are they always separable from the idea of artistic excellence. Useful amenities—amenities of convenience—are not necessarily distinct from agreeable amenities nor from the amenities of space and nature; a restaurant or an open-air market may have a fine 'natural' setting, and may itself contribute to that setting. Even

1. Le Corbusier, 'Ville Contemporaine'. The parks at the base of the skyscrapers.

2. 'Changing London' by C. R. W. Nevinson (1920). 'Towns have been built by a process of replacement and accretion going on for several centuries'.

3. Building the Empire State Building, New York, 1931. '. . . ever loftier skyscrapers—
   an American art form'.

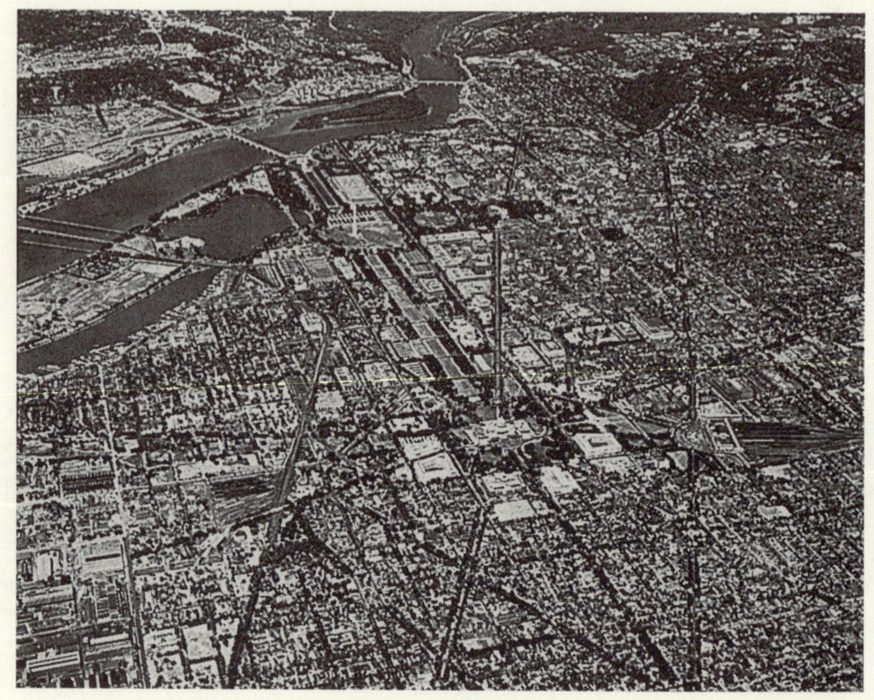

4. Washington, D.C. The Capitol, the Washington Monument, and the Lincoln Memorial. The White House is to the right of the Monument.

5. Swans on the *Witham*: central shopping area, Lincoln. 'Without the amenity of space and nature, there would be no time to stand and stare'.

6. Bath. 'What really let nature in was the planning of Bath'.

7. 'The Ashes of Phocion' by Poussin. '. . . the splendour of nature and the splendour of antiquity'.

8. The theatre at Manaos, Brazil. 'What is beneath the observer's feet is also part of the scene'.

prosaically useful amenities may sometimes be provided with an artistic content; Pevsner has argued that some of the best 'modern' British architecture is to be found in the stations of the London Underground built in the early 1930s, Arnos Grove 'perhaps more impeccably satisfactory than any other'. But the Commissioners, very wisely, have never much interested themselves in the usefulness of the merely useful, nor in the provision made for theatres, restaurants and the like. They have commented occasionally on the safety aspects of traffic arrangements, and frequently on the provision and location of car parks and on the routeing of by-passes. They have not infrequently suggested that there should be greater provision of housing in central areas, for it is people who give life to the town. Areas without housing, given over entirely to shops, offices and workshops, are dead areas when work is over; and likewise housing that is without any kind of agreeable or artistic amenity is a second-rate provision. A housing scheme can itself be agreeable, and even possess at least a touch of artistic quality; indeed, it ought to do so. The Commissions have always recognized this. But they were not established in order to encourage house-building, and it is therefore reasonable that most of their effort, architecture apart, has been in helping to create or preserve important examples of the amenity of place; appearance and atmosphere, space and nature.

To those immersed in the inescapable anxieties of employment, housing and traffic-flow, these may appear to be second-order problems. But to downgrade them in this way is a serious mistake. Beauty and amenity are among the highest values that we have; they provide the setting for a civilized life. This may sound ambitious or pretentious, but should not. One might think of amenity as a holiday setting, but it would be a holiday more cultural and less commercial than holidays now often are. One might depict it as a setting for leisure, but leisure suggests the twentieth century idea of leisure activities, which suggests in turn that something is being sold. One might describe it as a setting for agreeable idleness, except that idleness is sometimes held to be a sin. Perhaps what is most essential to public amenity is a negative: absence of pressure to move on. Without the amenity of space and nature, there can be no time to stand and stare: 'the freedom with which a person can walk about and look around is a useful guide to the civilized quality of an urban area'.[2] To some extent, amenity is an atmosphere. This atmosphere cannot be created by urban design, but may be encouraged by it. Thus there are many French cities and towns, as Gutkind observed, 'which have made a greater contribution to city planning than Paris . . . What is invaluable is the atmosphere, the spirit of Paris—the imponderables which belong just as much to the essential nature of a city as to its external appearance and physical form'.[3] The lay-out of Paris, along with the vast variety of interesting buildings within the city, supports and encourages, and is indeed essential to, *la vie parisienne*: the café life, the street markets, the artists with their easels by the Seine. Some British towns likewise possess amenity of this kind, at least in limited areas: Bath, which was an eighteenth century spa; Chichester, a prosperous market town; Edinburgh, which in the later eighteenth century deliberately set out to be elegant. In all of these, and in others, there is a glimpse of an ideal city, that city for which, according to the most enlightened opinion of the eighteenth century, there were four requirements: 'de belles constructions, de l'eau, de l'air, de la verdure'. To think of the city in this way is the first step to improving it.

No progress will be made, however, if we think of the beauty and amenity of the city separately from the citizens themselves. Urban beauty and amenity are to be enjoyed, in principle by everyone. And this was recognized throughout most of European history until the twentieth century by providing within the city a place of special assembly, an agora or square or market place, grander and more relaxed than the surrounding streets, where the citizens might meet and talk as well as carry on business. Such squares are adaptable, and they can be used for a variety of purposes; the most famous agora of all became at one time, we are told, 'the resort of all the idle and profligate in Athens'. Paved and formal squares have many uses, and the twentieth century has found them particularly serviceable as car parks. Every kind of amenity can be wasted or abused; that depends on the citizens. But the usefulness of city squares, as generally understood in the twentieth century, is not their real importance. What they provide that is irreplaceable is a sense of identity and a sense of freedom.

In the small towns of Italy, where near the centre of town the streets are often eight or ten feet wide, a square or piazza is invariably to be found, usually beside or in front of a church or some other public building. These piazzas are sometimes small and sometimes, as in Venice and Sienna, remarkably large, but whatever their size they give a feeling of liberation from the surrounding pattern of narrow streets and seemingly tall buildings. Entering them, one is suddenly free to linger and to absorb a little of the life and atmosphere of the place. There is a sense of enclosure and leisurely ease. And each of these squares with its surrounding buildings gives the city a sharper identity. It is the focus of interest and activity, providing the citizens with an image of the city to which they belong. The square symbolizes the city, and dominates it. This is obvious in small towns, but the same—or something very like the same—happens even in so large a city as Paris. There is no central square in Paris, but the *places* and buildings around the Louvre form a central group of such character and scale as to dominate even the enormous spread of the modern city.

Spaces like these also, of course, serve another function. They were planned to show off and to give emphasis to the civic and religious buildings around them. The Piazza del Campo at Sienna forms an almost theatrical stage in front of the lofty and imposing Palazzo Communale; at Bruges most of the principal buildings of the medieval town look onto the Great Market or the castle square; in countless small towns in England, France and Italy a square or market-place is the setting for the principal church and other important buildings. This means that we can stand back and see these buildings properly, and appreciate their style and proportions. And what is equally important, there is enough room to observe the relation between the forms of the various buildings; to note their uniformity or variety; to feel the effect of their size relative to one another and to the width and length of the square itself. The space that is laid out cannot be separated from the surrounding architecture, and is just as important.

We do not always recognize that many squares are elaborate and artistic entities, although not planned at any one time as they exist today.

> The unique relationship between the open area of the square, the surrounding buildings, and the sky above creates a genuine emotional experience comparable to the impact of any other work of art. It is only of secondary importance for this effect whether and to what extent in each instance specific functional demands are fulfilled. Obvious as this statement may be, in our age of over-rationalization the fact must be emphasised.[4]

St Peter's Square in Rome, St Mark's Square in Venice, the Place Vendôme in Paris and the Place Stanislas in Nancy are as much to be admired and in much the same way as the paintings of Canaletto, or Vermeer's View of Delft. Less can be claimed for less grand squares, but the same principles apply to them all. The Market Place in Cirencester, the Square in Kelso, are artistic open spaces, open spaces that are enclosed. There are also amorphous squares—Trafalgar Square is a good example; squares formed round a central feature, like the Piazza del Santo in Padua; and sequences of squares, as in Nancy. But whatever their form, they give a sense of space, a sense that can be ranked very high in the scale of artistic values. This sense, says Berenson,

> is something very positive and definite, able to confirm our consciousness of being, to heighten our feeling of vitality. Space-composition is the art which humanises the void, making of it an enclosed Eden . . . here there is more freedom, less is determined for one, although nothing is left to wayward fancy.[5]

City squares like those discussed above have little to do with nature, and are as much built as the Palazzo Vecchio itself. But they are open to the sky, and often provide views that are composed and sometimes distant. And this is as important as their social function, in allowing the citizens of the town to come spontaneously together, to trade, to talk, to see and to be seen. The public square is an artistic means—or at any rate it was an artistic means—of bringing the community to life.

Planned spaces of this kind were built in towns for centuries. And then, after the middle of the eighteenth century, the idea of having green spaces—spaces of nature—began to take hold. Almost every city now possesses some space of this kind, saved from being built on by the good sense of the citizens or the accidents of time. These spaces are useful, but they are more than that. For what would a city be that was all architecture, without open spaces, playgrounds, trees or parks? The simple answer is that it would not be much fun. And this is really an artless way of saying that it would lack amenity.

Some greenery was to be seen in seventeenth century cities, but it seldom amounted to more than a few carefully planted small trees and shrubs. But the park or pleasure garden made a fairly early appearance, set aside for sporting pursuits or to satisfy 'le goût de la promenade'. This taste already existed, both in France and Great Britain, in the seventeenth century: 'Promenade à pied, d'abord, pour laquelle . . . une place fermée comme la Place Royale suffire; ensuite, promenade en voiture, pour laquelle il faut de plus vastes espaces'.[6] Londoners frequented the Vauxhall Gardens in the seventeenth century, where there were trees, shaded walks and restaurants, and by the middle of the eighteenth century there were over a score of such pleasure gardens in the capital. Open spaces of a simpler and more rural character also existed. There was St James's Park, where Charles II used to walk with his spaniels and feed the ducks. Hyde Park ('greatness of style determines its beauty')[7] was another royal park, opened to the public in the 1630s; horse-racing took place there. Glasgow had its Green,

> A large, spacious piece of ground . . . walled in, except to the west, which is girded by the River Clyde. This piece of ground has a very excellent walk around it, and is the wall to the town . . . and here the gentlemen resort to follow their favourite amusement, the game of golf, which is universal throughout Scotland, as well as Holland.[8]

The first London squares were also created early, designed not for public but for private use: St James's Square, for instance, laid out in 1684, soon followed by Grosvenor Square and Berkeley Square. To begin with, these squares were not planted, and it is therefore somewhat of a poetic fancy to suppose, as has been suggested, that they enclose a little bit of country left behind in the course of urban development. But, like the squares themselves, it is a delightful idea.

What really broke the mould of the traditional crowded town and let nature in was the planning of Bath, by John Wood the Elder and

his son John Wood the Younger, between 1728 and 1767. This is, as
Helen Rosenau has said,

> a great achievement: by using a site crowning a hill, the Royal
> Crescent dominates the city of Bath architecturally . . . the shape
> of the combined Circus and Crescent achieves an effect of
> enclosure with variety.[9]

And at the same time one looks from Royal Crescent right across the
lawn in front, over the park and down to the valley beyond. The
country has virtually come into the town; and correspondingly the
Crescent itself is displayed and joined to the country. Thus Bath
combines French regularity with the Italian arrangement of using
sloping hillsides for gardens (common in Italy since the Baroque
period), along with English love of the countryside. Nothing after this
was the same. More and more planted squares appeared throughout
the nineteenth century; excellent examples are Charlotte Square in
Edinburgh and Blythswood Square in Glasgow. All of these are quite
different from the monumental squares frequently to be found on
the Continent, constructed for public display rather than for everyday
private or public use. Parks and pleasure gardens also became more
popular, and began to be 'landscaped' and 'improved'. Parks and
garden squares are an especially British phenomenon, but there are
plenty of examples everywhere. The land for Central Park in New
York was bought in 1853 in order to replace 'private pleasure
grounds', and the whole area was laid out afresh by F. L. Olmsted,
starting in 1858. There were winding paths and woods and a mall for
promenading, just as in London and Paris. There was also a lake,
which was at once stocked with swans brought from London and
Hamburg.

Landscaping was an English invention, first devised in order to
give a properly orderly but romantic setting to the great country
houses of the eighteenth century. The practice may have been derived
from the art of landscape painting, because the idea that an ideal city
should be set in an ideal landscape was well understood by many
artists of the seventeenth and eighteenth centuries. The paintings of
Poussin, in particular, frequently and splendidly illustrate this belief.
Poussin was keenly interested in architecture, and many of his works
can fairly be described as architectural landscapes. They combine the
splendour of antiquity with the splendour of nature. Groups of
handsome well-proportioned buildings, trees, fields, streams and
distant hills are brought together to provide a scene of perfect
harmony and permanence. In *The Gathering of the Ashes of Phocion*,
for example, the focus in the middle-distance is provided by a superb
temple, placed almost in the centre of the picture, and possibly based
on the ancient temple near Trevi, illustrated by Palladio. Other
buildings, very carefully realized, are grouped around, with the roofs

and domes of a handsome city on the skyline; and great trees embrace the composition, seeming to guard the town and its inhabitants, who appear to be engaged in entirely leisurely pursuits and to 'fleet the time carelessly, as they did in the golden world'. Later artists have likewise combined elegant architecture with trees and receding distances to form an ideal world beneath their golden skies. Claude's *Temple of Apollo* is as much tree and wood and far-away water as temple, while Turner's *Chichester Channel* or *Arth from the Lake of Zug* or *Rome from Mt Aventine* unite nature and buildings to form a magical and harmonious whole. Monet's *Quai du Louvre* is likewise a marvellous combination of trees and architecture, one of the most beautiful of all the paintings of Paris. Numerous other examples could be brought to mind.

Nature in the city, like space, has to be carefully managed. Even towards the end of the eighteenth century London squares did not have much growing in them. Trees were kept to the parks, which meant that they were usually well away from the houses. But that changed, perhaps because of Claude and Poussin, perhaps because of the great country houses and their landscapes by Repton and Humphrey Brown. The new ideas were stated by William Stark, a little-known architect and town designer, early in the nineteenth century; it is trees, he wrote, 'that enrich and give interest to the whole surrounding scene'. Trees are a part of nature; they have form, sometimes near-architectural form; they can stand for a century or more, symbols of life and stability; they provide colour, variety, even shelter. And in addition to all this, they are a support to architecture. Claude and Poussin, Stark observed, 'constantly combining trees and architecture in their work', showed 'that there could be no beauty where either of these objects was wanting'. Architects may be disposed to dispute this judgement, and with some reason. There are doubtless buildings and even groups of buildings that can stand alone, unrelieved by any natural form. But most architecture is helped by a little arboreal contrast and variety; that architects realize this is shown by the great frequency with which they include trees in their sketches and elevations. And it has to be added that there are a vast number of buildings from the sight of which the citizens should be protected or, if that is impossible, distracted, as far as possible, by trees. There are no doubt still some people who think that Princes Street in Edinburgh is a fine street, but that must be because they do not notice the architecture at all, except for the Scott Monument and Playfair's Royal Academy, neither of which they can very well miss. What they see are the trees and the gardens, flower beds and slopes of grass leading up to the castle, one of the most romantic and eye-catching views in Europe. The buildings that line the north side of the street are, with a few exceptions, best forgotten.

So much for the amenity of space and nature. But what can be said about the architecture that combines with them? What constitutes its artistic importance? Can any guide-lines be laid down? All those who think seriously about architecture agree that there are good buildings and bad buildings; that some buildings are aesthetically more interesting and more satisfying than others; and that the best architecture provides, for those who can appreciate it, aesthetic experience of a high order. It also seems possible to agree that a good building, like a good bridge, must satisfy three criteria: it must be well and securely built; it must be planned and arranged so as to work well and satisfy the users; and it must, at the very least, be inoffensive to the experienced eye. These three requirements may be summarized as soundness, efficiency and decency.

It is even possible to hope for agreement on one further point. Different buildings serve different purposes and should have different qualities. The broadest distinction is between monumental public buildings, which should have an air of dignity or even grandeur about them, and 'vernacular' or private buildings which appropriately appear to be more intimate or graceful or dashing. The distinction is of course not very distinct. Private houses can be modest or they can be grand, and appropriate designs are necessary; no one would expect a two-bedroom house in Pimlico to look like a scaled-down version of Frank Lloyd Wright's famous and much admired country house in Pennsylvania, Falling Water. Public buildings, on the other hand, may sometimes be simple and inconspicuous—there is no need for the Inland Revenue to advertise its presence all over town— or they may be elaborate and impressive; law courts, for example, should convey some idea of the importance and dignity of the law, although there is perhaps no need for them to look quite so lavish and intimidating as the new High Court Building in Canberra. But whatever purpose a building serves, it may be good or bad architecture. Grand buildings do not have a monopoly of artistic excellence, and perhaps too much has been written about them. Homes for ordinary citizens can also be admirable examples of design; such are to be seen in the eighteenth and nineteenth century terraces and crescents in Bath, Cheltenham and many other towns; in the streets of eighteenth-century dwelling houses in, for example, Stamford ('some of the houses here are very unspectacular, which can indeed be sometimes counted as a virtue'); [10] or in some of the inner-London borough housing schemes of the 1960s. We do not have to go to Italy to see good architecture.

At about this point, however, agreement begins to peter out. Soundness and efficiency, decency and suitability are not impossible to reason about; the first two can even be measured, which many people find reassuring. But what are the qualities that give a building artistic importance? In what circumstances are we to acknowledge that architecture is—or can be—an art?

In the forefront of what is artistic in architecture, there is style. The Greeks and the Romans built in what is broadly called the Classical style, and this was rediscovered in the fifteenth century. The buildings of Palladio are an early and brilliant adaptation and re-statement of this style, and it has never been lost sight of since; Inigo Jones established it in this country; Lord Burlington was a great exponent in the eighteenth century; and a good deal of American colonial architecture has a Classical derivation. But of course the Classical style is not the only style, and this fact has caused much heart-searching and confusion. The discovery that ideals of beauty are apt to vary according to time and place has made it appear that all norms in art are subjective and that what is good in architecture — usability apart — is simply a matter of taste. Without taking notice of the peculiarities of individual buildings, many different recognizable styles have been developed in Europe during the last five or six hundred years. We have had, to name only the most prominent, Romanesque, Gothic, Renaissance, Baroque, Classical and the International Style. Opinions about all of these styles vary. Walter Gropius, in a pronouncement of breath-taking simplification and self-confidence, once declared that Gothic was 'the last great and genuine expression in architecture'[11] before the International Style.

Style is an obvious and essential element in the artistic construction of a building. But we should recognize that whatever the style adopted by an architect it is the means of manipulating elements of still more fundamental importance: materials, proportions and variety; rhythm, scale and contrast; solids and voids, planes and angles. These are the heart of the art of architecture, and the architect's task, practical considerations apart, is to manage them. He must always aim for a satisfying relationship between volume and space, height and breadth, light and shade, and between the whole scheme and its details. The subject is of course immensely complicated, and treatises abound on the principles of architecture. These treatises are readily available. But sometimes they make it difficult to see the wood for the trees. The ordinary reader is bamboozled by displays of hyper-sensitivity, pedantic learning or searches for 'spiritual meanings and contextual reference'. So in order to expose the bare bones of the matter, let us adopt a very simple approach and say that there are two different ways of reacting to the appearance and style of a building; these we may call (with apologies for the terminology) the sensuous and the intellectual.

The first of these consists of our human response to mass and space, to proportions, sequences, shapes, colours, textures and the like. To some extent this *is* a matter of taste and of what we are used to; but it is not merely that. There are colours and surfaces, voids and proportions that naturally please the eye. And these visible contrasts or harmonies may in one case excite and in another soothe our feelings. Thus Greek temples are calm, whereas Baroque facades are restless; Regency terraces are elegant and urbane; the Gothic revival is solemn and serious; and the best twentieth-century buildings are light and full of freedom. Responses such as these are close to the pole of pure sensual experience. But at the same time these responses can be educated, not least in the direction of our noticing what is there. A good building is worth more than a glance.

> From the distance you appreciate the silhouette. You go closer, and it dissolves into a play of masses: wings, towers, stairs and porticos. A few more steps, now you enjoy the proportions of the facade, the balance between solids and voids. Quite near, now, and there is the elegance of the profiles to discover, the carvings of the capitals, the details of the cornices. Then you are standing at the entrance. There is the pleasure of a well-proportioned doorway. And then — the feel of the door-handle.[12]

What is beneath the observer's feet is also part of the scene. Rasmussen has written enthusiastically about paving:

> In Switzerland the cobblestone paving is exceedingly handsome . . . in a tranquil little square in Fribourg, for example, the beautifully laid pavement gives aesthetic pleasure to the eye and has its perfect foil in the uniform pale yellow limestone of the surrounding walls and the fountain.[13]

Also, the person who is accustomed to looking at buildings with some care and thinking about what he sees acquires an understanding of buildings and knows what to expect; and understanding and expectation are all but essential to aesthetic judgements. The better the understanding and the clearer the expectation in the beholder, the greater is his or her capacity for evaluation. 'The more limited and vague the expectations, the more accidental the aesthetic experience and the more poorly substantiated the evaluation . . . lack of definite expectations results in a hazy realization of the aesthetic object'.[14]

Previous knowledge and reflection are, of course, essential if we are to judge buildings not from the sensuous but from the intellectual point of view. In the higher reaches of the appreciation of architecture, indeed, this is a specialist activity. Even a well-educated taste is not likely to grasp — to take but one example — 'the religious significance of centrally-planned churches in terms of the martyrium tradition'.[15] But buildings can have meaning on a more accessible level than this. We connect the massive proportions of Durham Cathedral with permanence and the confident faith of the medieval church; the elegant uniformity of Bedford Square with the comfortable and commanding lifestyle of the eighteenth-century English aristocracy; the soaring shining wings of the Sydney Opera House with flying, sailing, singing. Moreover, we can sometimes see in buildings references to other buildings, and therefore to other scenes and other societies, if we know enough. Thus Chiswick House bears more than a passing resemblance to Palladio's Villa Capra (the Rotunda) outside Vicenza; the Mausoleum at Castle Howard is based upon San Pietro in Montorio in Rome, by Bramante, and the monument to Burns on Edinburgh's Calton Hill is derived from the monument of Lysicrates at Athens. This sort of knowledge may please us, and it enriches our appreciation of architecture. And finally, there is the possibility of appreciating the technical skill of the architect — or, of course, his lack of it. We can see that he has made good use of an awkward site, or has had to provide access for vehicles and has done so unobtrusively, or has turned a street-corner with the adjustment and emphasis that a corner requires, or has placed a staircase so that it is an interesting and agreeable feature to anyone entering the building. We might not be able to do these things ourselves; but we can appreciate them when we see them well done by someone else.

Looking carefully at buildings and trying to understand what they do and what they say and what problems they solve is thus a precondition of judging them. Thoughtful, well-informed and sympathetic examination may not lead us to like a building; but it should lead us to recognize its quality, including its aesthetic quality, if it has any. Complete unanimity of opinion is not to be expected. It has always been the case that differing views have been held by well-informed observers, within limits. For example, Colen Campbell detested the work of Borromini: 'How wildly extravagant are the designs of Borromini . . . where the parts are without proportion . . . excessive ornaments without grace, and the whole without symmetry'. Robert Adam thought the palaces of Palladio 'ill adjusted both in their plans and elevations'. Pugin railed against the Classical style of his contemporaries: 'No one can look on Buckingham Palace or the National Gallery . . . but must feel the very existence of such public monuments a national disgrace'. Voysey thought very poorly of the twentieth century's International Style: 'This new architecture cannot last'. These observations were made many years ago. But since 1930 matters have become a good deal worse. Novelty and experiment have been ceaseless, and 'isms have multiplied at a bewildering rate; we have had Productivism, Structuralism, Popularism, Post-modernism, Formalism, Romantic Pragmatism, Regionalism, and probably many others. Only twenty years ago Brutalism and tower blocks were all the rage. Unreliability of judgement among twentieth-century architects and architectural critics alike has become the rule. Thus Kenneth Powell recently pointed out that when the Tricorn Centre in Portsmouth was being completed in the late 1960s, Pevsner described it as 'a splendid composition . . . the form of the whole is highly romantic, with many planes and varied heights, and . . . a fascinating skyline'. But to Powell, in the late 1980s, the 'dank depths' of this concrete masterpiece 'constitute one of the most depressing, and even frightening, environments in urban Britain'; and what Pevsner so much admired is now *démodé* and half-deserted. Modern architecture clearly suffers from periodic enthusiasms and recurrent outbursts of novelty.

Novelty, indeed, is the key to the twentieth century, not least to an explanation of its architectural confusions. For over a hundred years before 1930, British architects did little that was remarkably new. British architecture was dominated by revivals and survivals. The most prominent of these was the Gothic Revival, advocated and pursued through several decades—not only for churches—with religious fervour. Its most famous products are Strawberry Hill and the Houses of Parliament. There was also a less passionate Classical Revival. For those who favoured neither Gothic nor Classical, buildings were designed in a vaguely Jacobean manner, or contained elements of the Baroque, or recalled medieval manor houses or Plantagenet castles. It was atavistic architecture, often heavily decorated. And, except for the sham half-timbering, it was all in stone or brick. To a country grown accustomed to these period pieces, 'modern' architecture came as a severe shock. Le Corbusier published *Vers une Architecture* in 1923, 'un livre passionant qui forme une extraordinaire catalyse de toute la pensée architecturale la plus avancée alors'.[16] He emphasized light, air and engineering. Far from imitating the past he did not even show it much respect, illustrating on the same page the Parthenon and one of his favourite cars, the Delage grand-sport; 'ce qui apparait comme une abominable provocation'.[17] Instead of complication there was simplicity; instead of elaborate enclosure there were open-plan rooms or working areas with large windows and balconies, providing 'le contact dedans-dehors, logis et nature'. In 1929 Gropius built the Bauhaus at Dessau, a factory-like building of concrete and glass curtain-walls, devoid of decoration, and in 1929 Le Corbusier built the Villa Savoie. Within a few years the revolutionary Continental influences which these buildings expressed began to enter Britain.

The trouble about extreme novelty—violent novelty might be a better phrase—is that it produces two extreme and opposite responses. Those who are against it, being fearful for the security of what they know and understand, condemn what is new and close their minds to any merit that the new ideas might possess; while those who like the new ideas become furious in their defence, and claim that hitherto nothing was ever done, or thought, correctly. As a result, there is exaggeration and misrepresentation on both sides, and judgement is unhinged. This is what usually happens when new ways of thinking are introduced. To take the most obvious historical examples, men were for long at loggerheads about the arrangement of the universe after the publication of Copernicus' *De Revolutionibus Orbium Coelestium*; there were violent disagreements about early man and the Bible after Darwin; and no one knew what to think about infectious diseases after doubt had been cast on the idea of spontaneous generation. With *Vers une Architecture* it was much the same. Le Corbusier and the International Style began an era of upheaval and dispute which, for reasons to be discussed in the following chapter, continues to the present day.

It must be recognized that the International Style or something like it was virtually inevitable once sheet glass and reinforced concrete became available as building materials. A radically new way of building was possible; and the demand for very large commercial buildings—mostly stores and offices—was also new. The new demand and the new supply complemented one another, and the first rectangular towers of glass and concrete, fifteen or even twenty storeys high, amazed the world and were hailed in many quarters as great architecture. But the aesthetic experience which they provided, and which such buildings continue to provide, was in fact of a low order. Astonishment at new technology and fascination with novelty have little to do with aesthetic experience. Mere novelty soon wears off. In themselves, tower blocks are too simple and too regular, too mechanical and unyielding in their lines and surfaces to provide much interest or elicit much human sympathy. But this is far from ending the matter, for modern architecture, the International Movement or whatever it may be called, has far more to offer than towers of steel, glass or concrete. There is nothing wrong with the modern style, if it is well done. Contemporary architecture for houses, offices or some kinds of industrial buildings uses new structural techniques that create a light and buoyant appearance; what is built no longer appears to be entirely closed in, but gives a feeling of openness towards the world outside; horizontal and vertical elements are reduced to their primary forms; walls become screens, and ornament is minimal. Architecture like this began to appear in the 1920s (Mies van der Rohe's German Pavilion at the International Exhibition in Barcelona in 1929 is sometimes cited as the first truly modern building), and at its best this style is indubitably very fine. It has little or no decoration, and therefore depends on mass, proportion, and the quality and nature of materials. It combines the precision and logic of engineering with an almost casual, sporting look. It is deceptively simple.

> In the hands of the great masters glass and concrete were deployed with classic simplicity to create patterns of lines and planes that can only be compared to abstract paintings of the period. The illusion of artistic purity could be sustained because of the way architectural photographs invariably portrayed new buildings: dazzling white concrete, cloudless skies, and no people in sight.[18]

For a short time, from about 1925 to about 1945, the International

Style, severe and unornamented, was hailed as one of the great inventions of the age, at any rate by large numbers of architects and architectural critics.

For several reasons, however, doubt and confusion grew and spread. Even the admirers of the new architecture soon had to admit that the utilitarian, no-decoration approach was apt to result in buildings which were 'rational to the point of extreme—almost forbidding—severity',[19] and after the war Pevsner felt obliged to defend the 'rather forbidding' appearance of the new style and its apparent 'lack of human warmth' on the dubious ground that this was a reflection of contemporary life, and to argue that representative examples of the style were usually offices and factories, not houses, because modern architects were designing for an age 'with nothing like the leisure for luxuries which patrons of the Baroque enjoyed'.[20] Admittedly he was writing in the dreary post-war years of make-do and shortages; but these were no arguments for a style that was supposed to have high artistic quality and universal appeal. A second source of trouble was that an architecture of straight lines and flat surfaces requires high-class materials and very careful detailing; buildings by Mies van der Rohe are outstanding in both these respects. But when the International Style is attempted in ordinary-to-poor materials, or, worse still, when the arrangement of planes and proportions—upon which the style so heavily depends—is mishandled by some designer who does not have the necessary skill, sensibility or design-time, the result is at best dull and at worst offensive. It is too easy to imitate the International Style and do it badly. To add to the confusion, the supporters of the new style laid a great deal of emphasis on function. Whatever was extraneous to the usefulness of a building was—or so they seemed to say—unnecessary. This was a reaction against over-ornamentation, but it went too far. And it was pushed still further by the fact that modern buildings are apt to be technically complicated. Many of them require lifts, central heating, air-ducting and the rest, and with the arrival of this more complicated technology the business of design began to be sub-ordinated, in many architects' offices, to management of the technology. 'Form follows function' was the catch-phrase. But architecture is something over and above the merely useful. If form follows function and has no life of its own, there is building but no art of architecture. And a number of twentieth-century architects have in fact confined themselves to building without architecture. They have not, of course, publicly subscribed to the idea that architecture should no longer exist; but they have supported it in practice.

Nor has judgement been made easier by flights from some form of functional simplicity to the opposite extreme, designs which surprise us indeed, but only because they appear bizarre, wilful, purposeless and perverse. Of this class, the outstanding examples are perhaps provided by the work of Antoni Gaudi, the savagery of whose ornamental invention[21] brought into architecture a strain of what looks very like insanity. These constructions have no antecedents and they have led to very little imitation; perhaps for the same reason that, as T S Eliot said, absolutely original poetry is absolutely bad. There is always room for originality and surprise in architecture, but not for too much at once. Good architecture without surprises is easy architecture, which soon fulfills our expectations; good architecture with surprises is more subtle; buildings with nothing but surprises, which simply set out to advertise themselves, can seldom, if ever, be classed as architecture at all. Such works, shot through by bombast and a straining for effect, may seem striking and original at first, but their attraction will not endure. In all good buildings, some of mankind's better feelings and nobler ideas are, as it were, made visible and comprehended in form, proportion and space.

Unfortunately, observations like these do not define good buildings. In spite of everything that has been written, artistic quality is beyond definition. There may be complete agreement — or as good as complete agreement — about the merits of what has been built in the past: before, say, 1900. But contemporary architecture is another matter. No one can be sure that a new building does or does not possess artistic quality. The opinion of architects, and of their critics, cannot be relied upon, and strident assertions about the excellence of this or that should always be treated with caution. What is hailed as a masterpiece in one year may be castigated in the next. The problems might not have become so serious if architects had been able to sort them out among themselves. But architecture, to a greater degree than any other form of art, and more so now than ever before, is a public business. The work of architects is constantly under scrutiny (although it is noticeable how few people ever stop for so long as one minute to look at a building), and there is much 'media coverage' of architecture. In a public competitive world the architects are bound to be influenced by the latest fashion, the loudest voices, the desire to do something different. They may be traditionalists or modernists, copyists of old styles ('sham architects') or so modern that they are post post-modern several times over. But they are all subject to the same pressures. It is probably no exaggeration to say that since 1950 there has been more talk, more building and more 'selling' of architecture than in all the previous centuries put together.

Architecture having developed so much into a public game with lots of prize money, no one can be surprised at the scarcity of unbiased and well-considered views about the quality of individual buildings. It is tempting to conclude, indeed, that architectural quality is a chimera. But this is not so. Architectural judgement is not a mere morass of personal preference and esoteric understanding. It is not the case that the opinions of any man, woman, child or so-called expert about the artistic merits of a building are as good as anyone else's. Although every observer can make mistakes and some can persist in them for a lifetime, there is such a thing as careful, informed, unprejudiced, experienced opinion.

When a new scheme comes forward, the first problem is to understand correctly and to evaluate the architect's plans and elevations. Understanding is not easy, because it requires both experience and imagination; experience in order to compare the drawings with other solutions of similar problems, and imagination in order to visualize what the scheme will look like when actually built. (Even architects are sometimes surprised when they see, in stone or concrete, the buildings they have themselves designed). Evaluation of the architecture is even more difficult, for all the reasons already discussed. But this is only the first stage of appraisal, because, whatever may be said for or against the new proposals, there are wider issues to consider.

The fact is that too much is heard about the styles and details of architecture, and not enough about the impact that is made by a new development, taken as a whole, upon the urban environment. Architects and their critics hold forth about the finer points of architecture, but the aesthetic effect of buildings, nine times out of ten, depends more than anything else on their mass and placing. Architectural design is important, no doubt, but its importance is usually overstated. This point was made almost twenty years ago by the Commission for England and Wales. The Commission was resisting the proposal by the (then) Ministry of Public Building and Works to build a high tower in Hyde Park for the Household Cavalry, and the Secretary to the Commission wrote a letter to *The Times*, which concluded with the following sentences:

> I hope it will be understood that this letter is not about architectural design. It is about something that matters even more—the basic sizes and shapes of buildings in relation to the places where they are to be built.[22]

This is indeed the prime consideration, especially because many modern buildings, being very large, have a disastrously diminishing effect on their surroundings, and do not deserve the attention that they attract. Masterpieces of architecture, like St Paul's Cathedral or the Glasgow College of Art, are to be observed for their own sake, from every aspect and in every detail. But most buildings play only a subsidiary role. Within our cities there are very few greenfield sites, and the problem that should receive most attention ninety nine times out of a hundred is how a building or a new development is going to fit in with what is already built, with the existing street scene or townscape. New work should preserve the scale of its setting, and its colour and texture and general outline should harmonize with its

surroundings. It does not have to copy what is there already, it has to
be *sympathique*. What we want is a fine town: a visually attractive
urban environment, pleasant to live in, not just a miscellaneous
collection of ill-related buildings, good and bad. Variety there must
be. But there should also be enough sympathy between building and
building to produce a harmonious and interesting composition,

> Where order in variety we see,
> And where, tho' all things differ, all agree.

This means that what we have to work for as a rule is not great
architecture—although opportunities for that may arise—but harmony
and decency. And that is a great deal. We want new buildings of
suitable character that will make a modest contribution to, and will
not detract from, the urban scene. Occasionally we may get more;
the trouble is, that we are so often supplied with far less. This is
sometimes the result of fashion, or of incompetence, but very often it
is because architectural assessments are too narrow in scope. Planning
matters as much as architecture. The lay-out of a city—and this
includes much besides its ground-plan—is at least as important to
almost everyone in it as the details of its architecture, and it is very
unfortunate that whereas architecture continues to be recognized as
an art, planning is widely regarded as mere office work, not very
important, not very skilful and not at all artistic. Which, unhappily, is
all too often what it amounts to.

The point cannot be too much emphasized that a few good
buildings will not make a good street or a good town, and that a few
bad ones will ruin everything. Sixty years ago Unwin said this about
Oxford:

> It is not enough to have regard only to the buildings of
> outstanding merit—the colleges, churches and the like. These
> may be preserved in themselves and yet be largely destroyed by
> replacing the harmonious background of simple but charming
> buildings, which were so common here fifty years ago, by blatant
> or merely incongruous examples of the modern lack of taste.[23]

Since Unwin wrote, examples of what he warned against have
multiplied at an appalling rate.

Badly designed and cheaply constructed buildings are part of the
trouble. Much of the rest is due to 'planning' that fails to recognize
that the agreeableness of a locality depends on the size and design
and colour of *all* the buildings, on the size and proportions of the
spaces round them, and on the landscaping. In a new development,
space and landscaping usually fare worse than architecture. Developers, acutely conscious of the high value of land, almost always want to
build as much as possible on any given site; but from the point of
view of everyone else this may be counterproductive. By coming too
close to adjacent buildings, or rising too high, a new building, even if
it is perfectly satisfactory in itself, may obscure or destroy the three-

dimensional quality of its neighbours' architecture, cut out light, or emphasize a visual conflict that might not otherwise have been noticeable; its own architectural appeal may at the same time be seriously reduced. Buildings, like people, need space, space to be seen and space to fit in. It was Degas who remarked that there is no such thing as the general effect. But while this may be true of a wall of pictures in an exhibition, which is what he was talking about, it is not true of a scene of buildings. Many buildings together combine to make a picture, and — to repeat a point — they need not be remarkably good buildings to make a remarkably good picture. Early in the nineteenth century Nash designed the stuccoed façades and colonnades of old Regent Street and Regent's Park. They were much admired in their day and their destruction has been often and long-lamented. But what was so good about them was precisely their general effect; 'mediocre as architecture, they were unsurpassed as man-made scenery'.[24]

The impression made by the buildings in a street, or in a whole town, is formed from a series of observations. This means, as Thomas Sharp observed many years ago, that one sees the city as 'a mobile thing . . . streets *move* as one is drawn through them even if one is drawn on one's feet';[25] and he described the High in Oxford as 'a harmonious grouping of dissimilar elements' set out along 'the fine bend of the street'. Certainly whoever walks along the High makes a marvellous progress. Once over Magdalen Bridge, the façades of Queen's College and All Souls come in sight; on reaching them the fourteenth-century spire of St Mary's is dominant, and more distant the spire of All Saints' (now Lincoln College Library). But the High is more than the sum of its most important buildings. Sharp described it as 'the greatest and most typical work of art England possesses',[26] full of harmony and complement. There are other streets of similar interest, variety and quality in other British towns. For example, the Royal Mile in Edinburgh leads downward from the narrow entrance-door and spacious esplanade of the Castle, past buildings which are all in stone, of varying heights but none less than three storeys and none over seven, some with gables to the street, some arcaded, a very few set back from the pavement, all with fairly small windows typical of the Scots vernacular style. Wide at first, the street is latterly quite narrow; and at the bottom of the hill, coming at last abruptly round a corner, one faces Holyrood Palace, some of it sixteenth- most of it seventeenth-century work, with massive castellated towers and an entrance with four Doric columns beneath an octagonal cupola surmounted by an imperial crown. The Palace is set in its open ground behind magnificent and elaborate wrought-iron gates made in the twentieth century, and backed by the green slopes of Arthur's Seat. The whole street, with the Castle at the top and the Palace at the bottom, built and rebuilt over four hundred years, is a dramatic unity, an extraordinary aesthetic and historical experience. Street scenes far less singluar than this, but full of interest and well put together, still abound in many British towns and villages. We still possess, scattered across the country, a great number of streets or groups of buildings, possibly built at different dates and in different styles, not all of the buildings individually of great architectural merit, which nevertheless form in each case an artistically valuable whole. The excellence and impact of these still-familiar scenes require neither grandeur nor precise historical connections nor the support of adjacent architectural masterpieces; but they must comprise a series of buildings that do not conflict with one another and that are in themselves broadly right.

One might suppose that all this was fairly obvious. But there are reasons why the design of a new building often takes little account of its integrative or disintegrative effect on the whole scene. Almost eighty years ago Unwin put forward an economic explanation:

> So long as each architect and each client thinks only of his own building, how individual and how noticeable he can make it, little progress in the total effect can be expected. Architects should be trained to think first of how their building will take its place in the picture already existing. The harmony, the unity which binds the buildings together and welds the whole into a picture, is so much the most important consideration . . . But the business man believes that he must shout if he is to live, and naturally desires his architect to do some shouting for him. The young and original architect, too, must become known if he is to secure commissions, and a little shouting in his earlier buildings may greatly aid him. But if we are to have beauty of surroundings we must set our faces against the development of such incongruities in our buildings as completely destroy the harmony of our street pictures. Harmony does not require monotony, but a proper relation between the different colours and parts.[27]

There is much truth in this—perhaps even more truth than when Unwin wrote it. But many new buildings clash with their surroundings to the advantage of no one. And this is because modern architects, it seems, far from being taught 'to think first of how their buildings will take its place in the picture already existing', are often taught nothing of the sort. Twenty years ago Sir Frederick Gibberd observed that 'the art of architecture . . . has tended to become withdrawn from the art of town design and has turned in on itself, the architect regarding his building as being an abstract composition with an existence independent of its surroundings'.[28] And more recently an eminent architect has told us that when he was a student,

> I was taught to look at buildings as perfect objects, consistent in all their parts, and with complete identities. We were seldom asked to look beyond the limits of buildings' walls, and were

never encouraged to wonder how these structures, merely by
their new presence, were to affect their surroundings.[29]
No wonder there is trouble! Architects concentrate on their own
buildings, and town planners concentrate on the economic and social
consequences of everything (and therefore on nothing in particular)
and inevitably the visible totality of a place, the local environment,
gets lost.

It must therefore be repeated that what makes a good building
depends to a considerable extent on what has been built there
already. In places of faint character, or poor character, the architect
can feel free to design almost as he pleases—always with the
qualification that he designs as well as he can. But in all other
situations he has to attend to the scale, form, texture and colour of all
the other buildings to which his will relate. It is obvious that we do
not put a black-and-chromium office desk with a surface of thirty
square feet in a small sitting-room with a Persian carpet and
Hepplewhite chairs; or a Victorian sideboard in a Scandinavian-style
dining-room; or a chandelier in the kitchen. Yet, in cities, greater
absurdities than these are to be found in streets and squares all over
the United Kingdom, thrust upon the notice of every passer-by. It
has even been said that few modern developments take proper
account of the quality of their surroundings. Certainly it is not at all
uncommon to see office blocks that are square concrete boxes wedged
between two Victorian buildings with Corinthian pillars and
complicated stonework, or to see glass façades twenty metres high
placed next door to something faintly Baroque.

The seriousness of the problem suddenly increased with the
invention—it is not too strong a word—of high-rise buildings. These
soon attained great popularity, first in the United States after 1920,
and then in the United Kingdom and other countries after 1945.
This is entirely understandable because, within limits and at the
expense of several competing advantages, such buildings can put a
very large amount of floor space on a given site. This is a valuable
characteristic where the price of land is high. But these structures
have serious disadvantages. They are expensive to build because
they require a carefully planned system of internal access corridors,
good fire protection, and lifts as well as staircases, and all these
provisions not only cost money but also reduce the amount of usable
space. They can provide high densities of development, but these
high densities have to be serviced by surrounding roads and parking
areas and are thus apt to impose large costs on other people. When
used to provide domestic accommodation, high-rise buildings have
been an almost unmitigated disaster, even when well supervised
(which they seldom are) and built with adequate and reliable lifts.
For office accommodation they clearly have their uses, but they are
apt to look boring, they can deprive one another of light and air, and

they may produce what Unwin in 1923 called 'a kind of vertical overcrowding'. Lastly, unless extraordinarily well designed and not too big, they are so much out of scale with older buildings that they destroy them aesthetically. It is worth noting that no tall buildings have been allowed in the centre of Paris, with one solitary and most unfortunate exception. True, disaster is not inevitable. Down-town Sydney has numerous modern high-rise buildings set amid nineteenth- and early twentieth-century buildings of a quite different scale and style; but because the new tall buildings are not very close to one another, and vary a good deal in colour, shape and height, they fit easily into the city and the overall effect is so far not displeasing. Crowded together, however, as they often are, such buildings create a dreary and overpowering effect. Smaller buildings, however elegant or interesting, begin to look absurd, and human beings to seem insignificant. If it is the aim of modern architecture, as Walter Gropius said that it should be, 'to let the human element become the dominant factor', high-rise buildings can seldom if ever be designed or approved by modern architects.

But height is only one of the problems. Architects of the present day are wedded to no particular style, and modern technology makes possible an enormous variety of unusual effects and novel solutions. Before the twentieth century, all European buildings, with few exceptions, were made of wood, brick or stone. To that extent at least, they all harmonized with one another. But now there are buildings which appear to be made entirely of glass, and on the other hand there is at least one building—the Beinecke Library at Yale— which has no windows at all, but admits a certain amount of daylight through two hundred and fifty concave panels of alabaster. There are aluminium-clad office blocks, and stainless-steel towers. The Musée Pompidou was opened in 1977 with escalators in polycarbonate tubes, external coloured ventilation pipes, external lifts, and other external services, and these features have been widely copied. The new Lloyds of London headquarters in Leadenhall Street (warmly commended by the English Royal Fine Art Commission) appears mostly to be made of glass and steel. It has a transept like the Crystal Palace surrounded by huge steel boxes and a jumble of external pipes, precipitous external spiral staircases, and an external column of rectangular lavatory capsules with porthole windows, each capsule 'plugged in' to the building and ready to be removed and replaced. It rather resembles the inside of an aircraft carrier, and most critics have likened it to Meccano. Whatever might be said for it in isolation, it is offensive and absurd beside its neighbours. The Renault Centre in Swindon has a pvc roof membrane which is held in place by an array of 'masts' which support cables which hold up the beams. It is painted bright yellow. Anxiety reached fever pitch when it seemed that Trafalgar Square might acquire something similar, a 'high-tech' extension to the National Gallery, described by one very important person as 'a kind of vast municipal fire station' which would resemble 'a monstrous carbuncle on the face of a much loved and elegant friend'.

Judgements like this are probably not entirely aesthetic or intellectual. Trafalgar Square, more or less as it is, has been there for a considerable time, and many people doubtless felt that they simply did not want to see it changed, or not drastically. In a world where so much changes so fast, there is a lot to be said for hanging onto a few familiar landmarks—physical or other—a few familiar shapes and styles. And this simple but important feeling sometimes combines with another, less simple but equally important, that buildings already in existence, whether they are beautiful or not, keep us in touch with the past, and are a valuable heritage. Here, indeed, is something of great importance, not obviously included in the ideas of beauty and amenity, and yet touching them both.

Concern about the past is of fairly recent origin, but nowadays it permeates European and American culture. Since the time of Descartes men have acquired a new habit of thinking historically. They have

> turned more and more to an investigation of the recorded story of mankind, bringing to that enterprise a remarkable attention to detail, an ever greater preoccupation with the factual event . . . To regard all things in their historical setting appears, indeed, to be an instinctive procedure of the modern mind. We do it without thinking, because we can scarcely think at all without doing it.[30]

It is therefore not surprising to find that the urge to preserve what has been left by history cannot be traced back beyond 1700.[31] Antiquaries—'We antiquaries', as Horace Walpole put it, 'who hold everything worth preserving, merely because it has been preserved'—were scarcely heard of before the second half of the eighteenth century. The Society of Antiquaries was founded in 1751, and at first its members concerned themselves chiefly with recording those British monuments that were thought fit to be set beside the monuments of classical antiquity, which had come to be greatly admired in, and sometimes removed from, Greece and Italy. Antiquarian studies naturally led to interest in and conservation of the fabrics. But it was not until the Society set up a Conservation Fund in 1854, at the suggestion of Ruskin, that concern for buildings of the previous centuries became at all active or widespread. This concern, however, proved to be a doubtful blessing. In the middle and later decades of the nineteenth century it was not so much conservation as restoration that occupied people's thoughts, with results which we regard today

as little short of disastrous. The Gothic style, translated into a
superficial and usually tactless imitation of the Decorated style,
became the only orthodoxy:

> Late Gothic, the Perpendicular and Tudor styles were decried as
> debased and degenerate; magnificent windows of the fourteenth,
> fifteenth and sixteenth centuries were torn out, and imaginary
> reconstructions of earlier and 'purer' styles put in their places.
> Scores, possibly hundreds of parish churches were so altered as
> to become to all intents and purposes unrecognisable . . .[32]

For thirty years lavish expenditure on ecclesiastical fabrics was the
true sign of repentance for previous neglect of religion. There is no
need to detail the mistakes that were made, but they were so serious
that one author has gone so far as to say that 'with few exceptions,
the ruins that Thomas or Oliver Cromwell knocked about remain
valid as evidence, so far as they survive in fragmentary condition . . .
but what happened to most of the cathedrals and to many of the
surviving domestic buildings was that the wells of truth were
poisoned'.[33]

Protests at what was done by Victorian restoration architects are
usually made on aesthetic grounds. Many old buildings are beautiful
as well as irreplaceable – their architectural quality is unique, and
they also possess historic interest. Thus doubly safeguarded, no
proposals are put forward, even in this barbarous age, to knock
down the Queen's House at Greenwich or the Customs House at
King's Lynn or the Glasgow College of Art or the Maison Carrée at
Nîmes or other similar structures. They are well-known buildings
and their merit is conceded. But with domestic buildings the situation
is not so simple. Domestic buildings do not usually advertise their
presence in the way that monumental buildings do. They are usually
not so noticeable, or so noticed. They are sometimes very discreet,
even humble – it may be part of their quality – and their artistic merit
is low-key. They are not connected with great events in history. They
are apt to be, in one word, unexciting. But so, in the same rather
superficial sense of the word unexciting, is a novel by Jane Austen or
a painting by Vermeer. Such works are quiet, subtle and urbane.
They are not instantly appreciated, and to an uneducated taste they
may appear dull. Yet discreet domestic buildings can have great
merit. Many towns have a perfect treasury of fine Georgian houses,
excellently proportioned; there are innumerable Victorian terraces,
handsome and well detailed; there are terraces of small houses – not
so often small single houses – in side-streets that are admirable
architecture. There are also – not now so discreet as once they were,
because everything round about them is new and different – older
houses such as one sees in Winchester or Norwich. And, leaving the
domestically discreet for the domestically monumental, there are the
grand constructions such as Carlton House Terrace in London or

Royal Crescent in Bath or Moray Place in Edinburgh. All this is a great range of architecture, in time, scale and style, and there is no question but that it adds not only to the visual variety of our towns and cities, but also to their artistic vitality.

Aesthetic conservation, however, is only one aspect of the matter. What was done by Victorian conservers destroyed not only the beauty and architectural purity of the buildings they worked on; it also destroyed their historical authenticity, their atmosphere. Old buildings bring before us, as nearly as can be, other manners and other ways of life. If we knew nothing about history, we would know only our own ideals and our own ways of doing things. And even these we would not understand properly, because we could not know their origins nor be able to compare them with alternatives — at any rate, not in our own culture. Documents and history books save us from being locked into the present. But documents and history books never entirely convince. Only a minority of people can envisage and begin to understand a previous age from the printed word alone. Who knows much about Henry VIII who has not seen his portrait by Holbein and been to Hampton Court? Who knows what there is to know about Shakespeare who has not visited his birth-place at Stratford, or Mary Arden's house nearby? Who understands Benjamin Franklin who has not been to Monticello? Who knows much about Edwardian life who has not visited a house by Lutyens? Even buildings that possess no great merit as architecture can link us strongly to the past. No one would say that Windsor Castle is a masterpiece, but it makes George IV and Queen Victoria real and understandable as nothing else can. Jane Austen's house, as a dwelling, is neither very attractive nor interesting, and the same could be said of the cottage in which Robert Burns lived and that in which David Livingstone was born; but these buildings are wholly of their time, and they bring history into the present with the force of reality. As Sir John Vanbrugh said, old buildings generate in us 'lively and pleasant reflections on the persons who have inhabited them, and on the remarkable things which have been transacted in them'. The eagerness of very large numbers of people to visit historic houses and other antiquities and relics of the past reflects deeper-seated needs than the need for entertainment. We live for most of the time and express ourselves almost always on the surface of life. But it does not require a Freud or a Jung to tell us that magic, religion and art, the ideas of death, passing time, and successive generations, touch chords of human experience which are fundamental and essential to complete human nature. At this level the advantages of visible history, apt to remain largely unperceived and unsupported by pure reason or quantitative arguments, are so great that it is hardly possible to overstate them.

Besides the aesthetic and the historical grounds for keeping some constructions 'that Time has been glad to forget' (along with others, more obviously serviceable, left over in the march of progress), two further arguments deserve a mention. The first of these is that old buildings provide, more than anything else, a sense of the continuity of life. What is done by ourselves and in our time is not very much, but whatever it amounts to it is a contribution to a long story. Previous generations have struggled with problems like ours, not always successfully, but win or lose there is a continuous development from the round houses of Skara Brae to the reconstruction of Covent Garden. The world is not made, it is being made. How far this continuous process of being made is synonymous with continuous improvement is not, for present purposes, the point. The point is that in a world where people tend, especially nowadays, to feel lonely, insecure and anxious, tangible evidence of the past is reassuring. There is nothing so flimsy and destructible as the present. And secondly, we take pride, with some justification, in the achievements of the past, and identify with them. We are encouraged, no doubt, by the thought that we have come so far and have survived innumerable catastrophes. And over and above this, we enjoy, when we see or enter an old building that is also a good building, an agreeable feeling of reflected glory. It was our ancestors—there is an element of ancestor-worship in it—who built Wells Cathedral; King's College Chapel, Cambridge; Azay le Rideau; the Palm House at Kew; the Town Hall in Stockholm—the list can be extended almost indefinitely, and as we will. How very gratifying to be associated with such achievements, and many humbler ones as well!

There are thus very good arguments for the retention of old buildings, even when these buildings are not of outstanding aesthetic or historic distinction. These arguments have often been ignored, and there is no doubt that far too many attractive and usable buildings from previous times have been knocked down in the past twenty or thirty years. 'The best service an architect can render to his client, in some cases, is to advise that a new building is not required but that the old one can be rejuvenated. Not only does this course often satisfy the client and the public alike, but it conserves resources.'[34] This is both true and important. Many a derelict warehouse of fine proportions has been successfully converted to provide flats, studios or small workshops; surprisingly secular uses have been found for many a church; a sixteenth-century laird's house in Edinburgh is now a paintings restoration workshop, and in Paris the exhilarating Musée d'Orsay has been created out of a railway station. On the other hand, we should recognize that in many cases heated arguments take place concerning the conservation of old buildings that are thoroughly undistinguished and ought not to be saved. Conservation societies and other special interest groups are sometimes inclined to argue as if there was no merit in a building but antiquity, and no such thing as progress. Cynical about progress we may be; amenity societies, it has been said, 'tend to favour preservation because they have (understandably) lost faith in what is sometimes offered in exchange'.[35] But we cannot afford to abandon hope. The world will go on changing, and our cities will have to keep pace. Old buildings that do not work properly are not good buildings. They are a liability. We cannot afford cities that are museums of liabilities. The way to preserve old customs, said Walter Bagehot, is to enjoy old customs. And the way to preserve old buildings is to make them a living, useful, enjoyable part of the cities in which we live. It is the life of the city that counts, and a truly beautiful and attractive city, sensitive to its heritage, is one that is nevertheless full of change and opportunity. The retention of old buildings is of the greatest importance to the cultural life of the city; but this retention must be a selective process, depending on the aesthetic quality of the buildings, on their history, and on their capacity for further use.

Thus historic interest is another value to be set alongside public amenity and artistic importance. It would be perfectly reasonable to say that public amenity should be defined in such a way as to include historic interest. But keeping them separate makes things clearer. So the ideal city has three constituents (apart from the citizens, who are of course the most important constituent of all): buildings of architectural quality, when possible of high architectural quality; historic interest; and space and nature.

An eminent author observed some years ago that men have been building ideal cities for hundreds of years—on paper. These efforts never end, because there is no formula for an ideal city; and there is no formula because the requirements and possibilities set by technology and circumstances change all the time. Nor will an ideal city be designed by a computer, because cities are made by those who live in them. Needs and preferences emerge and change and disappear; and the city, if it is a well-planned and well-managed place, adapts to them. It is altering all the time, and all the time it has to serve three purposes: it is a home; it is a stage for life and enjoyment; and it is a very large piece of capital equipment in the whole complicated process of production and exchange. From this last point of view, the production-and-exchange point of view, Le Corbusier in the nineteen-twenties was thinking along the right lines; a city, as he implied, is a machine; although to a lot of people it seems nowadays to be a machine for *not* living in. And after all, no one would choose to live in a machine—with all that that implies of noise, metal surfaces and general discomfort—unless it was very well disguised. So in practice the machine aspect is overlaid with homes, and these take up most of the space of the city. For those who live there they are the most important part of it. But the city as a stage for

living on, for the drama and enjoyment of the open air and public
occasions, is the third essential of civilized existence. Any city worth
the name has an art gallery, a theatre, a concert hall, restaurants and
the rest. But in addition, if we are to have a truly civilized city—not a
madhouse; not a place that is pretending to be a city without having
any of the facilities and practical amenities of a city; not a mere built-
up concentration of commercial opportunities—then we must attend
most seriously to the aesthetics of its architecture, to the visible
evidence of its past, and to its parks and gardens and open spaces.

NOTES AND REFERENCES TO CHAPTER 2
 1. See above p. 00.
 2. Colin Buchanan, *Traffic in Towns* (HMSO, 1963) p. 39.
 3. E. A. Gutkind, *Urban Development in Western Europe*, vol. 5
    (New York, 1970) p. 238.
 4. P. Zucker, *Town and Square* (Boston, 1959) p. 1.
 5. B. Berenson, *The Italian Painters of the Renaissance* (London,
    1952) vol. 2, pp. 88–9.
 6. P. Lavedan, *Histoire de l'Urbanisme* (Paris, 1959) vol. 2, p. 200.
 7. S. E. Rasmussen, *London: The Unique City* (London, 1948) p. 331.
 8. T. Thornton, *A Sporting Tour* (London, 1804) p. 23.
 9. H. Rosenau, *The Ideal City* (London, 1974) p. 122.
10. Alec Clifton-Taylor, *Six English Towns* (London, 1978) p. 108.
11. W. Gropius, *Rebuilding Our Communities* (Chicago, 1945) p. 45.
12. Leslie Wilkinson, quoted in, Suzanne Falkiner (ed.), *Leslie
    Wilkinson: A Practical Idealist* (Sydney, 1982) p. 99.
13. S. E. Rasmussen, *Experiencing Architecture* (London, 1959) p. 27.
14. S. Najder, *Values and Evaluations* (Oxford, 1975) p. 149.
15. Foreword by David Watkin in, Geoffrey Scott, *The Architecture of
    Humanism* (London, 1980) p. xxii.
16. Michel Ragon, *Histoire Mondiale de l'Architecture et de l'Urbanisme
    Modernes* (Paris, 1972) vol. 2, p. 88.
17. *Ibid*.
18. Alison Ravetz, *Remaking Cities* (London, 1980) p. 174.
19. J. M. Richards, *An Introduction to Modern Architecture* (London,
    1953) p. 83.
20. N. Pevsner, *An Outline of European Architecture* (London, 1948)
    p. 214.
21. A phrase coined by the authors of the *Penguin Dictionary of
    Architecture*.
22. Reprinted in RFAC for England and Wales, *Twenty-First Report*
    (HMSO, 1971) p. 26.
23. *Journal of the RIBA*, vol. 31, p. 617.
24. Kerry Downes, *The Georgian Cities of Britain* (Oxford, 1979) p. 6.

25. T. Sharp, *Oxford Replanned* (London, 1948) p. 36.
26. *Ibid.*, p. 20.
27. R. Unwin, *Town Planning in Practice* (London, 1909) p. 363.
28. F. Gibberd, *Town Design* (London, 1967) p. 10.
29. Romaldo Giurgola, 'A Place for Everything and Everything in its Place', lecture given in Canberra, Sept. 1982.
30. C. L. Becker, *The Heavenly City of the Eighteenth Century Philosopher* (New Haven, 1932) pp. 17−19.
31. Even educated 18th century travellers consciously helped to ruin the monuments they visited. When the distinguished naturalist Thomas Pennant came to the ruins of the cathedral of Iona in 1772 he found the altar in a much damaged state 'owing to the belief of the superstitious; who were of the opinion, that a piece of it conveyed to the possessor success in whatever he undertook. A very small portion is now left; and even that we contributed to diminish'. T. Pennant, *A Tour in Scotland and Voyage to the Hebrides* (London, 1774) p. 253.
32. J. Harvey, *Conservation of Buildings* (London, 1972) p. 174.
33. *Ibid.*, p. 175.
34. A. J. Gordon, unpublished paper.
35. RFAC for Scotland, Ninth Report (HMSO, 1983) p. 15.

CHAPTER THREE

The Extraordinary Nature of
The Twentieth-Century City

It often happens that we use the same words that our ancestors used to indicate objects that have changed out of all recognition since their time. A theatre in the time of Shakespeare was an enclosed courtyard open to the sky with two or three tiers of covered galleries and a bare projecting platform, supported by trestles, which was the stage; a hospital, until late in the nineteenth century, was a charitable foundation which, if it specialized in caring for the sick, was distinguished from other large houses chiefly by its overcrowding, its squalor, and its stench; even an item so commonplace as a road has changed completely, for until fields began to be enclosed in the 1750s a road was usually a rough, muddy meandering track over which wheeled vehicles could pass only with difficulty, if at all. It is the same with the city. The word has persisted; but that to which it now refers bears as little resemblance to the old or traditional city as the new *Ark Royal* bears to Nelson's *Victory*.

No great knowledge of the past is needed in order to assent to this proposition. But there is an important corollary. Just as cities and the life lived in them used to be very different from what they are today, so urban beauty and amenity were created in previous centuries in forms that quite often we cannot reproduce, and were supplied by institutions, or through social arrangements, that no longer effectively exist. Not much will be achieved, therefore, by hoping for a revival of past practices. The physical and social setting, the building technology, the traffic, the clients, and even many of the objectives of urban development have all altered, and what can be done in the twentieth century to create beauty and amenity has inevitably altered along with everything else. We therefore have to make a new effort, and a new kind of effort, to create or maintain fine and civilized cities. In order to do this effectively, we must first try to understand what cities used to be like and who built them and why; and then we must investigate the nature and some of the remarkable peculiarities of the twentieth-century city, asking in particular, why mere usefulness (along with much strenuous self-advertising) is so predominant in present-day schemes of development, and beauty so often conspicuous by its absence.

Until the later decades of the nineteenth century almost all cities changed, in so far as they changed at all, very slowly. Some of them, of course, grew faster than others, especially the great capital cities such as London and Paris, about which so much has been written. But the development of these and a few other national centres of trade and administration was exceptional. If we are to compare present-day cities with cities of the past, we should look back to some 'typical' or 'representative' towns or cities of, say, the middle decades of the eighteenth century, places that were important but in no way pre-eminent, such as Chester or Cheltenham or Newcastle or Carlisle. Such towns were then very much as they had been a hundred years before, and many of them changed very little in the next hundred years. Could we be transported back to them, they would seem to us most strange in three respects: they would be very small; they would be very dirty; and they would be very quiet.

This quality of urban quietness, which the twentieth century has almost forgotten, used to be taken for granted, and eighteenth-century travellers rarely mention it; but they mention it occasionally, and it is brought inescapably to our notice in hundreds of eighteenth-century prints. The High in Oxford, for example, is usually depicted as a street in the middle of which dons stand and converse, and their conversation is characteristically shown as taking place within earshot of no more than a few passing washerwomen, perhaps a lady with a parasol, and possibly a drover taking his sheep into the town. 'In such a setting the entry of the mail coach, or of a gig, was a dramatic interlude. Today the dramatic interlude, if there is one, would be a sudden lull in the stream of traffic'.[1] Streets in those days were for people as much as for carts and carriages. Children played in them; street vendors set down their baskets on the pavement (if there was one) and carried on their business, as they still do in China, or India, or Peru; and when a horseman rode by he made no more disturbance than the children, or the sheep, or the cattle, or the fowls (kept in back gardens or being taken to market), or the church bells. Noise there was, but not of bedlam; subdued, in the daylight hours only, and easily disregarded.

The filthiness of towns, on the other hand, was often commented upon, even in times much more accustomed to general refuse and excrement in public places than our own. All over the country nightmen and scavengers were apt to empty their carts into the streets almost as often as into the surrounding countryside (as they were supposed to do), while the accumulated filth of eighteenth-century houses was frequently thrown out of the windows into the street below; a visitor to Edinburgh found the resultant stench in the High Street 'intolerable'. It is not surprising that Robert Adam, in one of his letters, refers to 'stinking Edinburgh'. Everywhere streams and ditches were habitually treated as common sewers; in London the Fleet ditch was described in 1722 as 'a nauceious and abominable sink of nastiness'. Pigs, dogs, donkeys and other animals lived partly in the streets, and in the larger towns hog-yards and slaughter-houses were round every corner. We are apt to forget how novel it is to live in towns which, on the whole, do not smell. In London, even in the West End, and even in the later nineteenth century, the stink was sometimes so bad as to arouse comment:

> A correspondent likens the smell in Victoria Street, Westminster, to that of a charnel-house, and the smell in the Quadrant, Regent Street, on Friday and Saturday last was so like that of carrion, that we heard the question debated whether it . . . might not arise from some, unknown, carrion there. But this is not the only part of Regent Street which has recently been distinguished by a foul smell. The stench (arising from stagnant sewage according to some, from foulness of the roadway according to others) has been specially obvious to the passer-by about the centre of the street and between Oxford Circus and Margaret Street. In the latter place it was particularly disgusting on Saturday evening. Other streets in the west of London have been, and are, suffering from persistent stink.[2]

As for the size of towns, there are figures sufficiently reliable to show how small we would think them to be. But they did not seem small to contemporaries. Thomas Pennant, who travelled widely in Britain and France in the 1760s and 1770s and had, in the words of Dr Johnson, 'greater variety of enquiry than almost any man', described Scarborough in 1779 as 'a large town', adding that 'the number of inhabitants belonging to this place are above 10,000'.[3] When he visited Newcastle three years later he found it to be 'a vast town, situated on the steep banks of the coaly Tyne';[4] he had previously explained that the population of this vast town was 'near 40,000 inhabitants'. Another, slightly later, traveller, who knew Paris and Rouen as well as he knew many major towns in England, on one occasion journeyed as far north as Inverness, and wrote, 'Inverness is a town of considerable magnitude, said to contain about eleven thousand inhabitants. Some of the houses in it are tolerably built, but the streets are narrow and dirty'.[5] And lest any reader should conclude that only Scottish towns were dirty (which most of them certainly were) the same author says of Carlisle,

> The view of the castle, on entering the city, is fine; the town is large, the upper street wide and well paved . . . The ditch around the castle is a filthy stagnated pool; and this character of filthiness is equally applicable to the walks around the city walls and the general avenues.[6]

This 'large' town contained at the time not more than 10 000 people.

By comparison, London and Paris were enormous; but by twentieth-century standards even they were not very large. Reference is often made to Wren's ambitious plan for the rebuilding of London after the Great Fire of 1666. This is probably the most famous town plan that was ever produced. Certainly it is the most famous that was never acted upon; nor could it have been acted upon without drastic changes taking place in the ownership of land. No doubt it is a brilliant conception, and has been properly admired. But it was thought up in a few days for the rebuilding of a town which did not contain, within and beyond the city walls, more than 400 000 people, and may well have contained not many more than 250 000. Yet for those days London was a quite extraordinarily large town, the largest in Europe, except for Paris. Other cities which are famous in the history of town planning, such as Antwerp, Bordeaux, Edinburgh, Florence, Nancy and many others, were made great and beautiful in their heyday for populations of less than 100 000; even Venice in the third quarter of the sixteenth century contained only about 190 000 people — a figure never subsequently exceeded — and the architectural reputation of Sienna rests on what was built for a population of perhaps 30 000. If we could be transported back to any of these famous cities, except London or Paris, we would think them small, in many cases almost incredibly small. And their size in 1750 was usually not very different from their size in 1650, or even, in quite a large number of cases, in 1550.

Then, for reasons that are still not clear, everything began to change. Between 1800 and 1900 the population of the UK, which had grown slowly from approximately three million to approximately ten million in the course of four centuries, grew over ten times faster to reach more than forty million; or, to state the matter in a more striking although approximate way, six million people lived in England, Scotland and Wales in 1600, seven million in 1700, ten million in 1800 and forty million in 1900. The words 'population explosion' are not without justification. And changes similar to those that first started in Britain were soon taking place all over Western Europe. With people there came jobs. Whether it was the jobs that called the people into existence or whether causation was the other way round is still not decided. But certainly at the very time that population began to grow so much faster than before, new machines and new processes were invented and new machinery was put in place to employ the ever-expanding labour force: spinning machines, weaving machines, coal-fired blast furnaces, steam engines — above all, steam engines. For it was steam power that made possible the railways, and the railways made possible the mass transport of people and of goods that was the foundation of the new industrial towns. It is fair to say that the railway network in Victorian Britain was as important as the dark satanic mills, and more widely conspicuous. The towns grew by natural increase but mostly by immigration. People flooded into them from the nearby counties, from the

Highlands, from famine-ridden Ireland. Growth in some cases was phenomenal; the population of Manchester numbered 41 000 in 1774 and 270 000 in 1831. At the middle of the century the typical Englishman was still a countryman, but only just. Population exceeded 250 000 in London, Liverpool and Manchester, and half a dozen other towns had populations of over 100 000. Small towns were very common; the authors of the 1851 Census noted that 'a population [of boroughs] ranging from 2,000 to 7,000 is that most commonly met with'. But fifty years later eight towns, including London, had populations of over 250 000, and the figure today (misleadingly small, because so many towns merge into one another) is seventeen, with 39 others each in excess of 100 000.

The size of cities has important consequences. Until population exceeds a certain figure perhaps 30 000, perhaps 100 000 (it depends mostly on density and the means of transport) the idea of a central focus for the city makes good sense. Before they grew too large, almost all towns of consequence had such a centre: in Alnwick, for example, or Cirencester or innumerable other English towns, the Market Place; in Edinburgh the Mercat Cross and the Lawn Market; in Florence the Piazza della Signoria; in Venice the Piazza san Marco. These central places were the common possession of the town, dominated almost always by trade and the church. Everyone went there, at one time or another, in order to buy or to sell, to pray, to gossip, to assemble, to hear public proclamations. And because everyone went there, and because in any case the town was small, the poor and the humble rubbed shoulders with the rich, and all shared, within limits, a common experience and a common sense of belonging. In the modern city with a quarter of a million inhabitants or more, that is not possible. The old central place may still exist but the life has gone out of it, because most people live in the suburbs.

Suburbs are a modern invention. For several centuries, in a great number of important cases, the town ended and the country began at the town wall. Houses were squeezed into the limited area protected by the walls, and very few houses were built in the immediately surrounding fields. In the course of time town walls began to lose their military importance—this was noticeable in England by the middle of the sixteenth century—but almost everyone continued to reside within the town, because it was convenient, customary and indeed almost necessary to live where one worked. Artisans and merchants lived above or behind their shops, as artisans and merchants had always done, and poor people continued to live as near as possible to wherever they might have work. During the seventeenth and eighteenth centuries, as roads improved and highwaymen became scarcer, the nobility and the well-to-do increasingly built country houses within a day's carriage-ride of wherever they lived in town; but these houses, or villas as they were often called, were scattered, and could in no sense be described as forming suburbs. Perhaps the first development in England which had all or most of the characteristics of a suburb was on the Eyre Estate, north-west of Regent's Park, built early in the nineteenth century.

By 1821 St John's Wood contained several hundred cottages or villas, thickly sown towards the south, and gradually thinning out towards the north. The area had its own chapel, built in 1813–14, its own inn, assembly rooms, and pleasure-gardens at the Eyre Arms, and its own cricket ground. It was more than a cluster of houses; it had developed into a full-blown suburban neighbourhood.[7]

But this was exceptional. The outward movement from the closely populated cities was only beginning in Britain during the 1820s and the 1830s. The better-off moved first. Then, by 1850, clerks and other skilled men also were beginning to leave their place of work, and to dwell in neat rows of small houses in new estates. Some suburbs were grander than others, but all had one feature in common; dissociation, more or less complete, from the heart of the city. The heart of the city stayed where it was, but now, as far as most people were concerned, its beat was fainter. This situation has persisted, and as a result the modern city is not so much a city as an idea. Only a very few people – to take the most obvious case – live in London. Londoners live in Wimbledon, Hackney, or Hampstead, in Chiswick or Shoreditch, in Greenwich, Tower Hamlets or Kingston-upon-Thames. Considerable numbers of people work in central London and visitors go there. In London, as elsewhere, the central city continues to function, but it functions for the most part as a business facility, as an heirloom, to some extent as a symbol. These uses are important. Nevertheless, they should not be allowed to disguise the fact that the present-day city-as-a-whole, once population exceeds, say, 100 000 (transport has improved but densities have diminished), is scarcely a social and in some respects not even an operational idea.

Because of the suburbs, going to work is now synonymous with travelling to work, which used not to be the case. Commuting – the word was a scarcely-used Americanism in Britain before the 1930s – was first on foot, or by train, except for those wealthy enough to own a carriage. As the suburbs spread outwards, travelling by train became more and more general. The railway train was the marvellous innovation of the Victorian age, superb in technology, spectacular, universally useful. And to make matters still more marvellous, Victorian and Edwardian trains ran exactly to time. But the domination of the train was brief. Primitive powered road vehicles began to appear in Europe in the 1870s, in the late 1880s the manufacture of automobiles for a tiny but steady sale began in France and Germany, and in 1908 the first examples of the Model T

Ford (significantly described by Henry Ford as 'the car for the people, the car that any man can own') were brought from Detroit for exhibition in London and at the Paris Salon. By 1913 petrol-driven vehicles were common in every major city in Europe and America. Most of them were lorries or motor buses. Private cars were still too expensive to be widely owned, even in America where car-ownership had nevertheless reached the figure of 11 per thousand of the population, which seemed absolutely astonishing. In Great Britain the corresponding figure was an insignificant 4, in France it was 3, and in Germany it was only 2.

Technical progress accelerated during the war years, and motor vehicles multiplied. As soon as the war was over in 1918, motor vehicles of all kinds were seen to have become a necessity. Private cars in particular were no longer looked upon as a fad or a luxury but were recognized as an essential form of transport. In 1922 there were a million vehicles on British roads, approximately twice as many as ten years before, and one-third of them were private cars. Petrol engines were replacing horses, and the age of mass private transport wa about to begin. In the United States it had begun already. Raymond Unwin went there in 1923, and was aghast to find himself in a country that possessed twelve million motor cars, a considerable percentage of which were in New York. They choked the streets, and made movement of people, especially when the offices were emptying at the end of the day, excessively difficult. Unwin foresaw that they would continue to increase in number, and that they represented a threat to the amenity of cities, whether the vehicles were moving or standing still; 'the question of parking cars in New York already presents an unsolved problem'.[8] New York was not the kind of city that Unwin was used to, or liked, or for that matter had ever imagined. He found the traffic noisy and overwhelming, and he laid most of the blame on the skyscrapers, each with hundreds of office-workers ('vertical overcrowding') and on the private cars. In 1909 he had published *Town Planning in Practice*, which is an excellent book with a very wide coverage; yet he had not thought it worthwhile to mention road traffic. He was well aware, of course, that traffic problems could exist; they had for quite some time. Even eighteenth-century town-planners sometimes made allowance for them. A 1786 plan for Edinburgh, for example, provided for a large octagonal space where an important road was to cross the busiest street of the Old Town, and this space was in order 'to prevent the accidents to which both carriages and foot-passengers would be liable if the entry to so great a thorough-fare was at right-angles to the High Street'.[9] A hundred years later street accidents had become an everyday occurrence; perhaps ten per cent of the work of surgeons during the later days of Queen Victoria was on behalf of those who had been knocked down by a cart or carriage in the street. But by 1920 the traffic problem, like so much else, had changed out of recognition. Main streets in big cities had been crowded before, but now the rapid and continuous movement of vehicles and the provision of space to park them in became two of the city's prime requirements and principal problems.

Unwin—and he was not the only one—disliked and misunderstood the rapidly growing demand for modern road transport; 'a passing craze for incessant movement', he called it.[10] But it was not a passing craze. Le Corbusier understood the new developments much better, and rejoiced in them. But he too misjudged the situation. He loved the machine—'the great life of the machine has shaken society'—and no doubt he loved the immensely stylish cars of the 1920s such as Rolls Royce, Bugatti, Delage. It is small wonder if he did, for these were the most stylish motor cars that have ever been built. Sympathetic to modern machinery and not least to automobiles, he made what must have seemed generous provision for cars and other speeding vehicles in his city plans, especially in the Voisin Plan of 1925. But the flow of motorized traffic that Le Corbusier planned for soon became a deluge. Thousands of vehicles an hour rushing past his widely spaced towers of concrete would quickly have destroyed the dream. Instead of the town being, as he imagined, 'like a great park' it would have become more like a great parking-lot. And indeed, some town centres in America have been reduced to this, lofty towers rising from a wasteland of parked vehicles. Elsewhere, in every country, it has seemed to many people that the main impact of the motor vehicle, moving or stationary, has been to take over and dehumanize large areas of towns, leaving room only for offices, streets, car-parks ('the parked car is just another form of urban rubbish')[11] and, of course, the vehicles themselves. Certainly the motor vehicle is omnipresent. In Great Britain there were over two million in 1932, almost five million in 1952, twenty million in 1982; and usage has increased faster than numbers. But we scarcely need to be told how many of them there are, or how often they are used, because they are multitudinous, and they have obviously and radically altered and extended urban and suburban life.

New technology created the motor vehicle, and it has almost as much recreated the fabric of the city itself. During the past one hundred years technological innovations have revolutionized architectural design, and have greatly changed the whole business of building. Structural steel and re-inforced concrete are at the centre of the stage, and together they dominate twentieth-century architecture. Concrete itself is not a new material. It was used by the Romans, sometimes on a large scale, noticeably for the walls and dome of the Pantheon in Rome. Then it was virtually lost sight of as a building material for over a thousand years. (One trembles to think what the great cathedrals and palaces of the Middle Ages and the Renaissance would have looked like if concrete had been available—but perhaps the medieval builders would have been shrewd enough, and ambitious enough, to ignore it). Concrete began to be rediscovered in the early part of the nineteenth century, but its use was limited until methods were devised to combine it with iron or steel. Iron, made much more cheaply by new processes devised after 1750, was first used for structural purposes by engineers in the late eighteenth century. Nash used it, conspicuously and to the astonishment of his contemporaries, in the Royal Pavilion at Brighton as early as 1818. By 1860 Viollet le Duc was prophesying the advent of a new architecture dominated by steel and iron, and Labrouste had already applied some of the new methods to the Library of Saint-Geneviève in Paris, and to the reading room in the Bibliothèque Nationale. But brick and stone remained the standard building materials until it was discovered that steel rods encased in concrete provide a material which has the crushing strength of concrete allied to the tensile strength of steel; and this makes very wide spans possible. The changeover to concrete began in the 1890s, most of the pioneering work being done in France and Switzerland, and within a few decades concrete became the dominant building material throughout Europe and America. The designs for Tony Garnier's 'Cité Industrielle', made in 1904, are all based on the use of reinforced concrete, and Garnier subsequently carried out several schemes in Lyon, using this material, between 1910 and 1930. Le Corbusier's 'Ville Contemporaine', more showy but less realistic than the 'Cité Industrielle', likewise depended upon concrete; Le Corbusier, it has been said, with much truth, 'fell in love with reinforced concrete'[12] at the very start of his career. By 1925 many reinforced concrete skyscrapers had been built, several reinforced concrete houses and at least one reinforced concrete church. None of these was in the UK. British architects had some doubts about concrete. A writer in the *Journal of the RIBA* in 1924 acknowledged that concrete 'is *the* factor which must have the greatest influence upon the architecture of the future'. But, he added, 'reinforced concrete . . . demands a treatment entirely its own. The enormous facilities of the material will undoubtedly be a danger to its development in design'.[13] He was right. Although concrete has made possible may splendid buildings, buildings of lightness, simplicity and poise, it has some unlikeable characteristics: it is relatively cheap and is therefore apt to be used regardless of its appearance; it is apt to look horrible after weathering for a few years;[14]   and, as reinforced concrete, it makes possible the construction of very high buildings and of buildings with very wide spans. As a result, towns today are apt to have a drabness of appearance which in general they used not to possess, and they tend less and less to be dominated by church spires and more and more by tall, plain, rectangular, enormous concrete slabs and towers. These changes have been partly relieved, and partly reinforced, by sheet glass, produced by new glass-making processes that were introduced at the end of the nineteenth century. Until these new processes were perfected, large panes of glass were expensive and very large sheets could not be made. But when skeleton construction came in, buildings could be erected without visible vertical support, being enclosed not by load-bearing walls but by curtains of glass. Walls became windows. Curtain-walling appeared in the Bauhaus buildings by Gropius in 1925, and was a feature of the Villa Savoye by Le Corbusier in 1929. By the 1970s there were glass houses, suspended curving glass skins, and steel-and-glass office spaces; the Willis Faber Dumas offices in Ipswich show what can be done with glass and imagination.

All these urban developments and innovations—far more population, far more traffic, suburbs, concrete, skyscrapers, tower blocks, car-parks—all these have flooded down upon us in the course of a mere sixty or seventy years; and it is only when their novelty is realized and they are all added together that the extraordinary character of the twentieth-century city becomes apparent. Cities have existed for centuries, but they never much resembled the cities we have today. What we are accustomed to find in cities nowadays is almost entirely new, and it is for that reason that we have had to struggle for the last fifty years to devise new ways of managing cities, that we have had to graft new forms onto old forms, and to adapt old forms to new uses. This task has been very difficult. And it has proved especially difficult to retain (never mind to increase) the advantages and attractions which cities used to possess—their beauty, individuality and repose—while accepting the new materials, the new styles, the new traffic, and above all the new scale.

The task of adaptation and further development would not have been so difficult if urban novelty had been restricted to technical innovations alone. But the uses of the new buildings that have had to be built have also changed, more or less independently. As early as 1952 the Commission in London remarked on the number and size of new office blocks and power stations that were appearing all over the country, and on the problems that they posed:

> Their colossal size suggests a monumentality traditionally reserved for buildings of religious or other civic purpose. But neither office buildings nor power stations can claim high significance on an emotional plane, and to 'monumentalise' them is to debase the currency of architectural values and to incur the risk of rendering the buildings themselves ridiculous.[15]

Architects, however, were not deterred, and the effects of the technical innovations and the changes in demand were magnified and reinforced by what soon became the prevailing attitude among architect/planners towards scale. Architects of all ages have had a weakness for grandeur, but during the second quarter of the twentieth century this weakness became something like an obsession. The eighteenth century discovered the Picturesque, and the twentieth century has had the misfortune to fall for the Gigantesque. Buildings became wider, deeper, and above all higher. Land that had been the site of six separate buildings became the site of one. Fenestrations became uncountable rows of identical windows. Cliff faces became the rule, and massivity was all.

The gigantesque came in with Le Corbusier. He was the prophet of 'planning on a noble scale',[16] of 'enormous schemes of planning'.[17] His vision of the twentieth-century city was of soaring towers, immensely wide highways, great open spaces. 'Elements on a scale hitherto unimagined', he wrote, 'will achieve sublime effects'.[18] The materials of city planning were said to be 'sky, space, trees, steel and cement', and in his judgement they were to be used to create 'vast architectural perspectives . . . a dazzling mirage of unimaginable beauty'. The possibilities were boundless, because of scientific progress.

> Science has given us the machine. The machine gives us limitless power . . . We possess technology which is the sum of man's acquired knowledge. And armed with this technology . . . we can create *great works*.[19]

It may seem somewhat surprising to a later generation that these great works were not to be devoid of beauty, but would produce 'ordered delights'.

> suddenly you are at the foot of the first sky-scrapers. Between them there is not the feeble glimmer of light to be found in miserable New York, but enormous space. There are extensive parks, terraces of houses rise tier upon tier above the lawns, amid areas of woodland. Low buildings stretch out and lead the eye far away, along undulating lines of tree-tops. Here stands the central CITY, full of people, calm and serene, amid pure air, all noise muted by the foliage of the trees . . . We drive quietly on into the residential areas. The plan of the buildings, some set forward and some recessed, extends the architectural perspective. There are gardens, play-grounds, sports areas. The sky dominates everything, stretching away into the distance. The horizontal lines of terraced roofs stand out sharply, fringed with greenery that makes them seem like hanging gardens. Regularity of detail emphasises the firm outlines of the large masses of far-flung buildings. Softened by the blue haze of distance, the sky-scrapers raise their great geometrical planes entirely of glass. Reflected in these glass façades from top to bottom the azure sky gleams and sparkles. Dazzling spectacle. Immense but radiant prisms . . . As dusk falls, the glass sky-scrapers are ablaze with light.[20]

Certainly, he wrote well. He was to some degree a poet, and the more he talked about backing up his arguments with history and science and statistics the more he wrote poetry. But all his proposed schemes began with the immense and immensely improbable advantage of an extensive virgin site, and he always specified regularity and order everywhere, the same for everyone. In other words, he always wanted to control and order everyone, which is what architecture on a grand scale, and a good deal of planning, are very apt to be about. His vision of the twentieth-century city was in many ways splendid; but it was fatally marred by his passion for immensity, uniformity and strict order. Nevertheless, a whole generation was persuaded.

> Alors que les Etats-Unis continuaient à construire des grattes-ciel, grattes-ciel ayant honte d'euxmêmes puisqu'ils cherchaient désormais à rassembler aux cathédrales mediévales, l'Europe rêvait de cités babyloniennes, beaucoup plus grandiose que les rêves de l'Ecole de Chicago.[21]

Le Corbusier's drawings are likewise inspiring—sparkling white buildings of clear geometrical form rise into a blue sky, with roof gardens and balconies, freely spaced out in an open, lightly wooded landscape. In spite of the concrete and the geometry, there is a romantic charm about many of Le Corbusier's schemes; at any rate on paper. But always he thought big. He wanted, for example, to have an elevated expressway crossing Paris from east to west, and he wanted it to be no less than 120 metres in width. His Unité d'Habitation, built on the outskirts of Marseilles after the war, was planned to provide a completely serviced environment for 1 600 people living in a single building seventeen storeys high. The flats are entered on either side of corridors which are 130 metres long and artificially lit, the whole construction resting on a gigantic thirty-foot-high substructure of concrete pillars. The garden, or sun terrace, is on the roof. At Chandigargh, Le Corbusier's buildings, large as they are, are so far apart that even an ardent admirer of 'shafts of space' and 'routes of movement' has felt obliged to say that 'they fail to master the space they are in'.[22] Of much of Le Corbusier's work it might indeed be said, 'c'est presque l'alliance de l'architecture et de l'infini'.[23]

This exultation in grandeur on a heroic scale—not new in architecture or town planning, but now capable of expression in layouts and structures more colossal than ever before—is to be found also in the writings of many of Le Corbusier's followers. Sigfried Giedion, for example, in his often reprinted and highly influential *Space, Time and Architecture*, rejoiced in the fact that 'possibilities of a great scale are inherent in our period'.[24] He saw in the modern parkway or motorway, such as already existed in the 1930s in Connecticut and New York State, the scale of construction—and reconstruction—that should be aimed for by all enlightened architects and town planners of the later twentieth century. He wrote with lyrical enthusiasm about these new roads 'born out of the vision of our period', and his description of the delights of parkway driving bears just sufficient relation to subsequent experience as not to seem perfectly ridiculous:

> The road is laid into the countryside, grooved into it between gentle green slopes blending so naturally into the contiguous land that the eye cannot distinguish between what is nature and what the contribution of the landscape architect . . . Air views may show the great sweep of the highway, the beauty of its alignment, the graceful sequence of its curves, but only at the wheel of the automobile can one feel what it really means—the liberation from unexpected light signals and cross traffic, the freedom of uninterrupted forward motion . . . Full realization is given to the driver and freedom to the machine. Riding up and down the long sweeping grades produces an exhilarating dual feeling which is like nothing else so much as sliding swiftly on skis through untouched snow down the sides of high mountains.[25]

Here again we have that love of speed and machinery which had been so often expressed in the 1920s. And the reader of *Space, Time and Architecture* is further invited to admire the beauty of what are nowadays slightingly referred to as spaghetti junctions: 'the modern sculpture of numberless single or triple cloverleaves', overpasses, ramps and 'great bridges'. All this grandeur, of course, was in the countryside. But Giedion's point is precisely that it should not remain there. The parkways of the 1930s had not yet penetrated the city, but 'after the necessary surgery has been performed . . . the parkway will go through the city as it does today through the landscape'.[26] And this would be most suitable, not only because the parkway speeds the flow of traffic but because it coincides in scale with the skyscraper, and the city—the whole city, that is—'must adopt the new scale which is identical with that of its bridges and parkways. What really needs to be changed is the entire structure of the city.'[27] After all this, it can hardly come as a surprise to find that Giedion was a completely uncritical admirer of Haussmann:

> When Haussmann in the [eighteen] 'fifties undertook the transformation of Paris, he slashed into the body of the city—as a contemporary expressed it—with sabre strokes. Cleanly he drew the blade, cutting keen straight thoroughfares through the congested districts, solving his traffic problems by single daring thrusts. In our own period even more heroic operations are necessary.[28]

It is all very dramatic. It is also very revealing, because here we have the inescapable essence of Le Corbusier's message and that of his followers. Heroic operations are necessary; new construction and reconstruction must both be undertaken on a vast scale.

What does all this matter now? Le Corbusier and those who followed him had little influence in Britain in the 1930s and 1940s. It is true that the MARS Group (its best legacy the Highpoint One flats in Highgate, built 1935–6) adopted, or shared, many of the beliefs of Le Corbusier and the Bauhaus, and especially agreed with highbrow Continental opinion that the whole of the existing urban environment should be swept away as far as possible. These 'modern' views gained ground among British architects and town planners in the 1950s and 1960s.[29] But even so, the architects and the town planners and the developers failed to realize Le Corbusier's dream. It never was very practicable, partly because it had no connection with economic realities, and partly because it was so big. And if there was a time for it, in one or two places after the war, that time has passed. So why remember it now? The answer is that the dream still matters because the architects and the town planners and the developers have in fact done worse than not realize it; they have realized bits of it. Concrete, which was to make the city so white and gleaming, has become the commonest urban surface of the twentieth century and has turned out, on the whole, to be an artistic snare and a disaster. Instead of cheering us all up it depresses us. There is something peculiarly lifeless, dreary and brutal about concrete. When Le Corbusier himself used it in the Unité d'Habitation after the war he used it in a rough brutal style; and the New Brutalism was born. Highways, too, have been brought into town, some of them wide and sweeping; but instead of being lightly used, as in the dream, they are a torrent of vehicles. Full realization, as envisaged by Giedion, is certainly not given to the driver, and freedom certainly not to the machine. Tall towers have been built, some of them interesting and even elegant, most of them neither. A good number of them have had to be pulled down, soul-less and even uninhabitable. But in any case, where are the parks and the trees upon which the lofty towers look out in the Ville Contemporaine? Where are the compensating open spaces which Le Corbusier realized would be so necessary if tall towers were built? Where are the coherent street fronts that he imagined? The Barbican is an especially determined and large-scale attempt, by followers of Le Corbusier, to put the Master's ideas into practice, and the result is a trio of forty-three-storey triangular towers four hundred feet high, (and therefore not easy to see properly from the ground) which look down on closely surrounding concrete walls and walkways with a particularly repulsive finish, on a multi-storey car park, and on the sixteenth-century church of St Giles, Cripplegate, which appears as ill at ease and out of place as the people. No doubt the towers are, as has been said, of Piranesian grandeur; but the *tout ensemble* is not, and the general effect is cold, hostile and depressing.[30]

Failure to build according to Le Corbusier has been partly a failure of money; the kind of scheme that he imagined required many acres, or most likely many hectares, and finance to correspond. Development on such a scale is seldom possible. Consequently, we have tall towers set in asphalt car parks, or rising here and there from the heel of an old-fashioned pavement in an old-fashioned street. We have slabs looking out on more slabs. We have highways which speed the flow of traffic but which no pedestrian dare try to cross, and therefore the pedestrians, like rats, go underground, or cross on ugly concrete or iron bridges. Too much of what is new has been overwhelming in scale, and strikingly inhuman.

For many people, indeed, the inhumanity of the twentieth century city is its outstanding characteristic. People within it seem small, alien, vulnerable and unwanted. This is chiefly because of modern scale and the never-ending press of modern machinery, both of which strike at humanity. And there is a further important point, made forty years ago by Helen Rosenau. Rosenau pointed out that the enormously influential plans for ideal cities that were drawn up in the early twentieth century—by Garnier, Le Corbusier, Sant'Elia—were plans to solve certain technical problems, not human ones. Garnier and Sant'Elia designed with the avowed purpose of meeting the needs of modern trade and industry. Le Corbusier laid most emphasis on architectural form and on the rapid movement of vehicles—hardly surprising when one recalls his enthusiasm for the linear city which he described as 'fundamentally and inescapably a function of the transportation system, of storage needs, of merchandise handling problems'. The inevitable result of these approaches to urban design was that the essential human desires for security, comfort and reassurance, to say nothing of love, beauty and companionship, were pushed into the background. As Rosenau expressed it, these are ideal towns 'for robots who want to move, although no aim for this movement is apparent'.[31] Civic buildings are given the least possible emphasis in these cities—offices are the central focus of the Ville Contemporaine—and partly as a result the cities tend to have no recognizable centre or significance, and seem to be capable of indefinite outward extension. Even Garnier's concern for zoning—an immensely influential idea that was adopted by Le Corbusier—has not proved wholly beneficial. It separates work from housing, and may be said in this way to contribute to the fragmentation of life. And however desirable it was when manufacturing industry and pollution of one kind or another were practically synonymous, it makes much less sense when many industrial processes are pollution-free and industrial buildings are hard to distinguish from schools or hospitals—except that they are often architecturally more interesting. Dividing a town into distinct compartments is all very well on paper and may sometimes be necessary; but the process leaves very little scope for urban variety, and the interest and individual quality of places are seriously reduced. A great stretch of houses and flats followed by a great stretch of factories and warehouses followed by a great stretch of playing fields and open spaces—we have seen it so often and it is really not very interesting; the element of urban variety has almost completely disappeared.

Hopeful dreams about the twentieth-century city lasted until the 1960s. But long before then it had become obvious that the ever-expanding motorized cities suffered from serious disadvantages. The first efforts to change the direction of their development were made in the 1920s, in America, where cities spread further and towers loomed larger than anywhere else and the human situation was therefore worst. Some planners—Lewis Mumford was among them—conceived the idea that, in order to counteract the unfriendly anonymity of the big city, the community spirit of the suburb or small town should be revived by means of carefully structured neighbourhoods. This was 'Radburn planning', so-called after its first application at Radburn, New Jersey. According to its originators, there were two requirements. First, vehicles had to be kept out of the way of people, as far as possible. So there were to be local roads and pedestrian paths, altogether separate from the routes for through traffic. This proposal was not entirely novel. In B. W. Richardson's *Hygeia: A City of Health*, published in 1876, it had been suggested that all the houses should be built over arched subways, with communications to the city entering at the lower level, below the houses. This was to improve both safety and health. No regard was paid to the proposal at the time, but by the 1920s the desirability of some such scheme was vastly more obvious than it had been in the 1870s, and the idea of separating traffic from pedestrians was pressed enthusiastically. Secondly, Radburn planning involves the creation of physically distinct neighbourhoods. Each of these, containing 'a good mix' of a few thousand people (the figure varied from 5 000 to 10 000), should have its own schools, its own shopping facilities and its own parks, and each should be contained within wider through-roads with cul-de-sac roads leading into the neighbourhood itself. Planning of this kind reminds one of the seventeen *contrade* in Sienna, or of Rasmussen's view of London in the early 1930s as an assembly of villages. It tries to restore the atmosphere of humanity—rough and imperfect humanity, but humanity nevertheless—that survived in all earlier cities. It may even be said that this scheme to produce 'cellular neighbourhood developments' is not too far removed from trying to create a likeness of Howard's garden cities within the great city itself. It is as if Howard, and the city that he wanted to escape from—or rather, a subsequent development of it—have come together. But because neighbourhood planning requires fundamental changes in the road pattern it is of course very difficult to carry out, and has for the most part been confined to new developments, such as Coventry in the 1950s and, most recently, Milton Keynes.

Twenty years after the 1920s rediscovery of neighbourhood planning, dissatisfaction with the modern city had spread and intensified. Many people began to think that cities, far from being centres of civilization as they were supposed to be, were a kind of malaise; or that, if they were indeed a part of civilization, they should be included in what Stendahl once called 'the ugly spectacle of civilization'. Even some of those who had done much to create them, or had welcomed their novel twentieth-century appearance, began to have their doubts. In the early 1940s, as already noted,[32] Pevsner was defending modern architecture on the ground that if it looked joyless and dreary that was because it suited contemporary life. In 1945 Gropius, now in America, referred to 'the miraculous potential-ities of the machine', thus recalling Le Corbusier's triumphant declaration, 'The great life of the Machine has shaken Society'. But Gropius was far from triumphant. The machine, he lamented, had all but destroyed human companionship, and city streets 'have been degraded to mere traffic channels for lonely strangers'.[33] The building of neighbourhood community centres, he concluded, was now 'of even greater urgency than housing itself'.[34]

But the course of urban development was not to be so easily changed. Post-war housing was an immediate necessity all over Europe, and in Britain Government housing programmes received absolute priority. In the course of a few years public authorities became the greatest landlords of all time. About one quarter of all the dwellings in England and Wales, and about one third of all those in Scotland, have been built by Government, and if account is taken only of those built since 1945 the fractions are much greater. Thus it is public house-building that has come to dominate the structure and appearance of large areas of all British cities. As for the buildings themselves, they tended to become bigger if not always cruder as the years went by. The Corbusier-like slabs of the 1950s were succeeded after 1960 by tower-blocks of twenty to thirty storeys, 'notable townscape objects, notorious subjects of alienation and vandalism'.[35] The effort in the later 1960s to build half a million houses a year resulted in the adoption of patented building systems, mostly developed in France and Sweden, used for the rapid construction of high-rise blocks of housing. Many of these structures have now been demolished. They were riddled with defects, very few tenants liked living in them, and the deck-access style of design with open walkways on the different levels was an encouragement to thugs and criminals. After 1970, or thereabouts, there was not much confidence left:

In the first place, post-war buildings began to come to pieces: they blew up, collapsed, leaked, burnt out, had their roofs blown off. The spacious new houses and flats that people could not afford to heat suffered appallingly from condensation. In the high flats, the lifts failed and there was no one on hand to repair them: in the sealed office blocks, the air-conditioning failed or the external cladding fell off. Those who had the courage to employ expensive *avant-garde* designers found themselves at worst ruined or at best embarrassed by experimental technology that went wrong. Those who were forced to employ the cheapest found that 'cutting corners' could end in even more spectacular disasters. People began to look back with regret not only at the styles of the old architecture but at its comparatively safe technology.[36]

And this was a time when architecture was supposed to have come closer to engineering!

Thus cities and the problems faced by architects and planners have changed and changed again during the last fifty years. Some of the changes began in the nineteenth century but before 1900 they were not, in general, significant; many of them, such as motor vehicles, concrete and controls, have made their big impact only since 1945. The cities that we now work with are quite novel in character, an unprecedented hotch-potch, or amalgam, of the old and the new; where the new is often revolutionary, and in some ways dominant. We may be inclined to believe that beneath all the changes, which are so obvious, the city remains essentially the same. This is true only in the sense that we who inhabit the city are essentially the same. The great purposes for which cities are built—government, trade, convenience and pleasure—remain, in essence, unaltered, but the way and the appearance of life have altered very much, for all the reasons given above. In these changed circumstances it cannot be expected that beauty and amenity, if they are to continue to exist in the modern city, will be reproduced in the same form, or called into existence by the same means, as in the past.

In one sense, curiously enough, we do not often have the same power to make extensive improvements that our ancestors had. The intensity of land use in cities has increased so much that opportunities to carry out large-scale schemes of renewal are uncommon and are usually a good deal restricted by conflicting interests. Until as late as the middle of the nineteenth century, in most cities, expansion within the city centre, or quite close to it, was seldom very difficult. Building densities tended to be lower than they are today, and land, along with other forms of wealth, was concentrated in fewer hands. This made development relatively easy. During the Middle Ages, when many streets, squares and open spaces came to be laid out as they still exist, the Church, royal families and the nobility had complete possession of large areas, urban as well as rural, and built on them as they chose. The situation was not dissimilar in the seventeenth, the eighteenth and even the early nineteenth century. Thus Covent Garden (once monastic land) was planned by Inigo Jones in the 1630s on part of seven acres owned by the fourth Earl of Bedford. Equally accessible to Whitehall and to Lincoln's Inn Fields, in the very heart of London, it became and remained for a hundred years a fashionable place to live, and its arcades and coffee-shops were always full of people. At the end of the eighteenth century one of the Earl's descendants began to develop an estate which extended to no less than 112 acres just north of Oxford Street—what is now Bloomsbury—almost as close to Westminster and the law courts as Covent Garden itself. In the 1820s the Earl of Moray laid out his Edinburgh lands, thirteen acres in extent, so as to form the grandest element in Edinburgh's New Town, 'the whole development', as the Earl himself put it, 'governed by a single plan'. Even in the middle decades of the nineteenth century the railway companies did not find it too difficult to secure large areas in the centre of cities on which to build railway stations and extensive marshalling yards. Opportunities for unimpeded development on a comparable scale occur very rarely in our cities today. Our task is to repair, renew or extend these venerable artifacts, a little at a time.

This bit-by-bit process is full of conflicts of interest, and is at the same time a communal enterprise. It involves the taking of important decisions by scores of people; architects, developers, planners, surveyors, highway engineers and politicians are among the most prominent. And, in addition, those who take the decisions quite often work and negotiate amid protests by hundreds of other people; a current public enquiry in London sees the QC for the developer pitted against the City Corporation, English Heritage, ten conservation groups and a number of retail traders. The difficulties are usually greatest when old buildings are involved. Justifiable concern about the heritage of the past used not to be very lively, but nowadays conservation groups are strong. Developers, on the other hand, are inclined to regard old buildings as a nuisance, and it is not hard to understand their attitude. Many old buildings are in a poor state of repair; they may be difficult to adapt for a new use; they may be positioned so as to be in the way of the obvious plan of development for the area. But the difficulties in the path of retaining old buildings are usually exaggerated. Admittedly there are cases where the retention of an existing building would make the reasonable development of a site uneconomic. But such cases are not the rule. There was a time, twenty or so years ago, when architects were quick to declare that old buildings could be put in order and adapted only at enormous cost, or that they could not be saved at all; and the 'clean-sweep' town planners of that day were very ready to believe them. Many of us can remember pleasant old buildings, or whole rows or terraces of pleasant old buildings, or even distinguished buildings, which were knocked down in the 1950s and 1960s without any serious thought being given to the question of how they could be saved and what it would cost. That is less likely to happen nowadays for three reasons. Firstly, we have come to appreciate much more than we did the aesthetic value of these buildings, how irreplaceable they are and how special is their contribution to the urban scene; and this appreciation has doubtless been sharpened by the sad discovery that modern buildings designed to take their place are often dreary or offensive. Secondly, architects have given more careful thought in the last twenty years to the problems of restoration and renovation. Techniques have been improved and skills extended; and architects have come to see that renovating and adapting old buildings can present as much of a challenge to their skills and imagination as building new. Thirdly, we have grown much more clever and imaginative at finding new uses for old buildings. In Paris, for example, the Hotel de Sully is now occupied by the Caisse Nationale des Monuments Historiques de France; in London, Covent Garden has been redeveloped for a wide variety of uses; in Edinburgh, John Watson's Hospital, for a hundred years used as a school, has become a Gallery of Modern Art; and the ancient tolbooth in Kirkcudbright, dating from about 1580, is now occupied by the Department of Agriculture and Fisheries. Countless other examples could be given. Disused churches pose particularly difficult problems; nevertheless, there are church buildings now in use as community centres, restaurants, art galleries; and at least one provides excellent accommodation as an electricity sub-station. It must be stressed, however, that new uses may not appear the moment that old ones have been given up. Buildings, like people, may take a little time to find a new job. Demolish in haste, repent at leisure.

It also seems to be the case, unhappily, that present-day developers are seldom much concerned about beauty and amenity in general. This is no doubt part of the low standard of artistic education which commonly prevails. But it is especially important in the developer, or client as he used to be called, because nothing would happen without him. He is the originator and instigator of the whole business of building, and it is very likely that his ideas of what should be done will determine not only the nature but also the manner and style of the entire scheme, and even many of its details. Architects and planners may comment, invent, and adjust, conservationists may protest, politicians may make or extract concessions; but what is in the end built must suit the client. From the outset he knows, at least in general terms, what he wants, and also, although perhaps not exactly, what he is prepared to pay. Within the limits thus set, the architects and the planners must do their best. They have their limitations, as already discussed. But in thinking about the process of urban development it is essential not to underestimate the importance of the developer. The architect who is dealing with an unenlightened client/developer has obviously little chance of adding to the nation's store of beauty and amenity. If, on the other hand, the client is a person or a corporation or a government possessing educated taste and a sense of social responsibility, the prospects are much better. What, then, are the chances?

Governments have always been among the most prominent of all developers, and often they have been the most prominent. Many of the buildings that we admire today were built by Governments. But Governments of the past were not much like those of the present. Democratic processes and public opinion are modern ideas. Until the nineteenth century—in some countries until the late nineteenth century—Governments were autocratic and their overriding aim was to maintain their authority. So they built to impress, sometimes to overawe. Like it or not, many of the finest buildings and most admired urban spaces in the world were the product of tyranny and had nothing to do with the preferences of those who were obliged to pay for them. The Palazzo Ducale and the Campanile and almost all the other much admired buildings in Venice were constructed during a lengthy period when the affairs of the Republic were entirely in the hands of a strictly limited number of families who were assisted in the tasks of Government by a dreaded secret police. The Place des Vosges (originally Place Royale) was built by the flamboyant Henri IV with pavilions on the north and south sides for Henry himself and his Queen, the other dwellings to be lived in by the cream of Parisian society. The Champs Elysées and the Etoile as well as Versailles itself were brought into existence more for the glorification of Louis XIV than for the satisfaction of his subjects. The Place de la Concorde in Paris as well as the famous *places* in Nancy and Bordeaux were built to the greater glory of Louis XV. The nineteenth-century reconstruction of Paris by Napoleon III has already been mentioned.

In Britain, life was not so autocratic, nor building so grand. Similar ideas, nevertheless, were in circulation. In the later seventeenth century, when Holland was the rival that Britain strove to emulate and out-do, a small book appeared entitled *Observations upon the United Provinces of the Netherlands*. The author was Sir William Temple, ambassador to the Netherlands in the 1660s and 1670s. In his book Temple makes no reference to Dutch painting, scholarship, or science, three of the great wonders of the age, but he dwells admiringly on the beauty and even 'magnificence' to be found in Dutch cities, readily paid for, he tells us, by means of 'extream taxes':

> This makes the beauty and strength of their Towns: the pleasantness of their Walks, and their Crafts in and near all their Cities; And in short, the Beauty, Convenience, and sometimes Magnificence of their Public Works, to which every Man pays as willingly, and takes as much pleasure and vanity in them, as

those of other Countrys do in the same circumstances, among the Possessions of their Families, or private Inheritance.[37]
Temple further notes that 'all this Greatness' is a cause as well as a consequence of prosperity. Any kingdom or state, he says,

By the Magnificence of Courts, or of Public Structures; By encouraging beauty in private Buildings, and the adornment of Towns with pleasant and regular plantations of Trees; By the celebration of some Noble Festivals or Solemnities; By the institution of some great Marts or Fairs; and by the contrivance of any extraordinary and renowned Spectacles [can] invite and occasion, as much and as often as can be, the concourse of busie or idle People from the neighbouring or remoter Nations, whose very passage and intercourse is a great encrease of Wealth and of Trade, and a secret incentive of People to inhabit a Country, where Men may meet with equal advantages, and more entertainments of life, than in other places.[38]

Arguments like these met with ready acceptance in Britain, where commercial ambition was widespread and grandeur in public buildings and in the laying out of cities was not unknown. The Banqueting House in Whitehall had already been built, and it was, as Roy Strong has put it, a monument to the claim of the first two Stuart kings 'to be the representatives of God on earth'.[39] In Temple's own time, apart from the rebuilding of London after the Great Fire and the creation of the new St Paul's 'in the grand manner', improvements were made to St James's Park by Charles II, and the Mall was laid out as a broad avenue with four lines of trees. Late in the seventeenth century the Naval Hospital at Greenwich (designed by Wren for Charles II), was completed by William III partly as a memorial to his wife;[40] while during the eighteenth century large numbers of distinguished buildings were commissioned by Government, such as the Horse Guards, Somerset House (the largest public building completed in Britain before 1800), and Register House in Edinburgh.

If we ask how development was managed in the private sector, we find that attitudes were not dissimilar. Artistic order and confidence reached unusually high levels in eighteenth-century Britain. Wealth and influence were in the hands of one or two thousand families who constituted a well-defined and exclusive society, its members sufficiently educated to take an intelligent interest in everything, and sufficiently wealthy to get the best of everything that was to be had. Building was one of this society's principal interests. Enormously rich by comparison with the country at large, its members built to their own glory, and to impress everyone else. Noblemen, gentlemen and wealthy merchants built splendid town and country houses, and developed their estates, often with outstanding artistic success; and this was due in no small part to the learning and sensibility of these same men of property who commissioned the work. Thus Mavisbank

House in Midlothian was designed by its owner, Sir John Clerk, 'under the correction of one Mr Adams, a skilful architect', i.e. William Adam.[41] Chiswick House was designed by Lord Burlington for himself, and Burlington had been to Italy and had studied Palladio's villas in and around Vicenza. Hopetoun House as it stands today is largely the work of William Adam, who was entrusted with the project by Lord Hopetoun, 'a refined and cultivated young man of the World', who during a Grand Tour had studied the architecture of Paris, Rome, Venice and Bologna, and who was himself largely responsible for Robert Adam's important tour of Italy. The Palladian bridge at Wilton, 'one of the most beautiful structures imaginable'[42] and a marvellous solution to a very complex design problem, was designed by the ninth earl of Pembroke, assisted by the architect Robert Morris. These are far from isolated instances. Most eighteenth-century building that has endured was commissioned by men who fully understood what they wanted, and who shared the same educated taste as those whom they employed as architects. Classical forms were the basis of the eighteenth-century style. They had been introduced into British architecture by Inigo Jones, and, suitably adapted and scaled down to meet domestic needs, they provided superlatively elegant solutions to the building problems of a superlatively elegant age. They could be, and they often were, studied in Italy, both by patrons and architects. But gentlemen could also learn about them sitting in their libraries at home. Colen Campbell, who worked with and for Lord Burlington, published in 1715 the first folio volume of *Vitruvius Britannicus*, a book of illustrations of the best modern buildings in Britain, i.e. those designed in the Palladian style. By 1725 two further volumes had appeared, and the success was so great that when another edition came out it ran to five volumes. Giacomo Leoni, who was a Venetian settled in England, published the first complete English edition of Palladio's *Four Books of Architecture* between 1715 and 1720; three further editions appeared in the next twenty years. James Gibbs's *Book of Architecture* was published in 1728. Sir William Chambers published *A Treatise on Civil Architecture* in 1759, in which 'the principles of that art are laid down, and illustrated by a great number of plates'. A third edition appeared in 1791, 'greatly augmented'. James Paine published his *Plans and Elevations of Noblemen's Houses* in 1783. These books were vastly influential. The gentlemen who read them and then commissioned buildings for themselves were apt to know as much about good design as the architects and the builders, and many so-called amateur architects — Lord Burlington led the way — were as well able to design sound and elegant houses as those who belonged to the nascent architectural profession.

In town planning similar influences were at work. The schemes that we admire today were built for the wealthy, and often under their direct influence. Thus the New Town of Edinburgh was built for lairds and lawyers and wealthy merchants and other men of property; its lay-out was suggested by a little-known young architect called James Craig, but his plan was referred for adjustment and improvement to a number of gentlemen, among whom was Sir James Clerk, an amateur architect who designed and built Penicuik House, and Lord Kames, a friend of James Adam and author of a book on aesthetics now forgotten. In some cases the architect was himself the developer. John Wood the Elder was an accomplished and successful eighteenth century architect who was 'sole contractor' for Queen Square in Bath, a speculation which was so successful that he went on to design the far more famous Circus.[43] Nash, when building Regent Street, took the Quadrant in his own name and persuaded several building tradesmen to come in with him in the speculation; he acted as planner, architect, surveyor and developer. The architects and planners of those times worked for the wealthy and they worked within the framework of well-understood and accepted norms of design. Indeed, one is tempted to say that how to design in the eighteenth century was almost as well defined as how to behave. Yet in many instances—Bath is an outstanding example—the standard forms of the day were improved upon with genius.

In almost all respects the situation now is entirely different, both in the public sector and in the private sector. There is no 'rule of taste'. The division of labour decrees that those who know about architecture and town planning are architects and town planners, while the rest of us, although we are prone to have opinions, educated or otherwise, rarely have much genuine knowledge of the subject. The architects, unfortunately, cannot agree with one another about what is good architecture, and change their opinions every ten or twenty years; while those who commission or authorize important schemes can offer little aesthetic help, being government departments, regional or district councils, consortiums of developers, or business corporations. It is not easy to see much resemblance between any of these and the patrons of the eighteenth century. Few modern business men or public servants have studied the writings of J. M. Richards or Le Corbusier or Pevsner or Robert Venturi, nor have they travelled to Sweden or the Netherlands or North America in order to familiarize themselves with the most advanced architectural and town-planning ideas in other countries.

The results of this lack of artistic education are plain to see. Everyone knows how the public sector in Britain builds in the second half of the twentieth century. Ten years ago the Royal Fine Art Commission for Scotland described the position and deplored it.

> In its management of the public estate we should expect the government consistently to reach the standards established by its best developments. There should be a presumption of quality.

Instead, central government and government-sponsored agencies are notorious for the prominent ugly buildings which they commission or occupy. The quality of a nation will be judged to no small extent by the quality of its public architecture.[44]

Very rarely do British Governments or local authorities show much imagination when it comes to building. As a general rule, the public sector goes by precedent and plays safe. It likes to see itself as sound and inconspicuous, the backbone of the national life. Consequently, although responsible for a large part of the construction work undertaken in modern cities and therefore spending a great deal of money, central Government and local government prefer their efforts to appear economical, anonymous and unobtrusive. The grand gesture is not for them — not in the UK at least. They would never have approved, or paid for, the Parthenon. They vastly prefer dullness to any kind of extravagance; although occasionally something really good slips through the net, like the Burrell Gallery in Glasgow, or something remarkably bad, like the new British Library. Shortage of money is not much of an excuse, least of all for central Government. Fairly relaxed about spending a few tens of millions to speed the flow of traffic (sometimes unsuccessfully) or a hundred million for research into a new weapons system that produces no weapon, British Governments would think it ridiculous and irresponsible to spend more than seems strictly necessary on public buildings or bridges. 'What is the cheapest tender?' is the basic question asked by government departments, and sometimes it seems to be almost the only one. To pay more for something worth looking at, something that would add interest and distinction to the urban scene, is not for British politicians. They prefer to remain on or below the architectural — amenity poverty line.[45]

The private sector is more variable. Many of its difficulties arise because of the nature of modern commercial developments. The trouble is not that they are commercial; Royal Crescent in Bath, Regent Street in London and Moray Place in Edinburgh were all commercial developments. But these were carried out in order to provide homes for the rich, and they were not designed to be cheap. What we build today are housing estates for hundreds of families, and office blocks and supermarkets, and in most of these cases costs are held down as far as possible. This does make life more difficult for present-day architects, especially if, as is often the case with non-housing developments, the buildings are planned for an expected life of only ten or twenty years. Moreover, the modern developer is prone to be in a hurry, and this is one of his greatest weaknesses. He is typically bold but anxious. He is bold because it is his business to lay out a great deal of money in the expectation of a future profit, possibly several years away; he is anxious because right from the start he cannot be sure what the planning authorities are going to say, he cannot be sure what demand for his 'product' is going to be (hotel accommodation, say, or family shopping facilities) even during the next few years, and he does not know what his competitors will do in the meantime. As a result, he seldom has time to spare, which means that his architects seldom have time to think. And he is often inclined to put as much as possible on a given site, for as little expenditure as possible, which means that he builds too densely and too high; that the component parts of the scheme do not step down as they should; that they are too close together; that they are built to the heel of the pavement when they should be set back a little. No wonder that the general effect is dull and oppressive, that there is no sense of variety and space! As for artistic style, that usually fares no better. The aesthetic effect of a building must depend chiefly on the overall design, on the detailing, and on the materials used. Good architecture is not necessarily expensive, and expensive architecture is not necessarily good. But it is generally true that detailing, and *a fortiori* good detailing, costs money. A building with no projections and no recesses; with doors having no architraves and windows without visible reveals; devoid of columns, portals, mouldings or cornices — such a building is almost sure to want interest and liveliness. It might be helped — it might even be saved — by good textural effects.[46] Stone or brick can often provide a satisfying visual effect. Even concrete, if the climate is favourable and the surface is carefully treated — if, for example, it has a distinct pattern left by the rough boards of the wooden formwork — can appear reasonably lively and effective, although success is hard to attain unless the material is used sparingly in a really good design. But if every penny is saved so that a texturally poor material has no detailing and the surface is smooth, homogeneous and totally uninteresting, then the building, unless by a rare miracle of design, will look dull and poverty stricken, like a down-and-out standing at a street corner without an idea in his head. Nothing worth looking at can be achieved in architecture, someone has said, without a touch of extravagance. And it has to be admitted that good detailing and good facing materials are likely to raise the cost of construction of the average building by at least ten to twenty per cent.

Cheap building and over-building can in some degree be prevented by law, because minimum standards must be met. But these concern safety and the rights of others, not artistic quality or amenity. Provided that the legal requirements are satisfied, it is at the discretion of the planning authorities whether or not to approve a scheme. If what is proposed is clearly unworthy of the site, or overcrowds the neighbourhood, approval may be refused. But it is not obvious where to draw the line, and artistic standards in a locality may fall progressively. Aesthetically poor design can be discouraged but is not easily prevented; and some of those who could discourage it are doubtless deterred by the reflection that if a tasteless scheme is turned down a worse one may quite possibly take its place. Architecture and town planning in the second half of the twentieth century have not inspired public confidence.

It must be emphasized, however, that overbuilding and building cheaply are not essential to commercial success. Many developers know this perfectly well. While we have all seen buildings which, in the words of Robert Louis Stevenson, 'belong to no style of art, only to a form of business much to be regretted', it is equally true that there are commercial developers who believe, like Stuart Lipton, that 'good architecture sells'. Such men therefore want to support good architecture and to be seen to build well. This ambition needs careful guidance, because there is a risk that big companies will fall too easily for what is big, flashy and 'modern', unaware that they are commissioning second-rate schemes which will look completely out-of-date in a few years time. The Lloyds of London headquarters building is an example of this. But if a business enterprise takes an enlightened interest in the matter, it will appoint good architects and allow them sufficient time and resources to design something worth having. This is the origin of some of the most interesting buildings constructed in Britain since the war. In Edinburgh, for example, there is the geometrical Scottish Widows Assurance headquarters built in York stone and a chocolate-brown solar glass which harmonizes with Salisbury Crags in the background; in Glasgow the National Bank of Pakistan Building contrives to be at once elegant, cheerful, and unobtrusive; and the MCC Bicentenary Stand at Lords is an admirable example of 'high-tech' architecture.

The good examples show what can be done. But the general milieu is not favourable. The Royal Fine Art Commission in London has stated the position as follows:

> The scale and tempo of present-day development, the high value of land, and the commercial competition for the limelight, for the 'not-to-be-missed' building, all lead towards the exploit-ation of land, environment and people.[47]

That was twenty years ago, and nothing has happened since to suggest that the 'enterprise society' is doing any better. In London, indeed, the situation has tended to grow worse, partly because of the Government's failure to encourage businesses to locate outside the South-East of England; this has led directly to higher and denser building. Nevertheless, we cannot afford to despair. The whole enormous enterprise of building and rebuilding cities, where ninety per cent of the country's population lives, and where people's lives and thoughts and attitudes are influenced every day by the sight and sound and form of their environment—this whole enterprise is so important that we must not resign ourselves to taking whatever a developer in a hurry, or one ravenous for more publicity, cares to offer.

But why, it may be asked, when there are so many architects and planners around, all of them qualified, supposedly, to encourage better design, are second-rate developments so common? Why is professional advice so feeble or ineffective against the drive for profit at the expense of beauty and amenity? The answer, as far as the architects are concerned, has already been given. Architecture is at sixes and sevens. There is no longer agreement about what constitutes good design, and many architects seem close to believing (subconsciously, no doubt) that any modern building is as good aesthetically as any other. It also seems to be true that many architects are as much in the grip of the profit motive as the developers themselves. It pays to be noticed, so they design — for effect — the eye-catching building, with heavy horizontals (or verticals), all windows (or no windows), a smooth outline (or be-decked with cranes and window-cleaning machinery) and so on. All such constructions — and many have been built — suffer from the grave defect of exaggeration, what John Constable called 'an attempt at something beyond the truth'. While there are many very good architects working in Britain (probably born as much as made) those who speak loudest are not necessarily to be believed. And in any case there is no consensus.

What, then, of the planners? The ingenuous may suppose that even if the architects remain silent on the subject of beauty and amenity, the planners are sure to champion the cause. According to Raymond Unwin, it was the function of the town planner to rise above the practical considerations of so-called profitable development, and above the details of architecture; he even spoke of the town planner as artist. Surely there must be hope in this? It is the town planner's job (one would suppose) to ensure that new buildings are in the right place, that they fit as well as possible into their surroundings, that attractive and usable old buildings are not needlessly destroyed, that whatever is reasonably possible will be done to provide for the needs of pedestrians, to facilitate the movement of traffic, and to secure an optimal conjunction of buildings and pleasant open spaces. It is a tall order, admittedly; but town planners (as we have seen) have frequently claimed a remarkably extensive territory as their province. Could it be, then, that it is in the modern town planning department that our salvation lies?

Merely to state the idea in the last quarter of the twentieth century is to realize its absurdity. Professional town planning began with noble ideals, but it has had a sad history. Unwin, as a young man, met both Ruskin and William Morris, and he became a member of Morris's Socialist League in the search for 'a more ordered form of society'. He believed in 'the vision of the city', what he once called 'a beautiful city for all'. But the necessities of the time, above all the urgent need for more housing, to be built with the least possible delay, soon dominated post-war urban planning in Britain, and in 1925 Unwin conceded that 'since 1909 we have concentrated our main attention on the practical problems which have had to be dealt with'.[48] So beauty and amenity moved out, and planning law and politics moved in. This utilitarian phase was succeeded after 1945 by comprehensive planning. The idea now was that structure plans and regional planning would take account of 'the whole web of our socio-economic-spatial system and the changes that are happening within it'.[49] Planning horizons became boundless. But the farther they were pushed out the clearer it became that planners were not particularly competent to pronounce on the problems that arose. 'Given to prescribing oracular remedies'[50] in the late 1940s and early 1950s (a few continued this practice into the 1960s), the planners were soon discredited. 'We used to be so respected', a former President of the Town Planning Institute lamented in 1957; and twenty years later the Town and Country Planning Association conceded that 'public disillusionment with planning is so widespread that one does not even feel obliged to document it'.[51] Simultaneously, experience began to erode the idea that crime, delinquency and ill-health would progressively disappear if only the built environment could be made more orderly and more salubrious. The complicated character of social problems became better understood, and the built environment was seen to be only one of many influences at work. It is now acknowledged that the notion of environmental determinism 'has scant validity';[52] and most planners have given up talking about broad social and political objectives, and have returned to the more practical and more limited task of trying to determine the right uses of land, and the limits of reasonable development. This is essential work. But the disappearance of comprehensive planning has not been followed in most places by the return of serious involvement in questions of physical form and the quality of urban space. Twenty years ago Frederick Gibberd lamented that many of those who were engaged in planning could not be described as town designers; and the situation has not improved since then. The modern town planner is not concerned with form, colour and texture, as Gibberd thought he should be, but with densities, heights and access. Population data, income structures, unemployment rates, industrial prospects and housing regulations are uppermost in his mind.

Why is the professional planner so little concerned with the pleasantness of places and the appearance of things? There are two reasons. First, his freedom of action is severely constrained by the authority of his colleagues in the department of roads and highways. Streets now have to be surfaced and lit to a standard never before known; large numbers of parking places have to be provided and the access to them approved; roundabouts, flyovers, underpasses, traffic lights, halt signs, give-way signs, no-parking signs, parking meters and all the other transport-related paraphernalia of the modern city have been invented and must be put in place, in the names of speed and safety (a curious combination). These things are not a beautiful sight, but apparently we have to have them. One result is that many a promising scheme of development has been ruined by the inflexible demands of transport experts for wider roads, more signs or more generous car-parking.[53] The design of bridges suffers in a similar way. Bridges over railway lines must nowadays have parapets on each side one and a half metres high, they must be smooth, solid and without openings or other kind of foothold; the reasons for this may be compelling (they are to ensure safety and prevent vandalism) but the regulation is a guarantee of ugliness. In a rather similar way, the old bridges that look so fine in the countryside and are sometimes to be found also in towns—bridges by the great engineers such as Rennie and Telford, but also many lesser bridges built by men whose names are now forgotten—these ancient structures would not pass muster with the Ministry of Transport, if designed today; for it is a requirement of the Ministry that all bridge parapets rise to a height of one metre above the pavement, and many of the old ones do not. The requirements of transport officials and transport engineers are very absolute.

For this reason alone, the struggle for beauty and amenity must be hard. But the second reason why the modern town planner seems to be less than passionately concerned about public amenity and the appearance of things is that his artistic sensibilities—perhaps not very great at the outset—have become etiolated in the course of a training devoted almost entirely to planning law, social hierarchies and the like, with very little visual content. It was not always so. When the Town Planning Institute was founded in 1914, it was composed mostly of architects: even so eminent a figure as Lutyens was one of the earliest members. But architecture and town planning soon parted company. The planners strove for independence, and equality with the architects. The architects wanted to control town planning, and threw doubt on its existence as an independent body of knowledge, and as a genuine profession. Matters grew worse when, after 1945, the planners were suspected of using development legislation to limit the freedom of architects to design as they chose.

Whether blithely philistine or merely anxious to do their best, the main instinct of planning committees and their officers was to reject any design that looked modern or original, preferring those that were unexceptionable in every way. Though the architects could never in fact agree among themselves as to what made good or bad architecture, they were united to a man against this invasion of their professional territory by lay committees and ignorant planners who did not observe the same professional code as architects.[54]

These divisions persist, and it is not uncommon in universities and polytechnics for departments of architecture and departments of town planning to have as little to do with one another as possible. They select their students differently and train them differently. Maximum differentiation of the final product seems to be the principal aim.

Thus few of those who enter the planning profession today have much knowledge of art or architecture. They are mostly geographers, sociologists, in some cases surveyors. A town planner of an earlier day—he wrote several noteworthy books on planning but was never popular with his colleagues—saw the town as 'a thing of beauty, a work of art, an expression of man's dignity and civilisation'.[55] But few planners think like this now; few thought like it when it was written. Whereas architecture is frequently spoken of as an art, which it can be, town planning is seldom so regarded. And this is understandable, because the plans of today's planner are rarely more than ground plans, important certainly, but with little or no attempt to give ordered shape and proportion to spaces, or to bring buildings into a balanced relationship with their setting. Planning has become more a matter of administration than of creation. It has been institutionalized, and the planner, employed within the Government system, works to a stereotyped pattern. No doubt aesthetic values are not easily accommodated within a government office, but if the best urban results are to be achieved the attempt to accommodate them must be made, and made successfully. 'It is not enough', the London Commission observed thirty years ago,

> to invite private developers to submit their own schemes with little guidance from the Planning Authority, and then to accept the highest bid whatever architecture may happen to have been included.[56]

But this is what tends to occur, especially if, as is sometimes the case, the local authority is itself the developer, or is one of the developers. When local authorities sponsor a development and at the same time are responsible for assessing its quality and likely consequences, planning for an easy profit is the almost inevitable result. Such planning almost guarantees third-rate surroundings. And even good contemporary planning is unlikely to approve exceptionally bold and imaginative schemes (which in most cases may be just as well). What would happen today, for example, if someone proposed to build a large, exotic, frivolous, conspicuous, out-of-place pavilion designed in the 'Hindu style' (more or less) in a pleasant open space on the edge of a prosperous English town, 'every building contiguous to it . . . of a common ordinary English form and appearance'[57]—which is what Nash did for the Prince Regent in Brighton in the years after

1815? Or what planning authority would consent to the building of a large block of flats, with turrets and red roofs, five storeys high, vaguely in the Flemish style, at the top end of Edinburgh's Royal Mile and three hundred yards from the Castle gate, looking down upon the entire length of Princes Street? It can safely be said that planning consent would not be given. But this was built in the 1890s at the suggestion of Patrick Geddes; and—wonder of wonders—it is generally agreed that it does not look at all bad.

These criticisms do not mean that the modern planner performs no useful function. He will see to it that the relevant planning regulations are complied with—no small task—and he will probably have something to say about the land-use implications for the area; he is sure to give thought to problems of the flow of traffic and parking, although on these matters he does not have the last word; if shopping space is involved he will calculate the net addition to local shopping facilities and comment on the likely viability of the scheme; but that is often about all. Few developments nowadays start on the basis of an up-to-date set of carefully considered planning guidelines that pay much sensitive attention to the visual impact of what is proposed. In most cases there are no planning guide-lines at all, and provided that the scheme conforms to the zoning of the site, the planners are usually content to wait and see what the architects for the scheme come up with. It has been said, and with justice, that

> there are times when it is difficult to identify just what difference has been made to a development scheme (perhaps a very poor one) by the work of the local planning department. We look to planners to control what may be introduced into the public domain, yet we find many places where there appears to be a free-for-all.[58]

And yet planning is so important! The siting of buildings, and the spaces between and around them can contribute to the pleasure of the urban scene as much as the buildings themselves; sometimes more. 'If Washington has kept its beauty', Ada Louise Huxtable wrote, 'it is because of the spaciousness of its avenues, the pleasure of its parks, the vision of its plan.'[59] Siting and arrangement can triumph over the mediocrity of single buildings. And when the claims of architecture to be an art are as dubiously and erratically evidenced as they are today, urban design is more important than ever.

Where large and important schemes are concerned it might be thought that in these cases, at any rate, the planner would play a significant role. But if a scheme is large enough to involve far-reaching questions about levels of employment and the character of neighbourhoods the unfortunate planner is likely to find that he is no longer secure in his own office, for he is becoming involved in politics. Local politicians quickly acquire strong views on matters of importance to their constituents; and proposals for substantial urban development are always important. They affect large numbers of people, directly and indirectly. They bring gains to some, and impose losses on others. Identifying the gains and the losses, and hence the gainers and the losers, is a matter of foresight and calculation, and is part of the work of planners. But placing values on these gains and losses and weighing one against another is not a matter of investigation and calculation but is a matter of judgement. Such judgement is political.

> Planning is unavoidably and inherently a political activity. I mean that the decisions taken on such important matters as sewerage systems, housing, transport, schools and airports are *political decisions*. No matter how competent the supporting scientific analyses, or how sophisticated the simulation models, these techniques can test only efficiency, and, at best, only identify distributional consequences. Insofar as the outcomes of planned actions affect a reallocation of benefits and costs (and they almost always do), the problems they address can have no technical solutions—only political ones.[60]

This is so even in fairly straightforward cases. And whenever such great incalculables as beauty and amenity are at stake, judgement is almost everything.

There was a time when it was hoped that cost-benefit analysis would obviate the need for merely human opinion and argument concerning the net advantages of development. But such hopes were vain. It soon became clear that while costs can more or less be measured, the benefits derived from, say, a public park or a historic building have to be stipulated, and such stipulation has to be fed into cost-benefit analysis and is not provided by it. Thus the Roskill Commission assembled all available information and carried out all possible calculations about the proposals for a third London airport; yet its work was inconclusive. There were doubts about the implicit valuation placed on preserving the Vale of Aylesbury, and about other valuations. And the Commission's recommendation in favour of Stansted was summarily turned down by the Government of the day.

In the field of planning there is therefore no escape, in the last resort, from political decisions. And it is worth remarking that these decisions are especially difficult when they relate to schemes in an area where business is bad and unemployment is high. In these circumstances, it is easy for councillors to believe that any development is better than none at all, and to lose sight of the non-financial costs and the losses that may be imposed upon the community in the longer run. Third-rate schemes, possibly on first-rate sites, are given planning permission because there is or there seems to be no prospect of anything better. Such action may be justified. But many poor schemes have been accepted far too readily. The cost of maintaining standards is easily overstated. Authorities that try to control development in an enlightened way build up an agreeable and attractive environment, and this environment tends to draw in the better firms, those which pay good wages and which enjoy good prospects. The great efforts which have been made in recent years to turn Glasgow, for example, into an attractive city are a case in point. A more attractive environment, with better amenities, has drawn in many high-quality enterprises. Dreary crowded surroundings, other things being equal, attract only the third-rate. The policy of making life easy for the developer at the expense of beauty and amenity is a dangerous one, and in the longer run it may not pay off even in the strictly commercial sense. It is the downhill road to comparative poverty, to be recommended only to the justifiably desperate.

The presumption that almost any development scheme is better than nothing and should therefore be accepted is unwise. Politicians may not like to see difficulties put in the way of developers, but what is needed is not development at all costs and as fast as possible but a proper balance of considerations. It is the job of the planning officer who is involved in a new development to put his own views forward, and to try to help the politicians to see all sides of the question and to consider the matter from every point of view. In doing so, he may argue for more space, more elegance, more consideration for historic surroundings, more time to think. Unfortunately, his tastes and training may not be such as to enable him to give good advice on questions of amenity and aesthetics. And in any case his task is not an easy one, for those whom he has to persuade are his own masters. So politics keeps seeping in. Yet it is obvious that inadequate artistic advice combined with the political pressures exerted by interested parties do not make a sound basis for planning decisions.

Reasoning along these lines would surely have been familiar to Sir Lionel Earle. Pressure for more war memorials, doubtful advice from advisers—these led to the creation of the first Royal Fine Art Commission, and then the Scots Commission. Standing outside the system,[61] and therefore immune to financial and political pressures, have these Royal Commissions made much difference to urban development? It is a very large question. Some sort of answer can be given, however, by examining the work of the Commissions during the last quarter of a century, and by looking in particular at a few of the more significant cases commented upon by the Commission in Scotland.

NOTES AND REFERENCES TO CHAPTER 3

1. T. Sharp, *Oxford Replanned* (London, 1948) p. 29.
2. The *Lancet*, vol. 1 (1880) p. 851.
3. T. Pennant, *A Tour in Scotland, 1769* (London, 1774) p. 18.
4. T. Pennant, *A Tour in Scotland and Voyage to the Hebrides, 1772* (London, 1784) vol. 2, p. 302.
5. T. Thornton, *A Sporting Tour* (London, 1804) p. 220.
6. *Ibid.*, p. 278.
7. M. Girouard, *Cities and People* (London, 1985) p. 277.
8. *Journal of the RIBA*, vol. 31, p. 135.
9. James Craig, Plans for Improving the City of Edinburgh, in, A. J. Youngson, *The Making of Classical Edinburgh* (Edinburgh, 1966) pp. 117-18.
10. *Journal of the RIBA*, vol. 21, p. 615.
11. RFAC for England and Wales, *Twenty-First Report* (1971) p. 16.
12. S. Gardiner, *Introduction to Architecture* (Oxford, 1983) p. 117.
13. *Journal of the RIBA*, vol. 33, p. 275.
14. It does better where rainfall is less than 10 inches per year; for example, in the Middle East or central Australia.
15. RFAC for England and Wales, *Report* (1952) p. 4.
16. Le Corbusier, *Urbanisme* (Paris, 1980) p. 67.
17. *Ibid.*, p. 69.
18. *Ibid.*, p. 69.
19. *Ibid.*, p. 142.
20. *Ibid.*, p. 168.
21. Michel Ragon, *Histoire Mondiale de l'Architecture et de l'Urbanisme Modernes* (Paris, 1972) vol. 2, p. 136.
22. Edmund Bacon, *Design of Cities* (London, 1967) p. 219.
23. The reader may be surprised to learn that this comment was actually made about Bath. See, P. Lavedan, *Histoire de l'Urbanisme* (Paris, 1959) vol. 2, p. 199.
24. S. Giedion, *Space, Time and Architecture* (Harvard, 1941) p. 554.
25. *Ibid.*, pp. 551—4.
26. *Ibid.*, p. 559.
27. *Ibid.*, p. 579.
28. *Ibid.*, pp. 547—8.
29. For example, 'a gigantic programme of urban reconstruction' was recommended in Colin Buchanan's *Traffic in Towns* (HMSO, 1963).
30. One who works in the Barbican was recently reported as saying, 'Look at this building . . . we're suffering here from the imagination of someone with a desire to bury people.' *Daily Telegraph*, 28 Mar. 1989.
31. H. Rosenau, *The Ideal City* (London, 1974) p. 153.
32. See above, p. 57.
33. W. Gropius, *Rebuilding our Communities* (Chicago, 1945) p. 17.
34. *Ibid.*, p. 54.
35. L. Esher, *A Broken Wave* (London, 1981) p. 128.
36. *Ibid.*, p. 80.

37. Sir William Temple, *Observations upon the United Provinces of the Netherlands* (ed. G. N. Clark, Cambridge, 1932) p. 103.
38. *Ibid.*, p. 136.
39. Roy Strong, in *Spirit of the Age* (London, 1975) p. 69.
40. It was begun as a palace but was converted to a naval hospital. As Rasmussen says, 'Regarded as a hospital it is an absolutely fantastic building . . . but the vista from the Thames is marvellous'.
41. The statement is made by Sir John himself, quoted in, John Fleming, *Robert Adam and his Circle* (London, 1962) p. 33.
42. S. Sitwell, *British Architects and Craftsmen* (London, 1945) p. 134.
43. Wood marked out the sites and then sub-leased them to builders and intending occupiers, all of whom were legally bound to follow his elevations.
44. RFAC for Scotland, *Eighth Report* (1980) p. 13.
45. For example, floods in 1989 destroyed the stone-built railway viaduct over the Ness at Inverness. It was a B-listed structure, with five well-proportioned arches. ScotRail plans to replace it with a plain economical design of no interest whatever. It is taken for granted that this is the right thing to do.
46. 'As a general rule it may be said that materials with poor textural effects are improved by deep relief while materials of high quality can stand a smooth surface and, in fact, appear to best advantage without relief or ornament'. S. E. Rasmussen, *Experiencing Architecture* (London, 1964) p. 170.
47. RFAC for England and Wales, *Twenty-First Report* (1971) p. 12.
48. *Journal of the RIBA*, vol. 33, p. 44.
49. Peter Hall, in B. Goodall and A. Kirby (eds.), *Resources and Planning* (Oxford, 1979) p. 13.
50. Quoted in, Alison Ravetz, *Remaking Cities* (London, 1980) p. 207.
51. Quoted *ibid.*, p. 207.
52. The words are those of the National Capital Development Corporation of Canberra, which has had over fifty years of experience in developing a communally very expensive and extremely orderly and prosperous city. The pattern of social problems in Canberra is not like that elsewhere, but social problems abound nevertheless.
53. The 1947 Development Plan for Edinburgh, by Abercrombie and Plumstead, is a classic illustration of megalomaniac transport planning. A very brief summary of what was proposed, and what happened, is in the Appendix.
54. Ravetz, *Remaking Cities*, p. 200.
55. T. Sharp, *Town and Countryside* (London, 1932) p. 70.
56. RFAC for England and Wales, *Sixteenth Report* (1958–9) p. 8.
57. J. Farington, *Diary 1793–1821*, vol. 8, p. 197.
58. RFAC for Scotland, *Ninth Report* (1983) p. 17.
59. Quoted in, Victor Gruen, *The Heart of our Cities* (New York, 1964) p. 171.
60. M. M. Webber, 'Planning in an Environment of Change', in *Town Planning Review*, 39 No. 4 (1969).

61. Whether the English Commission, which now finances some of its activities from commercial sources, can any longer be described as standing outside the system must be doubtful. Its membership also seems to cause difficulties. It is ironic that in connection with the important Paternoster scheme beside St Paul's Cathedral Colin Amery has regretfully observed that 'There is no public body to act as an independent umpire'. *Financial Times*, 28 Nov. 1988. And yet that is precisely what the English Commission was set up to be!

9. House at Brno, Czechoslovakia, by Mies van der Rohe (1930). 'An architecture of straight lines and flat surfaces requires high-class materials'. This house incorporates steel pillars, steel furniture, Macassar ebony, rosewood and white leather, and a partition of five very large sheets of onyx.

10. The Stonebow and the City Guildhall, Lincoln; begun in the late 15th century and completed in the 16th. 'There should be enough sympathy between buildir and building to produce a harmonious composition'. How not to do it.

11. Water Desalination plant, Kuwait. (Water colour by
    P. Brunnen). Modern technology makes possible the Musée
    Pompidou, the Lloyds Headquarters Building, the water
    desalination plant in Kuwait and many similar structures.

12. The Rows, Chester (from T. Pennant, A Tour in Scotland, 1769).

13. Rolls Royce 'Silver Ghost', 1925. 'The cars of the 1920s were the most stylish motor cars that have ever been built'.

14. The Lever Building, New York (1952). 'Fenestrations became uncountable rows of identical windows'. Compare the Le Corbusier illustration.

15. 'We love the view. It helps to remind us that we're part of a larger community'.

16. Torness Nuclear Power Station: 'extraordinarily dignified and imposing'.

CHAPTER FOUR

Planning and Advising

What is to be said about the effectiveness of the two Royal Fine Art Commissions? Do they do much to guide development in the right directions? Or are they, like so many people, swayed by the latest fashions, or inclined to take too limited a view, or do they retreat into approving only what is orthodox and safe?

Critics of the Commissions are fond of pointing out that they have not put a stop to bad building. As they have no powers to stop anything, this is hardly a surprise. They are also censured for making mistakes. But even Royal Commissions are not infallible, and the seriousness of fallibility in this instance is reduced by the fact that aesthetic judgement is seldom a question of right or wrong. It is usually concerned with emphasis and care and proportion, with the balance between different claims and qualities, with the problems of how something could be improved; and here an experienced and not entirely professional body with no axe to grind is in a very strong and quite exceptional position. Two other points should be made, which the critics seldom seem to understand. Firstly, the Commissions are entirely independent bodies, and this independence is very important indeed. Neither Commission has anything to lose by standing up to the demands of developers, whether they are Government departments or big or small business in the private sector. Pressure can be put on local politicians or officials, sometimes even on national politicians and officials, but not on Royal Commissions. In the economic/political/artistic mêlée of development, no other consideration is as important as this. Secondly, the Commissions do not duplicate the work of other bodies, or of other persons, precisely because they take a wide view. Architects talk about architecture, planners talk about densities, traffic flows and so forth, amenity societies represent the interests of their members. But the Commissions, besides taking into account all these matters, must think about the interests of the public at large, and must also consider the urban-design aspects of what is proposed: those aspects which modern town planning in Britain now tends to disregard, but which may make or mar a scheme from the point of view of amenity and general urban effect. No one would pretend that the Commissions' task is an easy one, but there is no denying its importance. And in addition to their independence and their unique character, the Commissions have other advantages. Whatever kind of development is proposed, the Commissioners have seen comparable proposals before, practically or aesthetically better or worse, put forward in comparable situations. They can take an entirely fresh look at a scheme that may quite possibly have been thought up in a hurry. They are less inclined to the downright foolish or fanciful than many vocal persons because half of the Commissioners stand outside the professional pressures of fashion and competition. All these arguments, when taken together, provide strong support for the view that independent and wide-ranging expert criticism of new developments is not impossible, and should not be treated as useless, and that building better cities is by no means an idle dream.

The scope and the limitations of the work of the three Commissions mentioned in this book vary considerably. The Washington Commission has the smallest geographical field of action, and the greatest authority. The Commission advises on all Federal projects in the District of Columbia, and it is very unusual for its advice in these cases not to be followed. As regards public memorials, recent legislation has made approval by the Commission mandatory for their construction. This is a device, it has been said, for keeping down the numbers by making it more troublesome for would-be memorial builders to get through the planning process. In all other Federal cases the Commission's advice is apt to be taken for the simple reason that projects are submitted to the Commission before they go through the appropriation process in Congress, and no agency would want to risk the Commission's opposition to a project at this critical stage. The officers of the Commission make it their business to keep in close touch with the various Congressional committees that have final funding authority, and it is scarcely possible to advance a project contrary to the Commission's recommendations, unless good reason for such action has already been given. There seem to have been no instances in which the Commission has been simply ignored. In the private sector, however, the situation is quite different, for it is the Mayor of the District of Columbia who has the final authority over what is built. The Commission advises, but buildings disapproved of by the Commission have occasionally gone ahead with the Mayor's blessing. In spite of this, the general opinion is that the Commission's success-rate with developers and their architects is very high.

The two British Commissions, on the other hand, are expected to advise on whatever is important that is being built in the whole of England and Wales in one case, and in the whole of Scotland in the other. These are not only geographically extensive tasks, they also involve taking an interest in a vast variety of developments and re-developments. The Commissions have commented on the design and siting of power stations, factories, hotels, office-buildings, theatres, electricity pylons and sub-stations, super-markets, shopping centres, car parks, by-passes — the conglomeration of construction upon which a modern society depends, and which it inevitably sees every day and within which, in a sense, most people live is truly astonishing. Some schemes are large and some are small. The London Commission has recently advised on the proposals for Canary Wharf on the Isle of Dogs, comprising no less than 11–12 million square feet of development, and also on the design of telephone kiosks; the Scottish Commission has spent many hours over the design of enormous and costly structures for the New Trident Weapons System on Loch Long and the Gare Loch, and has also advised on lighting in the Main Street, Inveraray. Many of the schemes considered by the Commissions relate, in one way or another, to a building, or a group of buildings, of historic significance. Sometimes it is a question of demolition, more frequently of alteration or extension; but most often the question that arises is how far the visual amenity of historic buildings will be damaged by new building in their vicinity. In the majority of the Commissions' cases, however, historic buildings of special significance are not involved.

It is sometimes suggested that the attitude of both the Commissions is merely negative. This is not true. Both Commissions can and sometimes do put forward suggestions as to how a scheme might be modified and improved; examples of this are given in the following pages. But it cannot be too often repeated, as the Scottish Commissioners put it in their 1960 Report, 'that it is no part of the Commission's function to usurp the role of architect or planner by putting forward alternative schemes of its own'. Even if the Commissions wished to do this, they have neither the requisite time nor the resources. The Commissions' role is purely advisory, and this means that there are strict limitations on what either of them can hope to achieve. Even if the Commissioners could require alterations to be made in a scheme, the results would still be of limited value because, as the Commission for England and Wales pointed out almost twenty years ago, 'control from without cannot turn bad architecture into good architecture, because it cannot turn bad architects into good architects; and good buildings need good architects'.[1] The Commissioners' task is to help, and this they are well qualified to do. They have seen many schemes, for many different kinds of development; they know what is possible and what is not possible, what works well and what works badly. They do not, of course, know all the answers. But they have no axe to grind, and their advice is therefore disinterested, as well as expert. It need not be followed, but one would have thought that it would be wanted. Such, however, has not always been the case.

Although the Commissions have many basic similarities, there are substantial differences between the operations of the two bodies. In part, this is a matter of geography. The obligation of the Commission in London, to advise on significant developments throughout England and Wales, would seem, to an outsider, to be an impossible task. The number of Commissioners sitting in London is eighteen, and a meeting of the full Commission takes place every month. At this meeting the Commission divides into two, and each of these two 'examination committees' considers three or four schemes, upon which each of them reaches 'provisional decisions'. These are reported briefly to the full Commission later in the day, and may be queried. There are also a number of preparatory committees which likewise report their decisions to the full Commission. These arrangements save time, and thus make possible informal discussions of general issues with representatives of other bodies who are invited to visit the Commission; these visitors may come, for example, from the City, the BBC or the Ministry of Transport. The disadvantage of these procedures is that it must be the exception rather than the rule for any case to be considered in detail by the full Commission. And even with so much subdivision of work, the number of cases referred to the Commissioners must be small compared to the number that might reasonably be thought to deserve their consideration. There are approximately three hundred planning authorities in England and Wales, and a very great deal of development takes place every year between Land's End and Berwick-upon-Tweed. The staff of the Commission cannot easily know of all the significant developments that are taking place, and must in any event exercise a very selective policy as regards those developments that they do know about in order to restrict the number of cases presented to the Commission, and thus leave Commissioners with sufficient time to think about each of them in turn. There must also be difficulties about personal knowledge of the sites, which is very important. In dealing with so large and diverse a geographical area, it cannot be easy for a sufficient number of Commissioners to visit the sites of proposed developments, or for a sufficient number of Commissioners to be already familiar with these sites and the areas round about them. When the Commission was established in 1924 no one imagined that its duties would become so heavy or so widespread. The Commission has responded to its changing situation by internal division and sub-division, as already described, but the rational and efficient response to the pressure of work would be for the Government to change the system and have two Commissions, one for London and the 'home counties' (or even for London alone), and another for the rest of England and Wales.

Matters are made no easier by the fact that the work of the London Commission now goes farther than commenting upon cases. Increasing emphasis is now placed upon the need to exercise some general influence on 'aesthetic design and architectural standards', and the Commission recently listed ten courses of action in pursuit of better architecture in general, and an improved visual environment.[2] These include the publication of an annual Report, of circulars, and of occasional papers on such subjects as universities, prisons and architectural education; visits to different parts of the country in order to increase the Commission's influence in the regions; the establishment of closer links with English Heritage, the Civic Trust, and other bodies; and making a constructive contribution to the design of foreign embassies in London, and British embassies abroad.

As regards specific cases, the London Commission's advice has frequently attracted attention, but has by no means always been taken. Many proposals of crucial importance have come before it. Even before the war ended in 1945 the demolition of artistically important buildings already had enthusiastic advocates, and in 1944 — to cite a once famous example — the Commission was invited to comment on the future of Carlton House Terrace, 'the accommodation being incompatible with modern requirements'. It is hard to believe that the total destruction of this splendid Regency terrace, overlooking London's only great processional way, was ever seriously contemplated. But such was the case, and the Commission had to struggle for many years to ensure retention, and to ensure, moreover, that reconstruction of all the important elevations, where necessary, would be according to the original design. A few years later the Commission was arguing that the remarkable Doric Portico at Euston Station should be dismantled and re-erected nearby, so as 'to enhance the architectural effect of the new station'; but British Rail opted (not for the last time) for the pedestrian and the second-rate, and the Portico was destroyed. Another important case, which closely concerned the Commission throughout the 1960s, was the series of proposals to redevelop Piccadilly Circus. The Commission objected strongly to the height and bulk of the proposed buildings, and especially to a 435 foot high tower on the Criterion site which, as the Commission observed, 'would have disastrous effects on views from St James's Park, Trafalgar Square and elsewhere'. This time, good sense prevailed. But the Barracks for the Household Cavalry in Knightsbridge ('the skyscraper in Hyde Park') was built in spite of the Commission, which advised that 'a tower in this position is highly undesirable in its effect on the amenities of Hyde Park', and the building of the Hilton Hotel in Park Lane likewise went ahead contrary to the Commission's advice. Outside London, to take a couple of recent examples at random, the Commission was overruled on the matter of a remarkably crude International Conference Centre at Bournemouth ('a disgraceful design'), and it likewise failed to prevent the extensive demolition of listed buildings in the heart of Bromley, carried out so as to make way for 'an intensive and imposing development built primarily to satisfy the commercial requirements of the client', who was J. Sainsbury.[3] On the other hand, the Commission was able to help in a large number of other cases: it assisted in the improvement of the Market Square at Lavenham; it successfully opposed 'a wholly misconceived design' for a house for the bishop in the cathedral close at Salisbury; and it achieved a very valuable success in persuading the Anglian Water Authority to adopt a flood defence scheme which improved rather than ruined the historic setting, along the waterside, of the superb seventeenth century Custom House at King's Lynn. Indeed, the Commission has felt able to claim that 'fundamental improvements to the planning and design of buildings, following the Commission's criticisms, are not uncommon.'[4]

The schemes that have been considered by the London Commission are extremely diverse, but anyone reading the Commission's Reports must be struck by two features that persist throughout the work that has been done. First, the Commission comments on a great many extremely large, extremely prominent, and extremely complex developments. To mention only a few, there were the proposals for the wholesale demolition and reconstruction of Liverpool Street Station, which engaged the Commission's attention from 1974 to 1985; the Hampton site competition for the extension to the National Gallery, when the Commission gave cautious support to the successive designs by Ahrends Burton and Koralek in the face of 'widespread condemnation'; the Broad Sanctuary conference centre at Westminster, close to the Abbey; and—all in a single year, 1986—several schemes for redevelopment on London Wall, including a 32-storey block opposite All Hallows (an exceptionally fine eighteenth-century building), two schemes for the redevelopment of Spitalfields Market (a twelve-acre site), a scheme for improving Trafalgar Square, an outline brief for the seven-acre Paternoster Square redevelopment beside St Paul's, and the £100 million Royal Opera House redevelopment at Covent Garden, on 19 acres, which involves the demolition of listed and historic buildings and the construction of shops, offices, an underground car park, overhead bridge connections and arcading. With so much on its plate, it is astonishing that the Commission found time for anything else. The second feature of the English Commission's work deserving notice is the heavy concentration on London and the South. In the period 1971 to 1984 over 35 per cent of the cases considered by the Commission[5] were in London, and approximately 45 per cent were outside London south of the Wash. Thus only 20 per cent were in 'the North' (widely interpreted) and Wales. For the years 1985 and 1986 the figures were approximately

42 per cent, 41 per cent and 17 per cent. That a great deal of attention must be devoted to London is certain; London is far and away the largest and is also the wealthiest per capita of all British cities. But it would seem that attending to London, along with other places within easy reach of the capital such as Oxford, Cambridge, Brighton, Bath and Exeter, leaves insufficient time, or no time at all, for the many small but important developments that take place in the numerous small towns and villages of Lincolnshire, Derbyshire, Cheshire, Yorkshire and other English counties, as well as Wales.

In spite of these difficulties faced by the Commission, there can be no doubt about the importance of its work. Its value in 'stopping things' has been acknowledged, and so has the fact that 'had its advice been taken more often, London and England would be the better for it'.[6] It has not been afraid to swim against the tide. Its activities are well publicized and are well known in high places. Many of its pronouncements on architecture and urban design should have a wider circulation:

> Commissioners are consistently concerned about the materials which are used for projects and they are dismayed that the richness of materials is matched only by the poverty in craftsmanship . . . The spaces between buildings are of crucial importance and public spaces need to be made inhabitable, enjoyable and pleasant places to be in and attention paid to the creation of micro-climates. Urban landscape needs to be treated as a whole, and by comparatively modest means it can be radically improved by the use of such things as proper street furniture and the good design of railings, lights, etc. Buildings could be greatly improved by the better design of manufactured components . . . The commission is sometimes dismayed by the lack of imagination and inspiration of the architects and developers with whom it has to deal.[7]

The services of the Commissioners are unpaid (as are those of the Scottish Commissioners) and the Chairman, Lord St John of Fawsley, has calculated that their commercial value would be in the region of half a million pounds a year.

The Scottish Commission does not work on so grand a scale as the Commission in London, but, since its history and activities are better known to the author, they may be described in more detail.

The responsibilities of the Scots Commission are confined to Scotland, which has a population only about one-tenth as large as the population of England and Wales. The amount of development in Scotland is smaller in the same proportion — probably even smaller than that — and the duties of the Scots Commission are correspondingly more manageable. Whenever a new development of importance is proposed in Scotland, it is most likely that several of the Commissioners already know the location; and if a site is to be visited it is most likely to be in Edinburgh, Glasgow, Aberdeen or Dundee, and these cities are readily accessible to the Commissioners, who live in Scotland. During the last thirty years the Commission has probably never commented on a development planned to take place on a site not recently visited by two or more Commissioners. It is obvious that only a very small fraction of all the developments that take place in Scotland in the course of a year can be — or indeed should be — considered by the Commission. But none of genuine importance can escape the Commission's notice.

The Commission for Scotland has not always worked as effectively as it does now. Established in 1927, its first Report was not published until 1960. That Report lists over three hundred items which had been investigated since 1927, which is less than one per month. Almost fifty per cent of the items listed are bridges and tunnels, and of these almost a half are in the Highlands. A further twenty-five per cent are lighting schemes, mostly in small towns all the way from Langholm to Thurso; there is a handful of memorials, and a few general items include two stamp collections, the floodlighting of Edinburgh Castle and a proposal (supported by the Commission) to remove the deplorable portraits hanging in the Long Gallery in Holyrood House. This does not leave very much room for items of major importance, few of which seem to have come the Commission's way before 1950. The Report dates 'the establishment of the Commission's prestige' to discussions about the design of the new government office building on the Calton Hill, completed in 1936, known as St Andrew's House. These discussions (part of 'a fierce controversy') lasted from 1929 to 1934. The Ministry of Works, apparently careless of the fact that this was one of the finest and most romantic-looking sites in Scotland, made proposals which were regarded, not only by the Commissioners, as anonymous and utilitarian, strictly Office-of-Works in appearance and unworthy of the site. Two sets of draft plans were rejected before the Ministry finally gave way in 1933 and agreed to the appointment of an independent architect. The result, which the Commission 'unanimously approved', is one of those buildings which look better on the drawing-board than on the site; its style has not worn very well, and it has recently been described, not unfairly, as 'an assertive monumental mass'.[8]

Another major project of the 1930s was the Kincardine road bridge. The Commission was not consulted about this by the Ministry of Transport until most of the design work had been completed, and could therefore do nothing, because before 1953 it had no powers to comment on a scheme unless officially requested to do so. In the end the Commission was able to play 'some small part' in criticizing details, but in effect it was by-passed. Plans for the new National Library building in Edinburgh — an uninspiring structure outside, but good to use—were submitted to the Commission and approved in 1936.

After the war the Commission's level of activity saw some increase. Large electricity generating stations began to be built or rebuilt—Portobello in 1945 was the first—and the Commission was usually involved. It made suggestions for landscaping and planting at Hunterston, and likewise recommended tree-belts to screen the extension to the steelworks at Ravenscraig. Trunk-road lighting became important, and the Commission gave good advice about the design, size and colour of lamp standards, being 'at no time very happy about the use of concrete standards'. Bridge-building continued, and the Commissioners 'made a special point of stressing that the problems involved were not purely engineering ones, and in several notable cases . . . they were able to persuade the local authorities of the need to employ a consulting architect in addition to the constructional engineers with immense benefit to the resulting bridges'. In 1952 the Commission played a part in securing the rejection of the design for a new office building in the heart of Edinburgh's New Town—but was given no opportunity by the Corporation to see the revised design, which was built.[9] In 1955 a proposal was put forward to solve Edinburgh's parking problems by building an underground car park and bus terminal in East Princes Street Gardens. (Nothing was too barbarous to receive serious consideration in the 1950s). On request, the Commission was shown the plans, which it strongly disapproved, and it further stated 'that it would deprecate in the strongest terms any interference with the valley to the south of Princes Street'. In the face of much public criticism the scheme was abandoned. A few years later a proposal to remove the mound and trees in the centre of Randolph Crescent in Edinburgh in order to form a roundabout caused much controversy, but the Commission declared that it could find nothing objectionable in the scheme on aesthetic grounds—a declaration which it would be unlikely to repeat today. This scheme did not proceed.

Thus during the first thirty-three years of its existence the Commission gradually extended its efforts. It won some and lost some, which is to be expected. It usually gave good advice. But whether its reputation rose very high during these years seems doubtful. The Commission was poorly organized and administered. It did not meet regularly. Its secretary was only part-time and he had no staff whatever to back him up (typing was done 'somewhere else'). The office was wretchedly small and there were no display facilities. Site visits were a rarity and sketchy presentations by architects or officials were the order of the day. Important submissions were dealt with at a single meeting and often without the attendance of those responsible for what was proposed. There is no doubt that at this stage the Commission, while it may have been prestigious (and it was certainly cheap), was not a very effective body. Many of the proposals submitted to it were submitted only when significant changes of plan could no longer be made. And many important proposals were never submitted at all. In 1953 the Commission's powers were extended when it was given a free hand to comment on whatever schemes it chose. But in itself this was not sufficient to make much practical difference.

A new era began, however, with the appointment in 1957 of Sir Hector Hetherington as Chairman of the Commission. Sir Hector was a man of determination and ability, and he was not readily reduced to silence by uncooperative officials, evasive replies to letters of enquiry, or half-baked presentations. Then in 1962 the Commission at last acquired a full-time Secretary. With these changes the Commission may be said to have emerged from the larval stage of its existence. It now had an exceptionally good Chairman ('a splendid old warrior', one of his colleagues called him), a Secretary who had the time and the skill to enlarge the Commission's range of contacts with government departments and planning authorities, and it operated in an atmosphere of growing public concern about amenity — concern for what the Commission called 'the convenience and seemliness of our cities, towns and villages, and the beauty of the countryside'.

The modern Commission — the Commission, that is, since 1962 — has slightly enlarged its membership, and now consists of eleven members plus the Chairman. All are appointed by the Queen, acting on the advice of the Secretary of State for Scotland. The professional members — mostly architects, but engineering and town planning are also represented — usually number six or seven; no architect has ever been Chairman, but Sir Robert Grieve, Chairman from 1978 to 1982, was a qualified engineer and town planner. The Commission is served by a Secretary and two other full-time members of staff. Meetings are held monthly, more often if required, and usually last all day. Presentations are made by the architects, planners or other officials involved, and consist — or should consist — of plans, elevations, perspective views, and, in most cases, a simple block model. (Scottish architects, until very recently, have been averse to providing information that can be obtained — by themselves as well as by Commissioners — only from a model). The Commission's comments are usually sent to the relevant Planning Authority or Government Department about a week after the meeting has taken place; waiting for a response from the Commission is not something about which any architect or planner has ever been able to complain. If the Commission feels that the scheme is an important one and is going badly wrong, it may, as a last resort, report to the Secretary of State and ask him to intervene.

Most Planning Authorities co-operate with the Commission to the extent that they keep the Commission's officers informed about new proposals in their area; where this is not done (Planning Authorities are under no statutory obligation in this respect) the Commission is almost certain to find out through other channels. In fact, the Commission is likely to have a better overall idea of what is being planned in Scotland than any Department or person in the Scottish Office. Most proposed developments require no comment; either they are very small, or they are not to be built in or near 'a sensitive area' (implying—which is no more than a relative truth—that there are 'insensitive areas'). The task of deciding which out of a vast array of schemes is to be brought before the Commission falls to the Commission's officers, and the policy is to submit all projects which are reckoned to be of national importance (recognizing that not all such projects are large and not all large projects are, from the amenity point of view, of national importance) and as many others of secondary importance as the Commission's time and resources allow. This has meant in practice that during the last twenty years the Commissioners have considered three or four projects per meeting on average, or about forty to fifty projects a year. If more were to be submitted, the time that could be given to each would not allow adequate consideration, and either standards would fall or the Commission would have to be enlarged and given more resources.

Commenting on forty or fifty cases a year is made easier by the happy fact that some schemes are well thought-out, well designed, and well presented. Thus the Commission found little or nothing to criticize in the plans for the General Accident Corporation's offices at Perth, for the Pitlochry Festival Theatre, for the Royal Scottish Academy of Music and Drama in Glasgow, and in many other instances. (It is interesting to note that of the three schemes mentioned here the first was to be built for a large business corporation, the second for a private developer, and the third for a department of Government, namely the Scottish Education Department.) On the other hand, a great deal of time may be spent on very bad schemes which ought to be severely modified and on schemes which in the end are not built. In 1965, for example, the Commission helped to fight off a scheme to redevelop the Waverley Station area in Edinburgh by superimposing a complex of buildings which would have risen above the station roof and would have almost completely engulfed the North Bridge. Three years later British Rail were bent on redeveloping the Haymarket Station site, and were given consent for 'a suitably composed architectural group as a terminating feature looking west along Shandwick Place'; but what emerged from the architects' office was a thin, elongated 23-storey slab which had no axial relationship to Shandwick Place and could not by any stretch of the imagination be described as meeting the conditions; so the Commission wrote to the Corporation objecting that what was proposed 'diminished, almost to vanishing point, the possibility of achieving a satisfactory architectural solution', and, after a good deal of toing and froing, some fairly drastic modifications to the scheme were made. A very important case, which again involved British Rail, was the proposal to build a shopping centre on the site of the old Waverley Market on the south side of Princes Street. Battles had been fought before to preserve the view of the Old Town from Princes Street, and won. But developers never give up, and the initial design was for what would have appeared as a fifteen-feet-high building alongside the pavement, which would have blotted out the view for a considerable distance, and would have drastically altered the visual relationship of the Old Town to the New, which is so essential to the whole style and character of Edinburgh. Numerous bodies objected, and a public enquiry was held. With the help of information supplied by the Scottish Development Department's graphics group and by Strathclyde University, the Commission was able to demonstrate at the enquiry that a building which rose to near eye level—never mind to fifteen feet—would be visually destructive, and suitable alterations to the design had to be made.

There are also cases which look simple but which turn out to be worth a good deal of thought. Plans for Torness Nuclear Power Station came to the Commission in 1978. This was a large scheme by any standards—the main charge hall was 90 metres high and 130 metres long—and the final cost was £1.8 billion. Complex engineering works are nine-tenths determined by engineering considerations, and the 'architecture' is usually not much more than a skin erected around the engineering. Mass and disposition at Torness could not be much altered by the Commission, but the Commission was nevertheless able to make three important suggestions, which were accepted. Firstly, the intention that the walls of the main charge hall should slope inwards towards the top seemed to give the effect of a vastly overgrown bungalow, and the Commission recommended verticality; secondly, the colour of the building was changed to a pale grey-blue, with some details picked out in a contrasting colour; and thirdly, the building was lightened, both inside and out, by a large area, vertical as well as overhead, of green-tinted solar glass. The result—and most of the credit must of course go to the architects, although the Commission has a share—is a construction which, instead of being messy and ugly, is extraordinarily dignified and imposing, and which sits well and naturally with the stern landscape, the sea and the sky.

Commenting on schemes as they come forward is the main part of the Commission's work. But the Commission has become increasingly conscious of the need to improve understanding among the public— and, it must be said, among architects and planners as well—of the possibilities of better design. In order to do this, the Commission's

Reports, published every two or three years (limitations of finance prevent an annual Report), draw attention to successful schemes which show what can be done, point out the more serious failings in the worse ones and comment briefly on architectural and urban design problems of the day. Also, in every year since 1984 the Commission has mounted an exhibition, with models as well as photographs, illustrating the work of the Commission during the previous twelve months. Great importance is attached to these efforts, because the Commission is convinced that no noticeable improvement of design can be expected until there is widespread public appreciation of the best that is at present being done, and of what could be done, in the fields of architecture and town planning.

The task of advising the Secretary of State and local planning authorities about new developments cannot be described in general terms, because every case is unique. The same kind of problems recur, but always in different combinations, and with different emphases. The best way to give an idea of the Commission's work, therefore, is to present a number of important but on the whole not atypical cases. None of those that follow concerns a scheme which seemed from the first to be so good that comment was needless. None of them was withdrawn and none of them was called in by the Secretary of State. They give some idea of how architectural, planning and procedural difficulties can arise, and they illustrate most of the common pitfalls—such as overbuilding, not fitting in, conceding too much to traffic—which constantly present themselves in different forms and in different combinations. No two schemes are alike, and there are no simple rule-of-thumb solutions.

Taken together, these seven cases show something of the rough process of development. They show how far removed it is from an amicable meeting of minds, where a talented architect and an enlightened client envisage a scheme which would be a credit to the neighbourhood, and are encouraged to build it by far-seeing local politicians. Nothing like this ever happens; or if it does happen, it is a case in a hundred thousand. Development, on the contrary, is a struggle. Those who are involved have many different points of view and many differing objectives. Even when they have the same objectives, they tend to have different standards. As a result, the development process is a battle of divergent interests and differing opinions, in which few of the participants much care about the points of view of the others, or are able, perhaps, even to understand them. Beauty and amenity do not fare well in this environment; they almost seem out of place. The names of Howard or Wood, of Vanbrugh or Palladio, would mean nothing, or next to nothing, to most of those who take the decisions. It is all a far cry from the coffee-table volumes and the entrancing pictures. Great architecture and marvellous cities are often and readily written about, but the way towards them is a rough road of argument and compromise, much of it about the flow and parking of vehicles, and even more about the flow and making of money.

The conclusion must be that little is to be hoped for from architects, developers, town planners and politicians left to themselves. Experience shows that in the development arena a supine reliance on the easy, stereotyped solution is favoured by many, while others engage in the single-minded pursuit of profit, often excess profit in the sense of more profit than is necessary to get the job done. This combination is bound to triumph over beauty and amenity unless there is strong leadership in the cause of urban quality, and strong public support. If the nation wants better cities, the work of the Royal Fine Art Commissions is not otiose.

1. *St James's Square, Edinburgh: Comprehensive Development Area*

Towards the end of 1958 word reached the Commission that proposals were being made to redevelop the St James's Square area in central Edinburgh. Planned and built late in the eighteenth century, St James's Square was sited near the east end of the New Town, on rising ground just north of Robert Adam's splendid Register House — one of the finest buildings in Scotland — and almost in the shadow of Calton Hill. In the course of a century and a half the Square had passed from dignity to dereliction. But it occupied a prime location in Edinburgh, only a few hundred yards from the central government offices in St Andrew's House, close to Princes Street and to the railway station, and it and its immediate surroundings had become an extremely valuable and important property.

Learning that some redevelopment was proposed, the Secretary to the Commission wrote to the Town Planning Officer stating that the Commissioners would be very much interested to know what was intended. In reply, the Town Planning Officer explained that proposals had been discussed in outline form between prospective developers and the Corporation Planning Committee, but that these discussions were confidential. He stated, however, that the development was likely to be substantial and extensive; that the Corporation believed that a plot ratio of 4 : 1 or a little over would be acceptable; that he himself expected the Royal Fine Art Commission to be consulted; and that he would welcome the Commission's preliminary views on the preservation of the form of St James's Square, and on the prospect of building up to eighteen storeys or more above the level of the Square.

Over a year later, in January, 1960, the Commission was informed that the Planning Committee had recently considered a joint report prepared by the Corporation officials based on the provision of

Crown offices in St James's Square and the need to improve street routes and widths in the area. This report was said to include a recommendation that the Commission be consulted especially in connection with restrictions to be imposed in the interests of civic design on the height and mass of the buildings. Drawings and a model were shortly afterwards produced, and in April the Commission sent to the Planning Officer its first official comments.

The Commission made seven points:

1. the scheme appeared to provide a satisfactory line of development;

2. there was nothing intrinsically wrong with the proposals to build high;

3. there was nothing wrong with the proposed plot ratio of 4.5 : 1;

4. the grouping and juxtaposition of tower blocks would require later detailed consideration;

5. it should be borne in mind that at a later date the building adjoining the Register House back premises might be demolished, which would make possible an attractive alternative layout;

6. it would be highly desirable to make some adjustment at the junction of Princes Street and Waterloo Place in the interests of traffic and of pedestrians, provided that this could be done without impairing the architectural character of Waterloo Place;

7. consideration should be given to opening up the east side of Leith Street in order to take advantage of the view to the Calton Hill.

These comments may fairly be said to have given the Corporation a good deal of encouragement. Of the three disastrous features of the scheme as finally built, two were at this stage, although only in general terms, approved; its height and its mass. It may seem strange, today, that a group of thoughtful, experienced and highly qualified persons, deeply concerned about the beauty and unique character of Edinburgh, should have made such a dreadful, albeit provisional, mistake. But tower blocks were still approved—indeed, they were exulted in although not lived in—by almost everyone in 1960, and slab blocks were the new fashion; and in these matters the Commissioners were not yet swimming against the tide.

So the Corporation proposed that twenty-three and a half acres or thereabouts should be defined as a Comprehensive Development Area, zoned for general business, cultural and public purposes, with a small area of open space and possibly a little housing. The Secretary of State ordered a Public Local Enquiry. There were only a few objectors, none of whom had any criticism to make of the proposal in general, and at the end of 1961 Mr Ewan Stewart presented his Report. The Reporter's conclusion was that although the Corporation had made out a good case for the area in question being made a Comprehensive Development Area, the proposed amendment to the City Plan should be rejected. The reasoning was that although the proposals not concerned with roads were 'admirable' (and, one may add, very vague) those which did concern roads were definite, final and unsatisfactory. The Corporation had stated that its objective was 'to provide for the proper circulation of traffic within this part of the central area' and the Reporter's view was that its proposals for Leith Street did not do this. 'A lot was said on both sides', he remarked, 'about the traffic study which was just about to begin'. But the procedure of putting proposals forward first and carrying out a traffic study afterwards did not appeal to the Reporter; nor did he like the Corporation's attitude that whereas 'outside expert opinion at the very highest level' would be called for in relation to the internal planning of the area, no such expert opinion was required for the roads. In particular, the Reporter was dissatisfied on two grounds. He saw little or no progress towards 'the segregation of pedestrians from streams of moving traffic'; and he thought it 'a negation of the purpose of town planning' for the Corporation to insist on retaining the A-listed building at the corner of Waterloo Place and Leith Street while 'at the same time they say quite openly that they are perpetuating a bottleneck'. The implication was that either the building should go, or the traffic should be restricted.

With the advantage of hindsight (a vast and most unfair advantage) it is easy to be critical of this Report. Two aspects of town planning are distinguished, namely 'internal planning' (buildings and their uses) and 'traffic routes'. The Report says almost nothing about the former, which is entirely understandable because what the Corporation proposed in this sphere was 'flexible' and 'only a tentative suggestion'; indeed, the Reporter found the internal planning proposals to be such that 'the Amendment might well have failed on the ground of vagueness' had not the road proposals been so definite. Roads were the focus of attention, for the Corporation and for the Reporter; buildings could as good as look after themselves. It is all very much of the 1960s. Demolition was taken for granted. The problem of increased and increasing traffic was what had to be solved even if this meant re-routing vehicles and widening streets all over Edinburgh. And that old will-o'-the-wisp, the segregation of pedestrians from traffic, was high on the list of the Reporter's priorities.

Two alternative recommendations were made: reject the proposals altogether, or accept them subject to better traffic plans. In May 1962 the Secretary of State opted for the latter course, and told the Corporation to go ahead, 'in the general manner proposed', subject to the submission, within a year, of new proposals for dealing with the expected flow of traffic.

Frantic activity by the City Engineer began at once, and the production of his report in the spring of 1963 threw the city into an uproar. There were to be tunnels, underpasses and carriageways with eight lanes of traffic, all in the centre of Edinburgh. For some months it almost seemed that the streets of the ancient city would flow with blood as well as vehicles. The Commission was not involved. But before the end of the year it had been agreed with the Planning Officer that the Commission would be consulted about the brief, which would shortly be given to the developers.

When it arrived, the Commissioners found the Planning Officer's draft Brief to be very much in line with their own views. Apart from more technical points, the Planning Officer emphasized the following considerations:

1. the grouping and scale of new buildings should harmonize with related buildings of special architectural and historical interest, especially Register House;

2. the overall design should be to scale with the layout of the New Town;

3. heights of buildings should not exceed the top of the Calton Hill, should not alter the dominance of the Melville column as seen from George Street, should not destroy the architectural effect of Register House, and should not damage the existing skyline as seen from the Castle and from the Botanic Gardens;

4. there should be a series of open-space amenity areas linked through to Calton Hill;

5. external finishes should be such as to harmonize with buildings of special architectural and historic interest in and adjoining the development area.

The Commissioners found little with which to disagree; the most essential points, they felt, had been covered. They expressed anxiety about the prospective loss of corner features in streets that were scheduled to be widened; they thought that the revised plot ratio of 3.5 : 1 might be somewhat high; they foresaw serious and intransigent traffic problems; but the brief, as far as it went, drew little criticism. The Corporation was left in no doubt, however, that on three very important matters the Commissioners were uneasy. Firstly, they emphasized the extraordinary importance of the site; and then added — clearly in response to some ominous comment or aside — that while redevelopment must be financially viable, it was vitally important 'that all proposals should be judged primarily on the standards of civic design which they achieve and on their architectural qualities'. Secondly, they questioned whether the so-called competition planned by the Corporation (not to be run according to RIBA rules but to some strange rules of the Corporation's own devising) would attract top architects or be adjudicated by suitably qualified persons. And thirdly, they urged the appointment of an architect/planning consultant 'of international standing' to collaborate in the project.

These observations were passed to the Corporation towards the end of 1963. Towards the end of 1964 the Corporation supplied the Commission with a copy of their developers' brief, which stated (as had been recommended by the Commission) that the final choice of developer would be based on the architectural merits of the scheme proposed, but which contained scarcely one of the architectural or design guide-lines originally put forward by the Planning Officer in his draft brief. At about the same time the Commission became aware, informally, that the Corporation was considering a short list of three developers, namely Murrayfield Real Estate (architects Ian Burke and Partners), Hammerson (architect Sir Basil Spence) and Ravenseft (architects not known). In the event, Ravenseft did not submit a scheme but the other two developers did. On 5 November the Commission was informed that the Planning Committee had decided provisionally to pursue further the scheme by Ian Burke and Partners. Neither then nor at any other time was the Commission allowed to see the Spence scheme; although it was said that the Scottish Office preferred the Spence scheme and that his model illustrated a scheme of potentially high aesthetic merit.

At two successive meetings the Commissioners gave careful consideration to the Murrayfield proposals, preferred by the Planning Committee. They studied the photographs and model placed at their disposal, and they listened to the architect himself and to four senior officials of the Corporation (excluding the Planning Officer). They concluded that the scheme before them was almost entirely devoid of merit. The Commissioners found it difficult to believe, as stipulated in the brief and as confirmed by the Town Clerk Depute, that the scheme had been chosen on its architectural merits rather than on technical and financial grounds (i.e. more rentable space for less cost). They felt that the Corporation's procedures, and the brief, had limited the chances of obtaining the best architectural solution to the problem. The selection of competitors on financial considerations had severely restricted the range of possible architectural solutions; while the brief itself had tied down competitors in a needless manner and had prevented them from seeking comprehensive and imaginative solutions for fear of incurring disqualification. In particular, the Commissioners made the following criticisms.

1. It seemed likely that traffic congestion in the area would become worse.

2. The general character and scale and massing of the major elements was entirely out of keeping with the architectural traditions of Edinburgh, and the scheme failed equally to make a modern contribution to the beauty and amenity of the city.

3. The siting, massing and heights of the main slab block were entirely unsatisfactory, as was its relationship to George Street, St Andrew's Square and Register House. It would also ruin Edinburgh's skyline.

4. The main elements in the design—the hotel and the slab block accommodating the Ministry of Public Buildings and Works—were

unoriginal in design and displayed a discordant duality of architectural character.

5. The slab block was to contain the Secretary of State's 'prestige' office. But this was approached from Princes Street by way of a tunnel.

6. The four residential blocks close to Calton Hill created a wall of building. They were much too large, and their design was uninspired.

Similar very unfavourable views seem to have been expressed by a good many other people. The Commission had strong grounds for believing that architectural opinion in the Scottish Development Department, in the Ministry of Public Building and Works, and in the Corporation itself decidedly favoured the architecture of the alternative scheme by Sir Basil Spence; which had been rejected (so it was said) on the ostensible ground of a minor deviation from the Corporation's road pattern. What could be said for the Murrayfield scheme was (the Commission was given to understand) that it provided more efficiently laid out offices and possibly preferable shopping facilities. But as the Commissioners never saw the other scheme they could form no opinion on these points. What was clear to almost everyone except the Planning Committee was that it would be disastrous to build a 240-foot-high hotel on the site chosen, rising more than 100 feet above Calton Hill and five times as high as Register House; that the whole block of new buildings viewed from the Botanic Gardens would be equally disastrous, even hiding, from some viewpoints, Salisbury Crags and the top of Arthur's Seat; and that the stipulated amount of accommodation could probably not be provided in the St James's Square area without recourse to excessively tall buildings.

The Secretary to the Commission accordingly wrote to the Corporation informing them of the Commission's views. The Commissioners, he stated,

> regret to report their quite unanimous judgement that the present scheme falls far short of the architectural and civic standard which they regard as imperatively required by this notable site . . . It was their profound conviction that the architecture of this key development must be of the highest quality and should either derive from Edinburgh's outstanding architectural traditions or should create, in a modern architectural idiom of unimpeachable distinction, a third New Town which would give continuity to the City's historic sequence of orderly development.

> The Commissioners recognise that the site sets a difficult problem; and that the present suggested solution has the merit of ingenuity. But as a contribution to the City's unique architectural heritage, it fails.

There was, however, an even more fundamental difficulty, as the Commission recognized. The attempt to overbuild a central site derived in large part from the Scottish Office policy of centralization. A new office block had recently been built and occupied near the Grassmarket, and now it was intended to gather together almost all the remaining Departments of State into one very large block in St James's Square (plus, of course, a very large car park, for 700 vehicles). Centralization was fashionable, although the Government had recently taken steps to restrict office building in central London; it was supposed to promote efficiency. But public-sector centralization in the heart of Edinburgh, added to a new hotel and an extensive new shopping centre, was an excellent recipe for increased traffic congestion. And besides, there were areas in Edinburgh where a large new office block would not reduce amenity, and where acquisition costs and possibly building costs would be substantially less than in St James's Square. What was wanted was reconsideration of the centralization policy. Criticizing official policy is not a function of the Royal Fine Art Commission. But the matter was so serious that a draft letter was prepared in which the case for accommodating Departments of State somewhere else than in St James's Square was set out; and along such lines the Chairman of the Commission was to write personally to the Secretary of State. Whether or not such a letter was actually sent is not known. If it was, it had no effect. The Secretary of State and the Scottish Office remained on course to disembark all their available forces in the immediate vicinity of Register House.

In declining to approve the Planning Committee's chosen scheme the Commission had put the Corporation in a difficulty. The city fathers wanted the scheme; but they also wanted to be able to tell the citizens of Edinburgh that they had the blessing of the Royal Fine Art Commission. So they began to manoeuvre. The Commission received a letter saying that the Planning Committee could not understand the Commission's planning principles; that the Commission's views had been stated in very general and what were felt to be rather negative terms; that what was wanted was advice of a somewhat more constructive character, and suggestions in rather more detail, as to how the scheme could be improved. In short, the Corporation wanted the Commission to co-operate in tinkering with a scheme which, as the Commission had already made quite clear, it considered far too poor to be worth going on with.

Of negative criticism, Dr Johnson once said, there is no end. And it is quite true that the comments made by the Commission are often apt to seem negative. But it must be borne in mind that the Commission is not in the business of planning sites or designing buildings. Its job is to point out where improvement is possible, when possible. Faced with a mediocre scheme, the Commission has to decide whether to offer detailed advice (which may be ignored, or which may be so misinterpreted as to make matters worse, or which, to some small degree accepted, may lead to statements that the Commission 'approved' or 'contributed to' the resulting mess), or whether it should say 'try again'. The first course precludes genuinely radical improvement; the second may result in a fresh and better approach, but it may also result in the original proposals going ahead, dismally unaltered. The Commission had carefully considered the scope for improving the St James's Square scheme, and had decided that nothing worthwhile could be done with it. Not to be inveigled into co-operation, the Commissioners therefore directed the Secretary to reply to the Corporation's letter along the following lines.

The Commissioners reminded the Corporation that in December 1963 they had informed the Corporation that they were in substantial agreement with the paper on draft principles, tabled by the Planning Officer, and they remained in agreement. They referred the Corporation to that document, which appeared to have been first ignored and then forgotten. As regards detailed suggestions, it was pointed out that the matter was not one of detail, but of total conception. But, since the Corporation professed a need for further guidance, the Commission drew attention to three particularly unacceptable aspects of the scheme. Firstly, the office block was not a tower, as the Corporation said, but a vast slab dominating the whole site; it provided office accommodation on a scale detrimental to everything else. Secondly, the hotel (undoubtedly a tower) gave little promise of architectural quality, and jostled with the office block for dominance in a scheme that was in any case devoid of architectural consistency. Thirdly, the housing element, located on a site not pre-eminently suitable for domestic use, was far too high in relation to Calton Hill. What was needed was a radical reconsideration of the whole plan.

The Corporation remained as flexible as Salisbury Crags. Early in 1965 they informed the Commission that, on the advice of a sub-committee of the Planning Committee, adjustment of the scheme would be proceeded with; and they had the effrontery to add that this would be done in consultation with the Royal Fine Art Commission. The Commission replied to the effect that a satisfactory scheme could not be devised by means of piecemeal adjustment to some of the existing scheme's worst features; such a process would in all likelihood exaggerate the overall lack of architectural merit. The Commissioners declined to enter into any proposal that they be a party to any such attempt. They also recalled that they had never been given an opportunity to consider the alternative scheme which had been submitted to the Corporation, and expressed their willingness to comment upon it, if invited. Needless to say, no such invitation was ever received.

Having thus failed to secure the Commission's 'co-operation' (or what might be called its submission) the city fathers fell silent. Then, over four months later, they announced their acceptance of a revised scheme, once more by the same developers and the same architect. In July 1965 the Commissioners saw a new block model, along with some drawings and photographs; and after due consideration they informed the Corporation that they considered the general disposition, massing and heights of the major elements in this new scheme to be in accordance with the principles which they had agreed with the Town Planning Officer in November 1963.

There is no telling why the Commissioners replied in these terms, or what they really thought. Did they indeed find the new proposals promising? or was it just that the new proposals appeared a little less bad than the old ones? or did the Commissioners make a political judgement, calculating that as the Corporation was evidently determined to go on with whatever they could get from Murrayfield Development and Mr Ian Burke, the wisest course was not to stand aside but to save whatever might yet be recovered from the wreck? There is no knowing, although the last seems almost certainly to have been the case. The Commission almost said as much in a subsequent letter. And the new scheme was not, in fact, very different from the old. The maximum heights were only a little lower, and the massing, although better, was still overwhelming. In any event, what happened in the course of the next two years demonstrates how dangerous it is for the Commission to become involved in a scheme when they have no power to change it.

The first nod of approval from the Commissioners must have been given on very slender evidence, because it was only at the start of 1966 that they saw a site plan, four sketch views, and an aerial view that was conceded to be no more than indicative of the general massing of the offices. They were not impressed. They commented that the tower appeared already to have grown higher than in the original model, and that some other changes had been made which would require careful study. They thought that the block running south from the tower was too high, as was the tower itself, and that the scale of everything was so great that the proportions and modelling (still not seen in any detail) would require a very delicate touch. Seventeen months later, having been kept in the dark for this period, the Commissioners made their final effort; although by now it was quite clear that they were on a losing wicket. A letter was sent to the Scottish Development Department reiterating the Commission's view that the fundamental trouble was that the site was being over-built, and suggesting that the policy of centralizing government offices in the heart of Edinburgh might yet be reconsidered. They had gone along with the latest proposals, they said, simply in order to take as positive an attitude as possible. This letter did no good. The Secretary to the Scottish Development Department washed his hands of the matter, saying that it was up to the Corporation. On the same day that the letter was sent to SDD, another was sent to the Corporation. The argument about over-building was repeated, along with the expression of doubts about the alleged plot ratio of 2.75 : 1.[10] The Commissioners complained once more about the tower, a heavy bulky block half buried among surrounding buildings; and about the circumferential block, which, they said, would appear from Leith Walk as a lofty, featureless flat-topped wall. To improve these particularly depressing features they put forward several suggestions. The answer (three months later) was as the Commission must have foreseen. Almost nothing could be changed because of the need to accommodate Ministers and departments. What was now planned was entirely reasonable, absolutely necessary, and all (or almost all) in accordance with the original proposals. As for the architectural merits of the scheme proposed, this soothing phrase had disappeared from the Corporation's public relations vocabulary.

Thus the St James's Centre stands as planned, in spite of every effort by the Royal Fine Art Commission to change it. The Corporation never ignored the Commission. On the contrary, it sought to get the Commission on its side, and, when that failed, it neutralized it and then successfully ignored its advice (as well as the advice of its own Planning Officer). The Government's policy of centralization and the Secretary of State's passion to have a vast amount of office space and a suite for himself with a view of the Castle contributed materially to the disaster. But the responsibility for what happened rests squarely on the Planning Authority. Edinburgh is now disfigured and disgraced by a very large, very ugly, and obviously very cheap building which is a monument to the greed and bad taste of the Corporation, and to its lust for a very peculiar kind of glory.

2. St Leonard's (Arthur Street etc.) Comprehensive Development area, Edinburgh

Holyrood Park is a splendid natural open space, made all the grander by its historical associations. It lies only a mile or so from the very centre of Edinburgh. It is extensive, bounded to the north-west by the Old Town of Edinburgh and Holyrood Palace, while immediately to the south there rise the steep grassy slopes of Arthur's Seat and Salisbury Crags. The Park is dominated by Arthur's Seat, over 800 feet high, but the Palace, extensively altered and enlarged by Sir William Bruce during the reign of Charles II, commands almost equal attention, for it is very large, and its turrets and battlements seem at once romantic and remote. It was here that Mary Queen of Scots struggled for the loyalty of her unruly subjects, and it was in the Park that the Young Pretender reviewed his forces in 1745.

Two hundred and sixteen years later Edinburgh Corporation proposed to redevelop, as a Comprehensive Development Area, some twenty acres on the north-western edge of the Park. The site that they chose lies close to the Old Town. It slopes east towards the Park, falling some sixty feet to the level of the Palace itself. As part of the townscape the site is one of the most important in Edinburgh. The Canongate lies just to the north, the Palace is clearly visible only a short distance away, and there is a magnificent panoramic outlook across the Park to Salisbury Crags and Arthur's Seat. Likewise, there is a splendid view looking from the hills across the site to the city. The visual impact of any new development at St Leonard's was clearly of critical importance to the overall image of Edinburgh.

The letter that reached the Commission in the spring of 1961 referred to development at a density of 190 persons per acre, requiring the construction of 1 100 dwellings. These dwellings, it was stated, were to be provided in blocks of varying sizes, which would range from three to 25 storeys in height. In reply, the Commissioners asked for a model, and they then visited the site. At the end of November their observations were transmitted to the Town Council. They conceded that what was proposed would be acceptable in certain other areas of Edinburgh. But they did not think it acceptable on the edge of the Park. Five 25-storey blocks rising to a height of 377 feet above Ordnance Datum would intrude with disastrous effect into vistas which contributed greatly to the visual appeal of the city. The skyline of Edinburgh was, the Commissioners reminded the Corporation, of special importance; and from most points on a wide arc of vision that skyline would be seriously and adversely affected by what was proposed. The Commissioners also commented unfavourably on the siting and relationships of the six tower blocks (some of them 15 storeys high) set in two groups of three to the north and south of the site. In short, they could find nothing to say in favour of the proposals.

The Commission was not alone in these opinions. The Ministry of Public Buildings and Works likewise informed the Corporation that the scheme was a bad one. They reminded the Corporation that Holyrood Park was a highly important amenity, a grand open space enjoyed by large numbers of people, and they observed that tall blocks of flats by the edge of the Park would have an overbearing effect on both Park and Palace. They pointed out, moreover, that the five 25-storey blocks were to be located on the one and only part of the periphery of the Park which rose to any considerable height above the Park itself. Their location on this high ground between the Park and the centre of the city would ruin the views over the city, which were so much appreciated by visitors to the Park, especially the view of the Old Town stretching from the Castle down to the Tron Kirk, which would be largely obliterated. Re-siting the tallest blocks would improve matters. But somebody ought to start thinking about the importance of the amenities of the area.

Early in 1962 the Commission learned that the scheme had been withdrawn. But they also learned that revised proposals had been submitted by the City Architect and had already been approved by the Housing Committee, but only, so it was said, for the purpose of initiating discussions. The Commissioners found the new plan to be a substantial improvement upon the old. The overall heights were the same, but there were not so many very tall blocks, and the new layout did not interfere so badly with the fine views of Arthur's Seat from the city, or of the Old Town from Arthur's Seat. There were two long blocks which were criticized as unduly high and heavy-looking, but the new scheme was pronounced on the whole to be more in keeping with its environment. The Ministry of Works wrote to the Corporation in similar terms. Soon afterwards the scheme was withdrawn because of proposed changes in Edinburgh's road pattern.

In March 1964 an entirely new set of proposals, the third, reached the Commission. On this occasion the matter was said to be of some urgency (as the Depute Town Clerk cryptically observed, 'the question of urgency always seems to arise at the last minute') because the Corporation allegedly wanted to reach a decision in three or four weeks. As well as plans and elevations, a model was submitted, and some photo-montages, and the Commissioners again visited the site and adjacent view-points. This time opinion was divided. In the first scheme the tallest block had reached 377 feet, now the tallest block was a mere 277 feet. (It was, however, 200 feet long). Some Commissioners thought that 277 feet was still too high, but the Chairman did not want it to appear that the Commission was against tall blocks as such, and he felt in any case that the principle of having tall blocks overlooking the Park had been conceded when the Commission neither approved nor condemned the second scheme. So the letter that went to the Corporation expressed general approval and commented adversely only on the height and positioning of one block in the centre of the scheme.

Having considered these latest proposals as a matter of urgency, and having sent their comments to the Corporation on 1 April, the Commissioners waited until December for an answer. They were then informed that the Planning Sub-Committee had approved some revised drawings subject to any comments that the Commission might wish to make. The Commissioners studied the drawings but could find no alteration in the design of the block to which they had objected in April. On receiving this news the Town Clerk replied that the location and form of this block had been given careful consideration but had not been altered for four reasons:

1. any significant alteration in its form, providing the same accommodation, would reduce sunlighting values in other blocks;

2. it provided a visual link between the two tower blocks as well as a 'backcloth effect' to the other blocks and the existing church;

3. although 200 feet long and with a roofline only 230 feet below the highest point of Salisbury Crags it would appear unobtrusive and generally 'insignificant';

4. it could be reduced in height but this would further reduce the density which was already below that originally required.

In short, the whole scheme was a good one and there was no need to worry; 'the principal landmarks in the town,' the Commission was informed, 'would not be affected to any degree'. The Commission replied, in a very brief letter, that the scheme as it stood was not approved. Twelve months later they learned that the scheme had been withdrawn on the grounds that it was not economically viable.

Almost five years had passed since the first proposals to redevelop the St Leonard's area had been put forward. The Commission had raised difficulties about three successive schemes, and nothing had been built. A fourth scheme was now being prepared, and it became known that this also was a high-rise scheme. The Commission, however, was no longer so complaisant about high-rise buildings as once it had been, partly, perhaps, because it had a new Chairman. In the course of 1965 it had commented on a number of such buildings in several Scottish cities, seldom with approval; and in 1965 it had taken the view that a ten-storey block to be built for Moray House College of Education in the Canongate was inappropriate for that ancient thoroughfare. This opinion, however, had landed the Commission in a difficulty, because the Scottish Education Department argued that if the Commission did not object to 24 storeys on the St Leonard's site it had no right to object to 10 storeys in the Canongate. It thus began to be clear that the St Leonard's redevelopment case was a very important one, both in its own right and also because no general principles had yet been laid down by the Planning Authority for the design and siting of tall buildings in or near central Edinburgh. During 1965 however, the Commission itself drew up a carefully thought-out paper on precisely this subject. The conclusion reached by the Commission was that general height limits in the central area should be laid down but that 'if any proposal is put forward for a building that will offend against height limits the onus of proving that such a proposal is in the long-term public interest should rest squarely with the applicant'.[11]

So in the early weeks of 1966, with the fourth St Leonard's redevelopment proposal just round the corner, the Commissioners sat down to consider what best they could do. Their difficulty was that they had all along tacitly accepted the Corporation's line that tall blocks were in this case the only possible form of development, and they had accordingly restricted their efforts to arguing about the top fifty or a hundred feet, and about the positioning of the blocks. They had failed to condemn the enormously tall blocks proposed in earlier schemes, with the result that many Commissioners believed that as far as St Leonard's was concerned they could not now object to tall blocks as such. (Explaining this to SDD, the Secretary to the Commission ruefully added, 'It never pays to appease, does it!'). Perhaps the best that the Commission could now do, some thought, would be to press for an aesthetically tolerable high-rise development, even if that would mean a lower density than the Corporation aimed for. But after discussion this line of least resistance was given up, and when the fourth St Leonard's redevelopment scheme landed on the Commission's desk it received a distinctly chilly reception.

The 1964 proposals had included one block of 24 storeys and one block of 22 storeys with a maximum height of 277 feet above the Ordnance Datum; the latest proposal provided, *inter alia*, for three blocks of 25 storeys ('Messrs Wimpey's design numbered 1001') rising to no less than 431 feet, and increased the density from 125 to 132 persons per acre. In all, there was to be accommodation for approximately 2 000 persons. The Town Planning Officer thought that the scheme was acceptable, except for its height. His view was that no building on the site should exceed 380 feet above Ordnance Datum. The National Memorial on Calton Hill was 396 feet, the Tron Church spire was 413 feet, and the University had recently got away with building the Hume Tower in what was left of George Square to a height of 423 feet. A building rising to 431 feet looked, on paper, a bit high but not ridiculously so; why not get used to the technology and proportions of the twentieth century?

The Commission, however, had had enough. Yet another high-rise scheme, every bit as bad as those that had preceded it, finally produced the explosion. Without delay a letter was despatched to the Corporation repeating the usual arguments about scale and skyline, and adding that if this scheme were approved a most regrettable precedent would be set for other very large buildings in adjacent areas. It was therefore of the greatest importance that a block model should be produced for the whole area including the Castle, the Old Town ridge, and Salisbury Crags. And the letter concluded by raising, at last, the really fundamental point. The Commission had felt obliged at the very beginning to accept the Corporation's premise as to the required density, and equally the conclusion drawn by the Corporation that such a density could be achieved only by building a high-rise development. But now the Commission questioned these assumptions. 'No doubt', the Commissioners wrote, 'feasibility exercises have been carried out by the Corporation's technical staff at various times during the past five years to verify the continuing validity of these basic contentions? Could the Commission please be informed as to the result of these (putative) feasibility exercises? And what precisely was the maximum number of persons per acre who could be accommodated satisfactorily on the site if a 'low-rise' form of development were adopted?

Having despatched this letter—a great deal more systematic and sharper in tone than anything previously sent on the subject—the Commissioners sat down to review the position. There were, they decided, several fundamental questions that had still to be asked. What advice had the Town Planning Officer given concerning the aesthetic and amenity aspects of all these proposals? What planning principles had been used? What was to be done about landscaping? Had the possibilities of low-cost walk-up housing ever been investigated? Was it not true that the choice between a high-rise and a low-rise development was one of preference rather than necessity? What replies the Corporation gave to these and similar awkward questions is not recorded. But soon afterwards the Commissioners saw detailed plans and a limited site model, and they then made their formal comments on the latest scheme.

It was, they said, quite unacceptable. They considered that it neither made the best use of the opportunity afforded by the site nor did it take any account of the scale and character of the surrounding townscape and landscape. They were not opposed to high-rise buildings as such. But the proposed towers would establish an overwhelming new scale; they would dwarf the prominent but comparatively small Old Town and its ridge; they would challenge Salisbury Crags and intrude upon Holyrood Park; and they would interrupt or destroy a number of views and silhouettes which people came from all over the world to enjoy. The Corporation claimed that only a high-rise development could achieve the required density. But the density had fallen over the years from 190 persons per acre to 132. This quite changed the situation. The Commissioners were convinced that an imaginative and modern low-rise development could solve the housing problem and at the same time contribute to the amenity and visual quality of the area. On this windswept site there should be a compact development, with maximum enclosure, tucked into the hillside, but making full use of the fine view eastward, and preserving the existing skyline. And—evidently distrustful of the Corporation's ability or willingness to devise such a plan themselves— the Commissioners further informed the Corporation that they had already asked the Secretary of State for Scotland to arrange for a study to be carried out with the object of assessing the feasibility of their ideas concerning the proper redevelopment of the site. The letter concluded with the observation that a good deal of the trouble over the last five years had arisen from the failure of the Planning Authority to begin with an adequately thought-out development brief including amenity and aesthetic considerations as well as technical and financial matters.

Hardly had the Corporation had time to read this letter when they received one from the Ministry of Public Buildings and Works. It was very much briefer but the sense was the same. What was now proposed was considerably less satisfactory than what had been proposed in 1964. The Ministry would feel bound to raise objections to the scheme as having an adverse effect on the amenities of Holyrood Park.

Two months later, in May 1966, the Scottish Development Department produced the feasibility study for which the Commission had asked. The scheme was entirely for low-rise or walk-up forms of housing, the tallest blocks being six storeys, designed as walk-ins from high level. The focal point was to be the existing church with a shopping and community complex beside it, all integrated into a three-level square. The terraced blocks were to be at right angles to the slopes, and the rest of the housing consisted of maisonettes and stub blocks of flats. The aim was to provide good enclosure with glimpses of the Park, and minimum intrusion on the existing landscape. Five hundred and sixty-five dwellings were provided compared with the Corporation's 587, and density was 125 persons per acre. The Commissioners were well pleased with this imaginative alternative scheme which, as they truly said, had been produced with remarkable speed and efficiency.

What the Corporation thought can only be guessed at; what they did is clear enough. They procrastinated for two more years, and then instructed Messrs Wimpey to prepare a scheme based on the form of layout and scale of development set out in the feasibility study. What resulted, it is almost needless to say, was yet another third-rate housing scheme. The subtlety and spirit of the SDD proposals did not survive passage through the minds of Edinburgh Corporation and Messrs Wimpey. The number of dwellings provided fell to 455 while the tallest block reached seven storeys and the density rose to 140. The detailing of the buildings did not make matters any better. The Commissioners described the final plans as 'sadly pedestrian', which is putting it mildly; but felt that at any rate the worst had been averted. There was one more disappointment in store for them, however. At the end of 1970, when building was at last about to begin, the Corporation discovered that the vacant church on the site was in a poor state of repair, and that it would be a good idea to demolish it. The Commission pointed out that the church had been the key component around which the SDD scheme had been designed, visually and socially, and had the church not been in existence an alternative layout might well have been proposed. The Corporation then ordered that the church be demolished, and it was.

There is no doubt that this case ended as an important victory, albeit a limited one, for civilized town planning. High-rise developments were the fashion in the early 1960s, and if high-rise was good enough for Merseyside it was, in the eyes of Edinburgh Corporation, good enough for Holyrood Park. There is no evidence that the Corporation and its advisers had the slightest grasp of anything beyond numbers of dwellings, numbers of garages, densities and cost. There is no evidence that the word amenity meant anything to the Planning Authority at all. At one point in the struggle the Commission was in great danger of conceding too much to the alleged necessities of the situation; to the imperatives proclaimed by planners in the grip of the prevailing high-rise convention and unable to think of anything else. What saved the day was the pressure put on the Corporation by the combined efforts of the Ministry of Public Buildings and Works, the Scottish Development Department and the Commission. The SDD in particular made a determined stand against ignorance and vandalism.

Edinburgh's skyline has suffered a good deal since the mid-1960s; the St James's scheme, which the Commission was contending with in these same years, has been especially damaging. But at least Holyrood Park and the great natural setting of Edinburgh has been saved. No one who knows the city and appreciates it would think that unimportant. It was a French economist, not a local planner or politician, who said; 'la plus intéressante de toutes ces beautés . . . c'est la vue d'Edimbourg dans tout son ensemble, avec son couronnement admirable de montagnes'.

3. *St Enoch Station, Glasgow: Redevelopment*

Opened by the Prince of Wales in 1876, St Enoch Station and its approaches had been grandly conceived. They lay in the heart of central Glasgow, an area of Victorian prosperity and ambitious Victorian architecture. Over thirteen hundred of the city's oldest slum properties had been demolished in order to make room for the new prestige joint terminus, and the main line swept over the river Clyde to reach platforms approximately twenty-five feet above street level. The main feature of the station concourse was a great glazed arched roof 80 feet high and 504 feet long, with a span of 198 feet; and the nearby hotel, opened in 1879, was conceived as the largest and most impressive railway hotel so far built in Britain. All rail services were withdrawn from St Enoch in the summer of 1966, and the station and the hotel were closed.

The site is a most desirable one. It is very close to the main shopping areas of Argyle Street and Buchanan Street and adjacent to the fine and spacious St Enoch Square. It is moreover within a short distance of extensive recreational space at Glasgow Green, and the pedestrianized riverside walk lies immediately to the south along Custom House Quay. Local bus, railway and underground stations are located in St Enoch Square. The site is almost surrounded by the

Glasgow Central Conservation Area, and structures of national importance line the river frontage, including the Custom House, St Andrew's Catholic Cathedral, the late-Gothic Merchants' Steeple, and the Suspension Bridge; even the Underground Station in St Enoch Square is a distinguished piece of nineteenth-century architecture. The whole area is central, Victorian in character, prominent from the south side of the river, and, in 1966, much of it was slowly but surely deteriorating and subject to future redevelopment.

Towards the end of 1971 the Royal Fine Art Commission received a brief description of a proposed scheme for the St Enoch Station area. The Commission commented that what was wanted was a well-considered outline plan for the entire area between Argyle Street and the river. For such a plan to be possible, account would have to be taken of proposals for Custom House Quay, of decisions concerning the inner ring road, of car-parking requirements in the city centre, and of the relation of high-rise blocks to the townscape in general. The Commission recognized that the Corporation was under a great deal of pressure to hasten redevelopment schemes, but added that the acceptance of unbalanced and piece-meal proposals which made a totally inadequate contribution to the civic character of Glasgow (the scheme under consideration being a prime example of such proposals) would have very unfortunate long-term consequences. The British Rail Property Board, according to the Commission, should not be allowed to exploit valuable assets like the St Enoch Station site in such a way as to waste a great civic design opportunity. What was wanted was enlightenment and imagination. Soon afterwards, for whatever reason, the 1971 scheme was abandoned.

Three years and one change of government later, dispersal became the new magic word. The Heath administration had discovered that there was no room left to expand in central London, and plans were afoot to move several thousand civil servants to Cardiff, Glasgow, Teesside and other locations. According to official sources, the move to Glasgow and East Kilbride was to be 'a pretty big affair', involving 7000 employees in the Ministries of Defence and of Overseas Development. Because those to be moved expressed a good deal of reluctance to go to Glasgow, the Lord Privy Seal took the view that here was a challenge and an opportunity to do something really imaginative in the way of town planning. Office buildings to provide for the newcomers would not be enough. There would have to be shops, restaurants, recreational facilities, adequate car parking: an end to the Gorbals image and, instead, a living example of the new policies towards urban renewal. Finance, the Department of the Environment thought, need not be an obstacle. A comprehensive approach to replanning would win over the dissidents, and pay for itself in the long run.

Twenty-two months later (we have now reached September 1976)
the Property Services Agency in Scotland informed the RFAC that a
large office complex was to be built on part of the St Enoch Station
site to house Ministry of Defence personnel dispersed to Scotland,
and that a number of other sections of the site would be apportioned
to other developers. The Scottish Development Department (as well
as the RFAC and many other people) thought that this was perhaps
the greatest opportunity of the decade to contribute to good civic
design in Scotland, and expressed the hope that the planning
authority would take the best possible advice on the preparation of a
comprehensive brief. But the rumour soon spread that Glasgow
District Planning Department was doing little more than shuffling
land uses and brooding on roads and traffic; so already there was
reason to fear that a co-ordinated, unified development plan was
slipping out of the window. To do the Planning Officer justice,
however, he pointed out at this stage that the transfer of civil service
jobs to Glasgow was still by no means certain.

A confidential report on the proposed development reached the
Commission in November. The Ministry of Defence had at first
wanted 24 000 square metres of office space with a 'prestige' frontage
to St Enoch Square, but this had been modified to 22 000 sq metres
not overlooking the Square. This left a substantial part of the whole
site, fronting the Square and therefore very much in the public view,
to be developed separately. According to the Planning Officer, this
area would be used for the relocation of some of the 1 000 parking
spaces currently available at St Enoch plus approximately 700 new
parking spaces (more for local shoppers than for MOD personnel)
accommodated on four floors above a shopping level. The Commissioners were unhappy, to say the least, with these proposals. If a
building of the size required by MOD had to be built in the very centre
of Glasgow (why not in one of the new towns?), it was certainly
fortunate that it would have very little visual impact on St Enoch
Square and no direct link with Custom House Quay. But it seemed
to the Commissioners that a multi-storey car park above a line of
shops, looking across to some intricate architectural forms on the
west side of the Square, would be an unqualified disaster. The
suggestion was therefore made that the possibility of basement or
underground parking should be thoroughly investigated. The
Commission again stressed that a comprehensive approach to the
development on the St Enoch Square site was required. There could
be shops facing onto the Square with the main mass of building set
back; or the main face of the building (provided that it was not a car
park) could be on the line of shops, helping to enclose the Square; or
there could be a terracing-back of upper levels progressively to the
east, so as to make the building less dominant. (The MOD building

was expected to rise to nine storeys). It was also suggested that the Square would be improved if it ceased to be used as a bus terminus.

These observations were sent both to Glasgow's Planning Officer and to the Property Services Agency, responsible for all government buildings. The Planning Officer expressed sympathy for the idea of a comprehensive approach but emphasized that many bodies and many individuals had their own ideas of what should be done. On points of detail, he informed the Commission that the Region was not keen on having more shops in the area, and that the local traders considered that they suffered from under-provision of parking. Therefore parking took precedence over offices and shops. As for underground parking, that would not be considered for reasons of cost. And as for levels of parking above shops on the St Enoch Square frontage, that would be quite all right, if properly designed. The PSA took a rather different line. They agreed that what was wanted was a comprehensive or at least a cohesive approach, and they stated their intention to keep in touch with all parties contributing to the overall building programme. In any case, overall development was the business of Glasgow's Planning Department, although experience so far had indicated that the Department was chiefly interested in statistical manœuvring, with scant regard for genuine principles relating to amenity and civic design. Several storeys of car parking on the St Enoch Square frontage was regarded by the PSA with almost as much aversion as by the Commission; it would, they thought, however well designed, be totally detrimental to the scheme itself and to the Square.

For some months nothing very significant happened. The PSA felt that they were being placed in the position of having to lead the way in terms of basic building plans in the hope that all other developers would then be persuaded to contribute in an appropriate manner. The Scottish Development Department felt that the controls being exercised by the planning authority were totally inadequate to meet the situation and that a local plan for the entire area was overdue. The New Glasgow Society felt that the decision (taken in January 1977) to proceed immediately with the demolition of the A-listed St Enoch Hotel without anyone having a clear idea what was to take its place was damaging and foolhardy. The RFAC felt that the work on sketch models carried out by the PSA and the SDD was promising, and that if the Scottish Development Agency (now owners of the entire site) was pushed into the role of superintending planner it would be no bad thing; but that the District's commitment to a car park for 700 cars on the St Enoch Square site was a horrible mistake, made worse by the ruling that the 3.5 : 1 plot ratio excluded car parking and so opened the way to gross overbuilding.

For two years matters thus went smoothly on — or rather did not go on at all—until in March 1979 consultant architects came forward with outline proposals for the whole site. Besides the MOD building (now said to be in the wrong place) there were intentions to build a department store, multi-storey parking, unit shopping and office accommodation. The Commissioners commented that there was still not very much to comment on. The form of the MOD building was not yet decided, and the planning and design constraints for the entire site remained vague. But they reiterated their strong opposition to the building of a car park substantially visible from St Enoch Square, and again cautioned about the danger of overbuilding.

They need not have worried. Bad economic news reached Glasgow in July. The Government had reviewed the programme of Civil Service dispersal, and the number of MOD posts to be transferred to Glasgow was reduced from 4000 to 1400. No longer would the Ministry require half of the former station site; a quarter would do, probably less. Changes of policy of this sort, as one senior civil servant remarked laconically to another, are facts of democratic life.

This left the SDA in possession of a very valuable 16-acre site in the middle of Glasgow, on which they had so far spent £6m. They had to do something with it and they wasted no time. In May 1980 they submitted outline plans for a 250000 square feet office block for the MOD, shopping space to the extent of 260000 square feet, a 250-bedroom hotel above the shops, an ice rink, one hundred residential units and, as usual, 1500 parking spaces. The Commissioners, also as usual, were not very favourably impressed. The proposals, they thought, lacked consistency. They criticized some aspects of the layout, found some of the elevations (especially the cliff-like external walls that usually go with shopping centres) seriously unsatisfactory, and questioned the proposal to mix housing with blocks of multi-storey car parking at the eastern end of the site. They also asked, once again, that a new location be found for the bus terminal. Their main complaint, however, was that the material presented to them made possible no more than a few superficial comments on the architectural aspects. The Scottish Civic Trust, invited to comment at the same time, was a good deal more emphatically adverse in its views.

A large number of people were now seriously concerned. The SDA had given a new and welcome impetus to the idea of redeveloping the St Enoch Station site. They knew, like everyone else, that it was the most important city-centre site in Scotland vacant or likely to become vacant, and they recognized that suitable proposals for the area could, as their chairman is reported to have said, 'put new heart into the city centre'. But would the latest proposals form the basis for one of the most outstanding city-centre developments in Europe, as the SDA suggested? There was a lot of room for doubt. And, to be fair, the SDA was in a very difficult position. Glasgow

District, presumably because of their over-riding concern for jobs, had approved a brief which imposed virtually no conditions, except that there was to be a multi-storey car park for 700 cars on the prominent hotel site, and this they and their Planning Department stuck to in the face of strong objections from the SDD, PSA and the Commission. Glasgow's Planning Officer declined to consider the pedestrianization of St Enoch's Square on the ground that the Square was not included in the planning application; and as for the bus terminal, there had always been a bus terminal in St Enoch's Square, an argument unlikely to help the cause of urban renewal. The MOD building had recently shrunk in size, leaving the SDA with a much larger area to develop than they had expected; and only in the spring of 1980 was it revealed to them that the whole redevelopment (apart from the MOD building) would have to be commercially funded. This meant that the considerable shopping content, which would be the main revenue earner, had to be put at the western or St Enoch Square end of the site, while the eastern end, farther away from the busy streets and less attractive in its surroundings, was abandoned to car parks and some houses. The concept was entirely commercial. Commercial developers never have any time to lose. So as soon as they could manage it SDA put forward what were called outline proposals, but at the same time made it clear that they were not to be persuaded to make any basic changes in the overall layout. The RFAC considered, quite reasonably, that this made nonsense of 'consult-ation'. The general concept would not be altered whatever the Commissioners said, and to make matters worse they found that the information about massing and proportions was too vague for comment. To add still further to the confusion, business interests in Glasgow began to complain about the amount of shopping in the scheme. Imaginative new policies for urban renewal, so confidently looked forward to in 1974, seemed to have dissolved into calculations of profit, and the smoke of battle.

At this point the City of Glasgow, somewhat to most people's surprise, decided to hold an informal enquiry into the proposals, exclusive of the MOD building. The Report was made public in December 1980. According to the Reporter, the most important question discussed at the enquiry was whether or not the proposed development would bring about an over-supply of shopping accommodation in central Glasgow. He found that this result was most improbable. Car-parking, described as the second main subject discussed, was deemed to raise only one question: ought the existing traders in the area to be provided with new parking facilities before the St Enoch Station site ceased to be available as a car park? The answer was no. The 1 500 parking places now proposed were 'adequate to serve the needs of the development'. Questions concerning the architectural impact of the development were dealt with in a few lines. Such questions were 'matters of detailed design' and should be considered at a later stage. 'There was nothing to suggest that it was not possible to devise an appropriate and acceptable solution to the architectural problems which were raised.' An enquiry of this sort is clearly a commercial investigation and of no help whatever to anyone concerned about civic design.

Over a year later, SDA came forward with a revised scheme, and the Commission sat down to consider the matter for the seventeenth time. This time the proposals were radically new. The Ministry of Defence, which first had wanted half the site and then less than a quarter, had disappeared altogether, gone to Anderston. Shopping facilities upon which the Region and the Planning Officer had looked with little favour in 1977, had grown from 260 000 square feet (approved in 1980) to something between 340 000 and 450 000 square feet. There was also provision for offices, housing, a 250-bedroom hotel, parking for nearly 2 000 cars and an ice-rink. The various activities associated with the major building were to be enclosed within an enormous glass 'tent' wrapping round a multi-storey car park, and the plot ratios had been reduced. The Commissioners were concerned that so much new shopping space might cause traders to give up business in other parts of the city and thus spread dereliction, and that the sloping roof of the 'tent' fronting St Enoch Square might not do enough to contain the open space of the square itself. But on the whole they liked the scheme. It was, they commented, the most assured and encouraging scheme so far, and capable of satisfactory development. In particular, the multi-storey car parking was no longer obtrusive. They wished to be consulted again, when the design for internal and external street elevations became more detailed.

These comments were made in March 1982. During the next two years the development was still further delayed for two reasons. First, financial backing for it had to be found. The total cost was put at £40 million, and the SDA and Strathclyde Regional Council could not foot the bill themselves; but in April 1984, the Church Commissioners entered into an arrangement which solved the financial problem. Secondly, a consortium of developers appeared in the summer of 1982 with plans to build a shopping centre and other facilities on a three-acre site not far from St Enoch Square. The problem was whether both these developments would be viable and whether, if both were built, they would ruin shopowners all over the rest of Glasgow. Glasgow District Council wanted them both; but Strathclyde Regional Council called in the planning applications and ruled that only St Enoch would go ahead.

This delay gave time for the developers and their architects to mature their plans, and a final version was presented to the Commission in June 1984. The scheme had expanded somewhat, although it was basically the same as in 1982. The Commissioners thought that it had been improved. They thought the concept exciting, and on this occasion even went so far as to describe it as an inspired scheme. The glass 'tent' — four and a half acres of it — would, they noted, be very unlike its surroundings and would very much change the style of St Enoch Square, but this would not be a disaster. The chief difficulty was to imagine just what this enormous 'tent' would look like from various points of view in the public streets, and what would be seen of the buildings within the 'tent', about which there was no information at all. Would these buildings all face inwards to a shopping mall, and thus present to the street and to the public at large only their back premises and piles of crates and empty boxes? Or would care be taken to make these 'inside' buildings attractive and interesting when seen from the street? Would there be planting within the 'tent' to give a green-house effect? Would pedestrians have access at all times, and would there be adequate management? There were bound to be unanswered questions, but it now seemed that £40 million and a splendid site were going to be used to produce something over and above practical convenience, jobs and profit.

Over twelve years were thus required to sort out the St Enoch Station site. The *laissez faire* approach to planning adopted by the Glasgow District Council and its Planning Department failed to produce what it was obviously intended to produce — quick results. The one inflexible requirement of the planning authority, that there be a large multi-storey car park on the edge of St Enoch Square, was insisted upon year after year because established shopping interests in the city centre wanted it. But in the end it was given up. There was no need for the car park to overlook St Enoch Square, and in any case redevelopment is about how to shape the future, not about how to conciliate the present. The shilly-shallying about dispersal by successive governments was part of the great advance towards and then the great retreat from regional economic planning. The failure to produce a comprehensive plan for the area was perhaps not so unfortunate as it seemed at the time, because such a plan might not have made much difference. The forces of development are strong, and they appear where and when they will; there is no use looking too far ahead or too far around. Unified planning for the site was finally achieved because the SDA (a government agency) became its owner and energetically organized its development. And the Commission was able at the end of the day to welcome a plan which avoids most of the errors that the Commission had resisted over the years. It is true that the bus station still takes up a large part of the Square and that no one knows exactly how the enormous glass tent is going to merge into the area or exactly what is going to be built (and planted) inside it. It seems unlikely that the new construction will ever look as grand and purposeful as the old. But it should stay cleaner. And its influence should on the whole be enlivening and benign on the important area of Glasgow that surrounds it.

4. *Kessock Bridge*

The Kessock Bridge over the Beauly Firth immediately north of Inverness was opened by the Queen Mother on 6 August 1982. Almost ten years previously, in February 1973, the Commission had begun to express an interest in the design of this large and important bridge. But in order to understand what happened at Kessock it is necessary to look at an earlier project, and to go back to the summer of 1972, when the Commission was presented by the Scottish Development Department with the design for a bridge over the wild and beautiful Ballachulish narrows, in the west of Scotland.

Ballachulish is a fairly long and difficult crossing. The narrows are a navigable waterway, so there must be clear headroom of about sixty feet for shipping, while the construction of a bridge with piers would be difficult and expensive because of the depth of water and the speed of a tide race. The Scottish Development Department devised a single span 'conforming arch' design, and submitted it to the Commission. The Commissioners responded by saying that the arch was very large, heavy and inelegant and would be seriously out of scale both with its immediate environment and with the wider scene. They thought that there could be other solutions to the problem. They were sure—or so they said—that the Department had considered alternatives; but they would be failing in their duty if they did not ask to see the alternative designs that had been considered and to be informed of the disadvantages that had caused these alternatives to be discarded. The SDD replied that no other designs had been developed because, technically, there was no satisfactory alternative to what was proposed. A through-truss design might be possible, but it would cost more and its appearance amid the hills at Ballachulish would be deplorable. The arch that had been designed was, according to the Department, elegant and simple, and was the only fitting structure. It would contribute to the beauty of the mountainous landscape.

The Commissioners were rather surprised to be told so frankly that they did not know their own business, and that a bridge which they thought possibly suitable for an industrial area would in fact enhance the west highlands. So they replied to the effect that while the technical and financial aspects were not their business the aesthetic aspects were, and they did not agree that the arch proposed was elegant and fitting. They noted, however, that the work was to go out to tender almost immediately, so second thoughts on the part of the SDD seemed unlikely. But they expressed the hope that in the future means would be found whereby fundamental issues could be discussed and decided long before a design was ready to go out to tender.

Thus the conforming arch seemed inevitable, like it or not; the Commission, as in several previous bridge cases, had been presented with a *fait accompli*. But this time a surprise was in store. One steel fabrication tender submitted to the Department included the offer of an alternative truss design to be built at lower cost than the arch, because, the firm said, they had recently built such a bridge and had suitable erection plant lying available, unused. Here, surely, was a golden opportunity! So the SDD hastened to inform the Commission (although, as it happened, their letter was written a few days before Christmas and did not reach the Commission until late in January, 1973), and the Commissioners sat down to study the new design. They did not like it. They thought, in fact, that the Department had been right six months before in saying that a truss design erected at Ballachulish would have a 'deplorable' impact on the landscape.

It was now fairly obvious that the parties would have to agree to differ. The Commissioners had been presented with two designs, and they heartily disliked them both. The Department insisted that nothing else was possible. But the Commissioners remained unconvinced that this was really the case. They believed that from the very outset, several years before, the Department had failed to appreciate that what was needed in this instance was an exceptional design to match an area of exceptional natural beauty, and that the usual departmental procedures would almost certainly fail to produce such a design; as in fact they had. In spite of what the Department said, something far better was technically possible. In order to confirm this opinion a confidential meeting was arranged between Sir Robert Matthew, who was one of the Commissioners, and Sir Ove Arup, famous for his original and elegant solutions to difficult engineering problems. The message which Sir Robert brought back from his discussion with Sir Ove was that the Commission was indeed correct. Much more elegant structures were possible at Ballachulish, such as had recently been built in Germany and by Maillart in Switzerland. Either steel or prestressed concrete could be used, and the deck could be supported from either above or below, preferably the latter — which was what the Commissioners had always wanted. A fresh start was needed, and the job should be entrusted to a designer who had already proved himself capable of meeting such a challenge as existed at Ballachulish, or an international design competition should be arranged. Such a competition would enable Scotland to break out of the unhappy web of mediocrity into which her bridge designers had fallen.

This advice was to prove most valuable; but for Ballachulish time was running out. The Commissioners met once more, and spelt out their final judgement. They informed the SDD that neither of the designs submitted was acceptable, adding that while it was not for them to suggest engineering solutions they did not doubt that the required result could be achieved in a variety of ways. But the engineers in the SDD were not willing (or able) to think again, the Roads Division in the SDD had a timetable which no one could (or would) alter, and tenders had to go out. The Secretary of State was assured by his advisers that no solution significantly different from those already put forward was feasible. And the truss design (being the cheaper of the two) was in due course built. It looks cheap, out of date and dreadful.

The reverberations of this difference of opinion — or, to put it more colloquially, this row between the Commission and the Department, reached the highest levels. Indeed, they reached so high as to cause the Secretary of State to give an assurance to the Commission that in future, when major bridges were to be planned and designed, the Commission's views would be sought at the earliest practicable and sensible stage. And the Chairman of the Commission, in his reply, observed that the Kessock Bridge (believed to be already on the drawing board) would provide an excellent opportunity for devising more effective consultation procedures; and he added that the best way to overcome the limitations which seemed to be inherent in the Department's standard approach to bridge design would be to organize international competitions.

This letter was sent in February 1973. Three months later the Commissioners saw the design chosen by the Department for the Kessock Bridge. It was very good. Wheels must have turned, or heads must have rolled, long before the Ballachulish affair was brought to an end. All that the Commissioners could find to say was that they commended the design and had no further comments. Everyone must have been delighted. But alas, the happiness did not continue for long. When the tenders came in the Department discovered that to build the bridge of their choice would cost in the neighbourhood of £30 million, and £20 million would have been thought quite high enough. So a choice had to be made, either to go forward or back; back to the drawing board or forward to a competition. The Department decided to go forward, and organized a tender/design/ build competition to be judged in 1977.

In the 'Description of the Project' competitors were not only provided with technical information but were also given notice that 'the aesthetic quality of each submission will form part of the overall assessment'. The bridge was to be built 'in an area of outstanding natural beauty and the finished structure will dominate the scene at the entrance to the Beauly Firth as well as being visible for many kilometres from the south, east and west'. Designs would be judged on engineering and economic criteria, but the views of the Royal Fine Art Commission for Scotland would also be taken into account.

After discussions, six groups were invited to submit designs, three of these groups having a known preference for steel for the main span and three with a preference for concrete. The closing date for tenders was March 1977.

The Commissioners saw all six designs. Their view was that the quality of all the entries was very high, and that two were outstanding. Of these two designs preferred by the Commissioners, one had a considerable cost advantage over the other, and the Commission therefore assumed that it, of the two, would be preferred by the SDD, and its acceptance was accordingly recommended. The Department proceeded to examine the details of the various schemes, and after resolving some technical difficulties was able to let the contract for design and building in respect of the scheme recommended by the Commission. The contract cost was £17.25 million, which, taking inflation into account, was far below the figure allowed for in 1973.

The Kessock Bridge is a most elegant example of advanced modern engineering. Its design is a development of the Rees bridge built over the Rhine near Dusseldorf in 1966 and of a bridge built in Belgium ten years later. The deck panels are of steel, stayed by means of steel cables from twin steel pylons at both main piers, the cables arranged in harp fashion. The whole structure is remarkably slender, uncluttered, unassertive, and convincing. It is an exciting addition to the landscape around Inverness, visible from some parts of the town. Competitions do not always have a satisfactory outcome. But in this case a design was secured which combined aesthetic excellence with technical soundness and economic advantage. Bridge design in Scotland was put on a new footing. Both the Commission and the Department had reason to be pleased.

5. Extension to Old Course Hotel, St Andrews

The Old Course Hotel at St Andrews was designed for British Rail by an American architect in 1968. It is sited on what used to be a railway goods-yard, and is close to what was once the Stationmaster's house, now the Jigger Inn. More important, it is adjacent to the seventeenth fairway of the Old Course, one of the most visited and admired pieces of ground in the whole of Scotland. Furthermore, it is an extremely prominent object as seen by anyone approaching St Andrews from the west (which used to be a splendid view of the city), as well as to anyone on the Old Course or the Eden Course. The hotel as it stood in 1978 was rectangular in outline, extremely horizontal in emphasis with heavy protruding balconies at several levels, five storeys high, and built of random non-local stone and concrete. When proposals for its extension first came forward it was described by the Civic Trust as 'a massive and obtrusive block' and 'one of Scotland's least fortunate post-war design and planning decisions', and by the Commission as 'a massive isolated ponderous lump' and 'an architectural mistake'. Few people who had seen it thought otherwise.

The extension proposals which were put forward by British Rail in the spring of 1978 were for sixty self-catering time-share apartments, built to a height of two or three storeys, some south of the existing hotel and some in an extended straggling line along the old railway embankment to the east. There were also to be squash courts, and an indoor swimming pool. The citizens of St Andrews thought that this scheme was another outrage to be added to the first, and so did the Commission. In a letter sent to the District Council in May, the Commissioners recommended that, as the architecture of the hotel was 'different' from anything characteristic of St Andrews, the hotel should continue to be separated from the town by open space and no linking development should be permitted along the former railway line where it led towards the town. The number of apartments should be reduced from sixty to forty-five, nothing built near the hotel should exceed two storeys and nothing near the Jigger Inn should exceed one storey, and there should be extensive landscaping. These comments amounted to a complete condemnation of British Rail's proposals. But the Commission was aware that the area was already zoned for commercial use, which made outright rejection by the planning authority unlikely, and it was in any case anxious that something be done to 'mitigate' (the Commission's word) the objectionable visual impact of the hotel. So, 'without in any way condoning the design of the original hotel building', the Commission suggested that planting and earth mounding should be undertaken so as to soften the profile of the hotel, and that a suitably designed, low-lying development immediately beside the hotel, rising no more than two storeys, would soften its profile and improve the view of it, especially for visitors approaching St Andrews from the east.

Possibly as a result of these comments some improvements were made to the design, and in June the revised scheme was submitted to the District Planning Committee. The Director of Physical Planning for North-East Fife District Council was not too well pleased, and is reported to have said that the plans would not have spent longer than five minutes in his office had it not been for the planning permission previously negotiated between St Andrews and British Rail. 'It all boils down to a salvage job', he is reported to have said. But, in the light of the planning permission already negotiated, acceptance of the scheme was virtually inevitable. Permission was granted, but was made subject to a long list of conditions, which included the Commission's demands for 'a very detailed landscaping scheme' and a reduction in the number of housing units to forty-five. It is obvious that the Commission and the Director of Physical Planning saw eye to eye. Six months later the scheme was abandoned.

In 1982 a new application was made, this time not by British Rail. The proposal was for a 'stepped' extension projecting southwards from the hotel, starting at four storeys in height and reducing to two storeys. There were to be a few small shops, a small bathing pool, and forty-nine bedrooms on the upper floors. The Commissioners considered that these new proposals would do a good deal to change the hotel's stark appearance for the better. They asked for more tree planting; recommended the use of a matching natural stone for the walls, so as to make the extension seem as much as possible a better-designed part of the original building; and suggested that a pitched roof should be added so as to conceal the offensive tank-like construction which dominated the skyline. They also observed that the design success of the alteration could be even greater if further accommodation were constructed in a similar form on the north-western side of the hotel.

Planning permission was granted and construction began. Eight months later the developer informed the District Council that he wished to act on the suggestion that a similar extension should be built on the other side of the existing building. He moreover proposed that the long-since demolished railway shed should be reinstated. This would take the form of a new building which would house a Golf School and provide an under-cover practice area in bad weather, while at the same time it would re-create the original 'blind' setting of the seventeenth hole. The relevant proposals were approved by the Commissioners soon afterwards, with only a few minor reservations. The aggressive impact of the original building had already been much mitigated, they stated; these further additions would again improve the appearance of the complex, enhancing its visual impact with some much-needed sculptural richness. The work was completed in 1984.

No one could say that the Old Course Hotel in its 1984 form improves St Andrews. It provides accommodation; but it is grim and alien in a gentle and historical setting. Over the years it has been altered for the better, but not enough. Now, however, late in 1988, a proposal has come forward for further changes, planned by a firm of American architects for the hotel's new Japanese owners. The balconies are to disappear, and will be replaced by bay windows one above another, giving a vertical emphasis; a pitched roof will at last be added; there will be gablets here and there, the windows will be renewed in more old-fashioned style, and a number of 'greenhouses' will appear, one of them on the roof. These considerable changes—part of a very costly reconstruction—will give the hotel a quite new, slightly tudory look. The Commissioners thought that the new style, vaguely traditional but 'without recognisable architectural ancestry', would be welcomed in St Andrews, being less brutal. But they stopped a long way short of actually commending it.

This case is interesting not only because the Commission helped to retrieve, as far as possible, a horrid mistake. It has three other noteworthy features. Firstly, it shows how much can be achieved when the local planners and the Commission agree, and support one another against the forces of darkness, in this instance, British Rail. Secondly, it gives the lie to the idea that the Commission is always in favour of building less. Overbuilding is a common fault, certainly; but on occasion designs come forward which, in their setting, lack height, or extension, or emphasis, and on these occasions the Commission has not hesitated to ask for more. And thirdly, it shows to what a remarkable degree buildings can be changed, not always for the worse. A basically bad design can probably never be turned into a good one. But it may be possible to modify or conceal some of the worst features, and thus turn a bad building into something that is at least inoffensive, and which may even seem to many people not uninteresting.

6. *The Scottish Exhibition Centre*

The proposal that Scotland should have a national exhibition centre was far from novel when it came to the fore in the early 1980s. Such centres had already been built all over Europe, each of them a cluster of very large halls where a country could display to the best advantage for the inspection of the rest of the world, its products, technology and services. To find a suitable site for such a centre is not easy, and to build such a centre is a very costly operation. Towards the end of 1982 the Commission learned that the Scottish Development Agency had identified a suitable riverside site at Queen's Dock on the Clyde near the centre of Glasgow—a site that was large, level, unobstructed and with excellent communications—and that £36 million of public and private money had been got together by the SDA in order to build the Scottish Exhibition Centre. The Commission further was given to understand that a design for the Centre was approaching the stage at which consultation would be appropriate, and the secretary therefore wrote to the SDA asking that the Commission's advice be sought before it was too late for the design to be altered. In reply, the Commission was informed that only basic designs existed, but that consultations would begin at the earliest possible stage. This correspondence took place late in November, 1982.

Because the layout on the site and the layout of the buildings themselves became important matters of controversy, it is essential to form a clear idea of the Queen's Dock site. The whole area amounts to 64 acres alongside the River Clyde, and the surroundings are those of a once-great commercial port: wharves, cranes, warehouses and water. The site has approximately three hundred yards of river frontage, and is about one hundred yards across. The Clyde walkway runs along the riverside length of the site. The scene is dominated, in a most appropriate way, by the gigantic Finnieston crane, now derated but capable in its heyday of lifting weights of up to three hundred tons. This is the largest crane in Britain, a marvellous piece of early-twentieth-century engineering, one hundred and fifty feet in height. There is also an Italianate pumphouse and a rotunda (the entrance to a now disused tunnel under the Clyde), and these two structures along with the crane stood in areas paved with several thousand well laid granite setts. Except for these three items and the walkway, the area was, when planning began, completely open.

The Commissioners learned nothing more about the Exhibition Centre until a model and plans were laid before them early in April, 1983. To say that they were disappointed with what they then saw is to put it mildly. Their comments, sent to Glasgow's Director of Planning, begin with a list of desiderata for the new Centre: it must match in design the best of the items that would be displayed within it; it must act as a magnet for international buyers; it must give a new impetus to and set the standard for further redevelopment of Clydeside; it should be instantly recognizable throughout the world. But what the Commissioners found set out before them was an arrangement of two enormous sheds in parallel, with gently sloping roofs, and with a large greenhouse sandwiched in between, the whole located in the middle of the site, with extensive car-parking east and west.

The Commission disliked both the buildings and their location. Whatever was to be built should be built, they thought, in as close a relation as possible to the River Clyde and its walkway running beside it. The crane also should be made visually a part of the scheme. But what was proposed took no notice of the river, which gave life and character to the area, and left the crane, abandoned, at the further end of a vast car park. Car parking, indeed, dominated the area, and the proposals for landforming, landscaping and planting did not look as if they were going to provide what the Commissioners considered should be there, namely the semblance, at least, of a riverside park.

The form of the buildings attracted equally strong criticism. The two sheds were designed to contain five exhibition halls varying in size from 1 000 square metres to 10 000 square metres. All were to be served by gantry cranes. They were therefore not only very large in area, they were also very high. These space requirements undoubtedly gave rise to very difficult architectural problems, but the Commission argued for an honest external expression of internal uses, and suggested that five rectangular halls of different sizes could be linked by a common gantry spine. A design of this kind would provide an interesting variety of three-dimensional forms. As for the roofs of the sheds, these were not flat, and this the Commission was glad to see, but they displayed a number of incongruities, were monotonous and, inevitably, enormous. Pitched roofs on such large buildings, the Commission advised, should be designed so as to supply easily recognizable, memorable silhouettes rising above a flat site, a roofscape stepping up from the low elements (workshops or restaurants) to ridges or points above the level of the gantries. The greenhouse or glazed entrance hall likewise brought no joy to the Commission's collective heart. It was expected, according to the architects, to 'sparkle' and attract people; but the Commissioners thought otherwise. They compared it with the Kibble Palace, the People's Palace, or the 1967 Plant House in the Royal Botanic Gardens in Edinburgh, and found it wanting. The whole scheme, they said, was mundane. Comparisons with contemporary high technology architecture in various parts of the world showed it to be horribly out of date. Many recent industrial buildings built for firms which understood that design quality and prestige went together were outstandingly better. The whole scheme should be reappraised in every aspect.

This sweeping condemnation is said to have angered the SDA, but that body can hardly have been surprised by the Commission's observations; comments of a similar nature had already been made by the Civic Trust, the New Glasgow Society, and the Society for the Study and Protection of Scottish Architecture. All three of these strongly advocated that the Centre should be built nearer to the east end of the site so as to achieve a relation with the crane and the rotunda. Both the Civic Trust and the Society for the Protection of Scottish Architecture severely criticized the design of the buildings themselves; they left a lot to be desired, resembled carpet showrooms on a warehouse estate, and the roofs, extensively visible from the Clydeside Expressway, were unimaginative and boring. Excessive consideration for the users of motor cars and neglect of the Clyde Walkway were also mentioned. The views of the Commission were thus by no means peculiar to itself. What was peculiar was that the Commission did not see the proposals until 11 April, whereas the Civic Trust had been able as early as 13 January to request that the buildings should be located further to the east (a request which they found had been completely ignored when they again saw the plans in March).

By the end of March, however, the cat was beginning to emerge from the bag. In a letter to the Director of Planning dated 29 March the SDA let it be known that 'the present dynamic compaction which is well under way is based on the position [of the buildings] currently shown on all plans and indeed the programme of completion leading to the first exhibition in October 1985 would clearly be out of the question if the building has to be re-sited'. Compaction costs money, and cannot be done in a day. So talk of moving the buildings nearer the river or nearer the Finnieston crane was a waste of time, and had been a waste of time for several weeks before the Commission ever saw the plans. The decision had already been taken.

This did not unduly worry Glasgow's Director of Planning. He was not unhappy about the siting, because he thought that it provided good access for both cars and pedestrians. But he, like most other people, thought that the roof was a very feeble piece of civic design, and he reminded the SDA that all design details had to be settled to his satisfaction before construction could begin. If completion was to be before October 1985, building had to start in June; and the Director could not imagine, at this stage, that a building of first-class quality could be planned in all its details in the course of the following two months. It was now clear that the pressure of the timetable was against a satisfactory design. And this opinion he transmitted to the SDA.

The Agency responded to all its critics at the end of April. Its contention was that the design was basically a good one. What was under discussion was industrial architecture, and once a number of detailed points had been sorted out the scheme would stand up well in comparison with the National Exhibition Centre at Birmingham, Paris-Nord in France, the Bella Centre in Copenhagen and the Pal-Expo in Geneva. The two non-glazed buildings would have walls of composite metal cladding in bright red and roofs coloured silver, and they would thus produce a bright and lively effect in a very barren part of the city. Further consideration had already been given to details of the design, and changes had been made which would go a long way towards meeting the criticisms put forward by several organizations.

If the SDA really believed this they were doomed to disappointment. The changes which had been made did not do much to placate anyone, least of all the Commission. It was impossible that they should do so, because the Commission considered the design to be basically commonplace and dull. It is true that in its revised state it pleased the Commissioners a little better than before. It was marginally improved, they thought, with a little sculptural quality and some evidence of styling; but the glasshouse was a failure and the fundamental major weaknesses remained.

By this time Glasgow's Planning Committee was on the verge of taking a decision about the scheme. The Commissioners felt that the SDA was not going to listen to their objections and was determined to go on with a second-rate scheme, one which would advertise to the world that Scotland was very far from being in the van of aesthetic and achitectural achievement, and which would in fact give both

Glasgow and Scottish industry generally a name for mediocrity and dullness. They believed, moreover, that the Director of Planning shared at least some of their doubts and might not recommend approval to his Planning Committee. It was therefore decided to make a last effort to influence public opinion and the planning authority. The Commission restated its objections in a letter to the Director of Planning and released this letter to the Press. It was to no avail. On 17 May Glasgow's Planning Committee gave the go-ahead to the Scottish Exhibition Centre.

The Centre is now in use (the October 1985 deadline was met) and it may well prove serviceable and convenient. It may even prove adequate, provided that not too much is expected of it. Some may think, as some thought at the time, that the Commission was over-critical. But this was a national project, and its major purpose was to promote the sale of Scottish goods at home and overseas. Furthermore, it was a very large project on a prominent site, and the general concept of an exhibition centre lends itself to the provision of public amenity in pleasurable and even artistic ways. On both these counts it was reasonable to expect the Exhibition Centre to be an especially fine and civilized design. That it is, instead, especially old-fashioned, inartistic and utilitarian seems not to have been the fault of the official architects. They, it seems, assumed responsibility only after the broad outline of the buildings and their location on the site had been irrevocably determined somewhere within the SDA. The SDA is a commercial organization and its achievement on this occasion was to organize the financial backing that was needed. Once that was done, completion of the building as soon as possible became the over-riding consideration. For such an important national building a competition would have been appropriate, as was afterwards suggested in several letters to the Press. But that would have taken time. What those in authority aimed for was something commercially sufficient—at any rate in the short run—and that was their concept of the Centre. Their plans became public only when they could not be changed. And when they became public many local politicians could think only of the short-term advantage of having them at once put into effect. 'It is bad news for Glasgow', said the Glasgow *Evening Times*, 'that the Royal Fine Art Commission is trying to block and change the plans for the Scottish Exhibition Centre'.[12] And one councillor on the Planning Committee is reported to have said, 'We were told to rubber stamp the plans or else risk losing the whole thing'. Imaginative buildings cannot be produced in this way. It makes no sense to 'submit' plans for the consideration of the Royal Fine Art Commission for Scotland or anyone else if nothing can be altered.

7. Dundee Waterfront Development

This scheme first came to the notice of the Commission late in 1983, when the SDA and a developer were preparing plans. What struck the Commission from the outset was the extraordinary prominence and high amenity value of the site. It is long and narrow. But it extends for approximately one mile along the shore of the River Tay, just south of Dundee, and affords superb and unimpeded views southwards across the river to the shores of Fife, over two miles distant. Secondly, the site is prominent from the south. The Tay is crossed a little to the west of the site by the 1888 railway bridge and the new road bridge, opened in 1966. This means that anyone approaching Dundee from the south, either by road or rail, sees the city rising behind the site, and whatever is built there must be for many visitors a major part of their first impressions of Dundee. For at least two reasons, therefore, this site, which had been largely derelict for many years, was of major importance.

The visual advantages of the site, however, were not matched by its convenience. The waterfront is cut off from the city by the railway, the road system is complicated and makes life very difficult for pedestrians in the area, and the elevated pedestrian walkways which joined the site to the city were longer and more repulsive, when Commissioners first saw them, than such walkways usually are. Commissioners described the locale as confusing and depressing. It was clear that the site deserved and required well-designed and well laid-out buildings, but the Commissioners were not reassured when they saw the recently built hotel and sports centre just to the east, dreary buildings with poor relation to the river; these earlier schemes, they observed, 'must be taken as serious warnings'. (The hotel was known locally as 'Colditz'.)

The proposals which reached the Commission late in 1986 were for a £30 million development. There was to be a Heritage Centre, with one of Captain Scott's ships, the *Discovery*, as the chief attraction, in the small harbour at the east end of the site; offices; a Leisure Centre with night club, restaurant, pub and twenty-four specialty shopping units; a ten-screen cinema; then, two hundred metres further west, a Tesco supermarket of 67 000 square feet; and another two hundred metres beyond that, 30 000 square feet of warehousing. There was little architectural information, but all buildings in the Leisure Centre were to consist of a single-storey ribbed concrete wall, four metres in height, surmounted by a reflective glass wall nine metres high and inclined at an angle of 77°. There were to be some covered walkways, some canvas awnings, and two atria of pyramidal form. The general effect, in spite of the atria which were small, was of a very long, low, glass building of unvarying height. A 'promenade', two metres wide, ran between the Leisure Centre and the river, and much landscaping was promised. Parking was provided at ground level for over 1 500 cars, and this took up the spaces between the Leisure Centre, the supermarket and the warehousing. No information about the form of these latter elements was available.

Many people in Dundee doubted the wisdom of this scheme. There were vacant buildings in Dundee and there were other vacant sites, at least one of them large enough for a supermarket. *Discovery*, it was argued, would be more suitably berthed in the historic dockland area of the city. The promise of 1 100 permanent jobs on the waterfront might be illusory, for the most likely effect of the new supermarket was further decline in the secondary shopping areas and especially in the ten-year-old Overgate Shopping Centre. These arguments were well rehearsed, and the Chief Planning Officer for the District submitted an admirable Report setting out the pros and cons. What chiefly struck the Commissioners, however, was the planning strategy proposed for the site.

Here was possibly the finest vacant waterfront site in Europe, and the proposal was to divide it into: Leisure Centre, 200 metres of parked vehicles, supermarket, 200 metres of parked vehicles, warehousing; with a two-metre-wide 'promenade' in front of the Leisure Centre. The road was a major problem. When planning began, the road ran the full length of the site along the water. In order to bring the site and the waterfront together, £5 million were to be spent on re-routing the road so that it bent away from the water half way along, and led into the city from the back of the development and not the front. This cut the site into two parts, east of the road and west of the road. The developers then located the Leisure Centre and its car park along the water, east of the road, and everything else to the west, on the other side of the road. The Commissioners objected very strongly to this development strategy. They thought it 'inexcusably wasteful' that an open south-facing riverside should be occupied largely by car parks, and even more largely by a road for vehicles entering or leaving Dundee at speeds frequently over thirty miles an hour. They also took exception to the idea of warehousing and a supermarket standing prominently amid acres of car parking; these buildings could be expected to make no architectural contribution to the scene, and might invite scrappy and messy development around them. They therefore suggested that the road should be moved to the north of the site for its whole length, freeing the riverside from traffic; that there should be three floors of car parking 'conveniently positioned' behind the other buildings; that the supermarket should have something of the nature of traditional shop windows instead of the usual 'blank and therefore deadening external walls'; and that there should be space for strolling and sitting by the water, and 'generous planting, including trees'. If this were done, the Commission argued, the view of Dundee from the south would be 'of the riverside quay, surmounted by continuous, reasonably low waterfront buildings, and the city stepping up the hill behind'; and a park-like area by the river would be added to the amenities of the city.

This advice reached Tayside Regional Council at the beginning of November 1986. But the Council was already under pressure, both from the SDA and from the developers, to accept the supermarket proposal as it stood. The developers seem to have made it clear from the outset that they wanted a quick decision; and the bait was not only the jobs to be created but also the Heritage Centre, which they would fund. This Centre, it was claimed, would give Dundee 'a new image'. It was a package. So the Council, a few days after receiving the Commission's letter and against the advice of their Director of Planning, voted for the supermarket. Three weeks later they granted outline planning consent for the whole waterfront development, and the scheme was 'under way'.

It was now clear that the Director of Planning was not the only person who thought that the scheme was a mistake. Many objections began to be heard, and one Councillor observed that the city's image 'would hardly be enhanced by fast-food shops, a disco, a cinema and a pub surrounding the *Discovery*'. The Secretary of State, whose powers were limited because this was an Enterprise Zone, gave notice that he would not intervene, but added that 'he expects the developers and the planning authority to take careful account of the Commission's views in considering the detailed layout and design of this development'. Thus supported, the Commission returned to Dundee in August 1987 (by which time the objectors had collected, it was said, 13 000 signatures against the scheme and were demanding a public enquiry), and began the first of several lengthy discussions.

The question of the road was soon settled. Many more millions of pounds would be needed to make further changes, and the money was not available. So the Commissioners proposed that nothing of any importance should be built where it would be in the way of re-routing the road at a later date. They then posed two 'over-riding questions': 'Is this scheme designed to benefit to the maximum extent from being on the waterfront?' and 'Does it make an architectural contribution to the waterfront?' If the answers to these questions were no, then, the Commissioners stated, 'either the use of the waterfront site cannot be justified for the purposes proposed, or this particular scheme needs to be redesigned'. Three criticisms were made especially clear. Firstly, no change had been made in response to earlier complaints about large areas of surface car parking which isolated the three parts of the development and took up riverside space; there should be decked and basement car parks to the north of the buildings, as far as possible out of sight. Secondly, there should be some provision for housing, even if the housing was to be built at a later date. And thirdly, the waterfront walkway was far too narrow to constitute a genuine amenity, and after joining the road it was continually interrupted by parking spaces; it should be mainly, if not exclusively, a promenade. Two further comments were made: the opportunity should be taken to have shops and restaurants facing the river and thus enjoying a view almost as fine as the view south from Princes Street (the conservatory effect of the proposed glass walls was therefore welcome); and the *Discovery* should be given, as far as possible, a real and not a sham harbour setting, with real stone, real ships' chandlers, real oyster bars, and real pleasure boats in the offing.

These criticisms and suggestions were of varying importance and they met with a varying response. But on the fundamental strategic planning issues the answer was simple: no. The developer flatly refused to alter the car-parking arrangements; above-ground or below-ground parking would cost more money and the budget was very tight; and in any case, a supermarket provided only with decked car parking would be bound to fail. As for not building where the road might later be relocated, that likewise was impossible. Tesco wanted the supermarket where the plan indicated, across the road from the Leisure Centre, and it could not be moved. Suggestions that in that case the supermarket's ground plan could be altered from a square to a rectangle so as to leave open the needed space were likewise turned down; Tesco, the Commission was informed, would not agree to anything so unusual. The response on housing and the harbour was more conciliatory. Efforts would be made to keep the old masonry of the harbour, and housing would be borne in mind; but no plans appeared. The Leisure Centre, on the other hand, was much improved in the course of a few months, thanks to the skill of the architects and their willingness to co-operate. Buildings were moved back from *Discovery* to give more space, and the same was done on the south front, creating a terrace approximately fifty metres wide and fifteen metres deep overlooking the river; and the original two metre wide 'promenade' (perfectly adequate, according to the developer) was altered to eight metres (six metres once past the Leisure Centre). The atria were enlarged, and re-design on ground and first floors opened extensive views of the river. These changes were very welcome, for they began to give promise that the Commissioners' vision of an extensive, conservatory-like development, low but not monotonous, with trees and planting and genuine leisure space round about, all linked to the river, might at least in part be realized.

So Tesco and the developer got what they wanted. They conceded almost nothing. They were in a very strong position because they were providing over £3.3 million for the Heritage Centre, the SDA was helping with over £5 million chiefly to relocate the road, and

several hundred construction jobs were certain to be created in the
short term. The developers' general plan was all worked out: neither
the Commission nor the local planners nor the local amenity societies
had been involved in devising the scheme. (If decked car parking
had been proposed earlier the plans might have been altered.
Commissioners were entirely unconvinced that such parking could
not be afforded or that it would keep customers away). Councillors
were much afraid that any attempt to make radical changes to the
scheme would result in the departure of the developer and would
cause the SDA, as it was euphemistically put, 'to reassess its position'.
The question for the Regional Council therefore was not 'Is this a
good scheme?' but 'Should Dundee take what it can get, risking
economic damage elsewhere in the town, or should it leave the
waterfront derelict for another x years?' Councillors took what they
could get, possibly wisely. But what they got was not a bargain.

No doubt it is never possible to secure an ideal scheme. The
Dundee Project has serious defects. Nevertheless, what is going to be
built is a good deal better than the scheme as first proposed. This is
the outcome of what seemed at times to be a severe struggle between
the Commission, along with the local planning officers and probably
numerous Councillors on the one hand, and on the other a developer
who evinced no serious interest in either amenity or architecture.
The Commission might have refused to be associated with the
scheme, but this would have left the planning officers and the
Councillors to fight alone. What is now needed is a serious effort to
design suitable buildings for the supermarket and the warehousing,
good planting, and as genuine a setting as can be contrived for
Captain Scott's *Discovery*.

NOTES AND REFERENCES TO CHAPTER 4
   1. RFAC for England and Wales, *Twenty-first Report* (HMSO,
      1971) p. 11.
   2. RFAC for England and Wales, *Twenty-fourth Report* (1987)
      pp. 12-14.
   3. *Ibid.*, p. 26.
   4. RFAC for England and Wales, *Twenty-second Report* (HMSO,
      1985) p. 25.
   5. Excluding roads, bridges and street-lighting schemes.
   6. Gavin Stamp, in the *Spectator*, 13 Nov. 1982.
   7. RFAC for England and Wales, *Twenty-fourth Report* (1987) p. 17.
   8. Fiona Sinclair, *Scotstyle: 150 years of Scottish Architecture* (RIAS,
      1984) p. 88.

9. The Sun Insurance Office at the corner of George Street and
   Frederick Street.
10. It later turned out that the plot ratio was actually 2.98 : 1.
11. This paper led the Corporation to commission from Lord Holford
    his Report on 'High Building Policy for Edinburgh'.
12. *Evening Times*, 16 May 1983.

17. St James's Square, Edinburgh

18. St Leonard's development area, Edinburgh

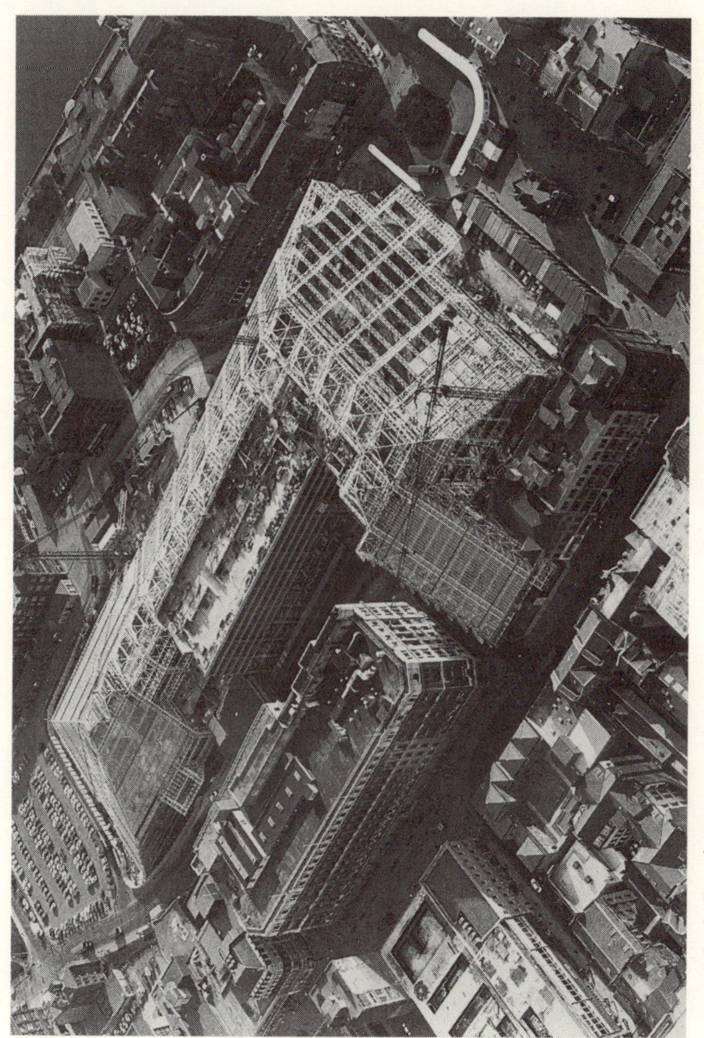

19. St Enoch Station, Glasgow

20. Kessock Bridge, Inverness

21. Old Course Hotel, St Andrews

22. The Scottish Exhibition Centre, Glasgow

23. Dundee Waterfront Development

24. Crafts Museum, Frankfurt, by Richard Meier (early 1980s).
'Good buildings can be and have been built in the later 20th
century'.

CHAPTER FIVE

Money: A modest proposal

Why, when we are so much better informed than our ancestors and command the skills and resources to do so many marvellous things, do we fail so often and so badly to build what is pleasant or beautiful? That there are technical and social reasons for our failure no one can doubt; the most important have already been discussed. Incompetence on the part of architects is often suggested. This can be a contributory factor, but is seldom, in important cases, the principal one. If the architect is working for a client who wants a good building and is prepared to pay for it, and if the architect himself is not bent on self-advertisement and glory (which is a most serious occupational hazard for architects) good buildings can be and have been built in the later twentieth century. The successes show what can be done. Most of them may not be marvellous, but at least they do no harm to the visible environment, and some of them are very good. When things have gone wrong for other than technical and social reasons, we can almost certainly trace the trouble to one or more of three causes: too much hurry at the planning and design stage; over-building; refusal to pay for anything not strictly utilitarian and necessary.

The last of these three is clearly a matter of economics; the scheme needs more money, and more money put into it would—or could—save it. But the other two likewise, although not so obviously, are founded on economic considerations. Overbuilding is caused by trying to derive the maximum possible profit from a given ground space. The more houses or flats that are built per acre, the more there will be to sell or the more rents there will be to collect; the higher the building the greater will be the floor space to let, other things being equal. It is true that a less congested development which provides less usable space may prove, by being less congested, to be more attractive to the occupants, and may therefore command higher rents or prices than a more congested development. Unfortunately, the financial advantages of building less densely or less high are not easy to judge, and the pursuit of maximum profit and not just sufficient profit inclines most developers to put as much on a site as the authorities will allow. Likewise, too much hurry at the planning and design stage is caused by thoughts of profit and loss. The developer who owns or rents a site is losing money as long as that site remains unused, and he therefore wants it to be developed as soon and as quickly as possible. And if he owns or rents no site but sees that some new service or commodity might profitably be provided if a suitable building were built, he is anxious to set about building without delay, because someone else may think up the same idea and forestall him, or circumstances may change in some other way, and the opportunity will be lost. Profit, it has been said, is the reward for getting there first, and in this sense business men are always in a hurry. This has serious aesthetic consequences for the simple reason that good design takes time. A site and a brief that present no problems are rare indeed. For any but the most straightforward building there is usually more than one possible basic design, and for complex developments on city-centre sites the possibilities are almost endless. Experience shows that it is not at all difficult to take quick decisions and adopt the wrong basic approach. And even if the correct decisions are taken at the beginning, the result is likely to be very unsatisfactory unless a great deal of further careful thought is given to second-order problems. Someone once said that the basic design of Rolls Royce cars is nothing out of the ordinary; it is the development and refinement of their design over several years that makes them exceptional. With buildings it is much the same. The basis has to be right; but the process of development and refinement is just as important, and this process takes time.

We must therefore face the brute economic facts. Although it is true that better architecture and more amenity need not in every case cost more, they are quite likely to do so. More money, either to pay for time spent on thinking harder, or to pay for better materials or better detailing or whatever, will not necessarily improve the situation, but the situation is most unlikely to improve without more money being spent. We can have more amenity and better architecture if we are prepared to pay the price. Beauty, an eminent authority has reminded us, is a flower; but money is everywhere.

This is in one way a fortunate conclusion. We need not suppose that architecture and town design are bankrupt, or that forces beyond human control condemn us to the dreary gloom of a second-rate environment, relieved only by flashes of what is good that has been saved from the past. We can build far better if we choose. What we have to do is to ensure that in important cases—not necessarily in all cases—sufficient money (which may on occasion mean sufficient time) is spent on new developments to produce at least a tolerably satisfactory result. We must also ensure that the maximization of profit is not regarded as the sole serious consideration. Brilliant designs cannot be had to order, but the offensive and the desperately dull could be ruled out.

In looking for improvement, those developments that are financed by the public sector present at once the least and the greatest difficulty. The difficulty in this case is least, because putting more public money into public developments, where that would be appropriate, is a straightforward political choice. Modern western Governments are awash with money, and where the sums involved are relatively small it is simply a matter of priorities. But for this very reason the difficulty is also greatest, because of two deeply entrenched habits of thought. Firstly, the British public has a long and lamentable record of acquiescence in second-rate design. A lot of education of public taste will therefore be needed, and this is not going to be easy. Efforts to improve the situation are always being made, but more efforts are always needed. Soon after the 1939–45 war ended the London Commission warned that 'a sounder knowledge of aesthetic considerations' and a sharper appreciation of their importance were going to be required if ill-considered developments and 'bad art' were to be avoided.

> It is feared that unless quality of design is looked upon as a responsibility no less important than quantity of construction, and architecture as no less important than engineering, the country will once more suffer irremediable harm and the face of England will be further ravaged by ill-conceived development and bad building.[1]

These were wise and prescient words. Exactly what the English Commissioners feared has happened, and if matters are not to go on in the same way for the next forty years appreciation and understanding of architecture and urban design will have to improve. Fortunately, the situation is far from hopeless. It is probably true that the war, along with the post-war years of shortages and utility schemes, debased public taste. But it now shows signs of recovery, and a much wider interest in questions of amenity and design is taken today than was taken twenty or thirty years ago. Also, the rapid change of the public's attitude towards conservation—from indifference to enthusiasm in thirty years—shows what can be done. The second habit of thought that stands in the way of improvement is the presumption by central and local government in Britain that it is their duty to build as cheaply as possible. The maximum amount of accommodation (or volume of traffic movement) at minimum cost is invariably their aim. This is not traditional policy, but it has become the established way of doing things during the last five or six decades. A fundamental change of attitude is therefore going to be required, and the idea that public buildings—or at least some public buildings—should set a high standard of excellence in design and finish will have to be accepted at Westminster and elsewhere. Such a change is not impossible; we must not fall into the mistake of thinking that bad habits cannot be altered. We should remember that central and local government was responsible for many fine buildings erected in Britain in the nineteenth century. This fact has been lost sight of in the fog of disapproval of Victorian architecture in general, which has only recently cleared away. It is now commonly recognized that a large number of distinguished public buildings were erected in the last century, buildings such as the British Museum in London, the National Gallery in Edinburgh, the Manchester Town Hall, the Birmingham Law Courts, and, above all, the Houses of Parliament. The Houses of Parliament are indeed a masterly work, although it used to be the custom to ignore or deny this simply because they are neo-Gothic in appearance. In addition to these and other outstanding buildings, there are a great many nineteenth-century law courts, custom houses and public offices which are of first-class design and construction. There is a tradition of fine, well-built public buildings in this country, some of them contemporary and some of them of advanced design, and what is required is that this tradition be revived. A radical change of present policy can be imagined, and it could be made effective.

So let us suppose that it became the strongly expressed view of the community that public buildings in prominent situations should always reach a commendable standard of design and construction, and should not in any circumstances look nondescript or cheap (as so many of them do); and that in appropriate cases they should aim for genuine architectural excellence; and that public amenity in the form of space and trees and gardens and the proper arrangement of buildings should take a high priority among the innumerable objectives of public expenditure; then government would have to bend to the weight of public opinion, and although the situation would not be completely transformed (because public expenditure is only a part of total expenditure on construction) it would be enormously improved. Indeed, it could be argued that no other single change in the building and re-building of cities could be equally beneficial. If the State set a good example the improvement would be very great, and it would become easier for others to build well. A Government bent on reducing public expenditure (even if only as a proportion of GDP) might object to this policy, but it is the duty of Governments to act in the public interest, and to do what only they can do. To leave beauty and amenity to private enterprise is an abnegation of public responsibility. The great economist Alfred Marshall correctly observed that while in normal circumstances each private individual can look after his own affairs, 'the State alone can bring the beauties of nature and art within the reach of the ordinary citizen'.[2]

Pushing private developments to a higher standard is quite a different matter. It is no use appealing to the altruism of developers. The profit motive is the driving force of capitalism, and the developer who does not put his own interests first is unlikely to remain long in business. He might be persuaded to make some minor design improvements, to pay more regard to the long run and less to the short run, to act in the hope that a less utilitarian scheme would bring a better return, to be satisfied with a good although not a magnificent profit; but he is constrained by market forces and probably in the majority of cases cannot, by himself, do much. Some form of subsidization is therefore the only possible solution. But subsidization is a dangerous game. Costs are very apt to escalate, and it often seems to be the wrong people who reap the benefits. In order to maximize the impact of the subsidies and to limit the overall cost, it is evident that assistance could be given to only a small number of developments. Even so, the idea of using public money to help finance private developments sounds as if it must be open to serious objections, and it is not at first sight obvious how subsidization could work, or how it could be justified.

In spite of appearances, the subsidization case is strong, and the arguments for it are both familiar and simple.

Architecture — and urban design also — is a form of art. There is sometimes reluctance to recognize this, because in two important respects architecture and civic design are unlike familiar art forms such as painting or poetry, sculpture or music. Firstly, what is created is for everyday use. But this should not lead us to a false conclusion. What is for everyday use need not lack artistic quality. Pottery and Persian carpets, although they may not rival the range and majesty of the works of Beethoven or Shakespeare, can be artistic none the less. A beer mug by Keith Murray is an *objet d'art*, and very useful too. However 'useful' or 'useless' an artefact may be, that is no guide to its quality as a work of art. Architecture, whether in the form of a home or a mausoleum, can be very high art indeed. One has only to think of the Parthenon or Lincoln Cathedral or Little Moreton Hall or Castle Howard or the Sydney Opera House to realize what a superb achievement a well-designed and well-executed building can be. Art and usefulness may seem hard to reconcile, but there is no contradiction between them. The second difficulty is the obvious one that buildings are business, and architects and planners are members of two organized professions. This must seem artistically odd, and for those architects and planners who have genuine artistic aspirations it is in many ways very inconvenient and sometimes perplexing. But again, we must not allow one truth to obscure another. Architecture is necessarily business, and so is civic design. In spite of this, the end result can be a thing of beauty and a joy forever, and this is what must always be kept in mind.

The next step in the argument is obvious. Governments subsidize art. The amounts handed over in this country are by no means small, although they are smaller *per capita* than in many other European countries. The grant to the Arts Council for 1987-8 is £138.4 million.

This is used to support an enormous range of activities all over the country, including drama (£26.2 million), music (£22.7 million) and dance (£10.8 million). There are some notable individual beneficiaries; the National Theatre is subsidized to the tune of £7.8 million, and the Royal Shakespeare Company receives £5.2 million. Money also goes to the British Film Institute and the National Film and Television School. These sums come from central government, and they are set to rise. In 1991–2 the grant to the Arts Council will be £168 million. Local authorities also make grants to support artistic activities, and at present these exceed £180 million per annum. Many activities are supported by both central and local government; this year, for example, the English National Opera is to receive £6.7 million from the Arts Council plus £1.2 million from Westminster City Council. These subsidies to the arts are often questioned, and the present Government is not too fond of them. The Government is also trying to persuade those in charge of artistic enterprises to put more effort into selling the product, and to try to find more money from sponsors and private donors. But even if this policy proves to be reasonably successful, it seems most unlikely that government subsidies will cease to exist. The balance between public and private subsidization may change, but the arts will continue to be non-self-financing. This situation gives rise to many difficulties and often to a good deal of recrimination. The geographical distribution of the subsidies is at present distinctly odd, and the cost-effectiveness of the system is not easy to determine. Financial support seems sometimes to be misdirected and in other cases it may merely encourage extravagance. But if all subsidies to the arts were withdrawn the general level of artistic performance in this country would almost certainly decline. So the arguments that go on are very little about whether those who go to see *Hamlet* at Stratford-upon-Avon or listen to the music of Delius at the Festival Hall should or should not pay the full cost; they are almost entirely about who should pay the subsidies, and who should receive them.

Architecture and town design gain no advantage from this national policy. Although its benefits extend to almost every kind of activity which could conceivably be described as artistic (and sometimes to activities which are merely eccentric or worse) architecture and town design are left to pay their own way. This may be the result of historical accident. It is certainly not logical, for two reasons.

The first is, that the national Government concedes the point that architecture is important, even going so far as to spend large amounts of public money on the upkeep of interesting or attractive buildings — provided, with very few exceptions, that these buildings were built by our ancestors, preferably remote. The Ancient Monuments Act was passed in 1913,[3] and central government action in the field of conservation dates from that Act. The body that was first set up was principally concerned to record structures that had existed prior to 1707. Not until 1938 was the date altered, and then only to 1815. There is now no terminal date. After a time, physical conservation was seen to be equally or more important, but expenditure was limited and progress was slow; by 1933 there were only 173 historic structures in government care, among the most notable being Stonehenge and Rievaulx Abbey. Since 1945 a series of Acts has enormously extended the scope of government-directed and government-financed conservation. In 1983 English Heritage took over from the Historic Buildings and Ancient Monuments Commission for England (there are separate Councils for Scotland and Wales) with powers to purchase, or to make grants or loans for the maintenance, improvement or repair of buildings of historic or architectural interest. In the present financial year English Heritage has a budget of £71 million, of which £64.9 million comes from central Government. But all of this is strictly for the past.

The second reason why it is anomalous that architecture and town design are not subsidized as contemporary artistic activities is that they are and in the nature of things must always be a very public possession. It is a commonplace that architecture is the most public of all the arts. Buildings and open spaces are always on display. For better or for worse, their contribution does not have to be sought out, one does not have to pay to see it, and in many locations it is almost impossible not to notice it. This public character leads directly to a series of considerations which are very familiar in economics, and which, moreover, make the subsidization of architecture and town design far easier to advocate than the subsidization of any other kind of artistic activity.

Economists are fond of imagining a world in which there is perfectly free competition, with many individual buyers and many individual sellers and a vast amount of standardization and everyone free to trade with everyone else. In this imaginary world, every consumer pays a fair competitive price for what he consumes, and every producer meets his own production costs. But the real world is much more messy. Some producers do not pay for all their costs of production, and a large number of goods and services do not lend themselves to provision through a competitive market but have to be subsidized or provided free of charge. This has nothing to do with assistance to those on low incomes; that is a separate matter. It has to do with the character of some goods and services, and it means that free provision and subsidization are common procedures, and, in appropriate cases, perfectly defensible. They do not form an occasional aberration from the healthy rule of leaving every kind of enterprise to make a profit, but operate throughout the economy. Some people disapprove of subsidies or free gifts, and some profess to disapprove of public expenditure of almost every kind. But subsidies and 'free gifts' are almost as much the rule as the exception, and there are very good reasons why this should be so.

In order to clarify the issues, let us consider how frequently costs of production are imposed upon other people. Reports appear almost daily about farms or factories which discharge poisons into rivers which kill fish or plants and thus injure fishermen and possibly others who live and work along the banks; or about chemicals sent into the atmosphere from factory chimneys which destroy trees and vegetation, sometimes — but not always — at a great distance; or about heavy lorries which slow down other road users and cause cracks to appear in the walls of houses at the side of the road. In all these cases and numberless others like them the total production costs incurred are greater than those that are met by the producer, and someone, somewhere, has to find the difference. These arrangements are manifestly unjust, and legislation may be needed to redress the balance.

The opposite situation is not so widely advertised but is just as common. Some benefits, if they are to be provided at all, must by their very nature be available to everyone, whether everyone would be able and willing to pay for them or not. The obvious example is defence. Defence, if there is any, is for everybody. No citizen in the modern world can opt out of being defended. It requires a lively imagination indeed to picture a country running its armed forces on a subscription basis and issuing instructions that non-subscribers (once identified) were, in the event of attack, to be abandoned to their fate. So defence is provided via taxes, without any particular charge. The situation is much the same as regards some kinds of important services which individual consumers could pay for, and which would come to them individually, but which would not be paid for by a sufficient number of people to make proper provision possible. It sounds complicated but is quite simple. Suppose that protection from infectious diseases had to be bought privately. History shows — and current events are again showing — that a lot of people take a remarkably care-free view about infectious diseases. Many would prefer not to pay for protection, and as a result diphtheria and meningitis and other serious diseases would be able to get a grip on some parts of the population, and endanger everybody. It is the same with fire protection. A fire next door is a first-class hazard, and if the fire services are on a subscription basis and your next-door neighbour has not subscribed, you are probably in a lot of trouble. It is considerations such as these that lead to fire brigades, fever hospitals, sanitation and other advantages of life being paid for by means of taxation, and not directly by consumers. It is difficult to apply the 'normal' principle that he who benefits should pay, and public provision becomes necessary. The same sort of difficulty arises where consumers are limited in number but cannot be identified. Lighthouses used to be a popular illustration of this principle. Who would build a lighthouse and hope to charge shipowners? In unusual circumstances it might be possible. But, in general, once a lighthouse has been erected, no passing ship could be excluded from its benefits, and therefore no private operator would be able to make consumers pay, and recover his costs or make a profit. In all these instances we are dealing with goods or services which are a public possession, and which, for one reason or another, have to be provided by government. Such goods are conveniently and intelligibly described as public goods, because they are designed to confer benefits simultaneously on a number of people, and these benefits cannot easily, or could not at all, be charged for.

Not unlike these public goods—and here we come closer to the problem of subsidizing architecture and town design—are objects and activities that are designed for some private purpose but which unavoidably provide uncharged-for and unchargeable benefits to other people. A fairly trivial example is a well-kept garden that can be seen by passers-by. The garden is looked after by its owners for their own enjoyment, but it gives pleasure to other people also, and no charge can be made. Business enterprises likewise can sometimes 'give away' unintended benefits to the public, or to other producers. A distinguished economist[4] has proposed an agreeable illustration of these 'external economies', or 'uncovenanted benefits' as the jargon goes. Suppose that a farmer turns horticulturalist and gives his land over to growing apples. After a few years there are new acres of orchards and apple blossom. Suppose, also, that in this area there are beekeepers. Because of these new orchards the bees are able to find nectar more easily than before, and more of it. The production of honey increases, as do the beekeepers' profits. The beekeepers pay nothing for this improvement in their situation, and the orchard-owner is none the worse off; he may even be helped by extensive cross-pollination. The public benefits as well. Instead of monotonous fields of corn and potatoes, there is the interest and visible attraction of pink and white apple blossom in spring, and, for the poetic, the suggestions of mellow fruitfulness in autumn. Advantages of this kind can also be found, occasionally, in advertising. Advertisements are created in order to sell the product, but some of them are entertaining or decorative in their own right. Television commercials are sometimes amusing (although not very often); and there can be genuine artistic quality in the design of posters—those by Toulouse-Lautrec are the most famous of all. It is not hard to think of other examples.

The conclusion to be drawn from all this is obvious. A well-designed building is a public good. Its commercial usefulness may be accounted for in financial terms by the business that is handled within it, but its aesthetic appeal is given away to every passer-by. To subsidize a building of high artistic merit would therefore be every bit as justifiable as to subsidize an opera. Indeed, it would be a great deal more justifiable because of the number of people affected. It is pretty clear that existing subsidies to the arts are subsidies to the few. In 1983 the Royal Opera sold 249 000 seats, but because many people attended more than one performance it is thought likely that fewer than 50 000 members of the public were involved. The corresponding figure for the Royal Ballet is only a little higher, just over 50 000, and even at the Royal Festival Hall it is calculated that fewer than 100 000 individuals accounted for all ticket sales. These are very small figures; and no one supposes that those who buy seats for opera, ballet or concert performances are a representative sample of the population. By contrast, a new office block in the centre of a big city, or a large shopping development in the suburbs, is sure to be seen by thousands of people every day. These buildings have a mass audience, made up of citizens of every age and from every walk of life. Architecture and town design are public arts, and they should be recognized and supported as such. It is no use objecting that no one is sure what good architecture is; no one is sure what good opera is either; even well-executed traditional performances have their limitations and their critics. Another possible objection is that the Government would be embarking on a new and strange course if it undertook to spend public money on artistic amenity and what might be popularly described as 'improving the view'. What lies behind this objection is the attitude that artistic amenity is not of much importance anyway. But the direct answer is that the Government does something very like this already. In the spring of 1987 the Minister for Agriculture announced that in the country's five so-called 'Environmentally Sensitive Areas' grants of up to £80 per acre would be available to farmers who undertook to farm in ways that conserve and improve the countryside and its wildlife, and to avoid modern 'industrial' farming techniques. Any agreement entered into by a farmer would limit the number of livestock and the number of times grass could be cut for hay or silage; would ban pesticides; and would require the proper maintenance of hedges, ponds and reedbeds. Some months later it was announced that grants of up to £120 per acre would be available in eight new Environmentally Sensitive Areas. In Breckland, the maximum grant is available to farmers who undertake to leave a six-metre-wide strip of land round the edges of fields for wild flowers and other vegetation to grow, and not to spray, irrigate, sow or damage the strip. Late in 1987, 1 400 farmers had applied for grants, and £12 million had been budgeted for these areas. This policy probably commands a very large measure of public support. But how typically British it is that concern for the appearance and amenity of the countryside (where few people live) should be supported with public money, while the appearance and amenity of the towns (where most people live) is left to be fought over by architects and their clients, planners, amenity societies and two Royal Fine Art Commissions with no effective powers!

As a matter of principle, therefore, there are no good arguments for leaving things as they are. But in practice, we will be told, the difficulties in the way of change are insuperable. Who would decide which schemes were to be subsidized, and to what amount? How would projects be selected for favourable treatment? What safeguards would there be against architects and developers manipulating the system so as to reduce costs to themselves and pass an undue share of them on to the taxpayer? These are far from idle questions. But the problems which they raise can be solved.

It is self-evident that the selection process has to be kept out of the hands of politicians, as far as possible; it must not become a scheme of political bargaining and patronage, either national or local. It is equally true that it must be kept out of the hands of architects, at least to the extent that their voice does not predominate. This may seem hard and even unreasonable, but having a lot of architects on the selection committee would be like having too many cooks in the kitchen. As has been said already, architects are professional men but they also have — or should have — artistic inclinations. This makes for a doubly unquiet profession. Viewed as a business, architecture is very competitive, and rivalries are often strong; and at the same time, the actual design of buildings is apt to cause fierce professional criticism and artistic animosities. So architects are somewhat wary of one another. And to make matters a good deal more serious, fluctuations in 'expert' architectural opinion have been severe during the last fifty years. There have been too many different 'movements' some of them with extensive social and ideological underpinnings; all sorts of 'styles' have had their advocates, and detractors; praise and denunciation have often been expressed in extravagant terms; and the public, less prone to enthusiasm and less easily seduced by mere novelty, has grown distrustful. So while the opinions of architects must be heard in the selection process, these opinions must not be decisive. They should be treated with qualified scepticism. They must be set alongside the opinions of planners (who are more in the nature of administrative men), landscape architects, painters, designers, and other persons who are less committed to the artistic world but who have nevertheless demonstrated some knowledgeable interest in the planning, appearance and amenities of cities.

The reader will notice that this proposed membership of a selection committee (for such it would be) is along the same lines as the membership of the Royal Fine Art Commissions. This makes good sense, because the kinds of skills and the kinds of judgement required to advise on new projects in general are the same as would be required to pick out the best and most important of them. The simplest way of doing things, therefore, would be to add the task of selection to the other duties of the Royal Fine Art Commissions. The Commissioners have extensive knowledge of present-day architecture and planning, they know the difficulties and the possibilities, and the staff of the Commissions are extremely well-informed about current schemes and those 'in the pipeline'. The alternative would be to set up parallel bodies, possibly with some overlap in membership, and to require the officers of the present Commissions to supply the new bodies with the necessary information about proposed developments.

What would be the criteria for selection? Out of all the hundreds of new proposals that reach the Commissions every year, how could a choice be made? Obviously there could be no rules, except that developments recommended for subvention would have to be prominently located; developments in small towns or villages, or in back streets, which would not be seen by large numbers of people (unless, of course, they were in areas of outstanding architectural interest), would not have a prominent public character, and would therefore not justify subvention. Apart from prominence, the only requirement could be that the new development must make a significant contribution to the neighbourhood in terms of aesthetic quality or public amenity. It would be important to make clear that in the selection process no one architectural style would be assumed to have a monopoly of aesthetic quality. A good building can be 'modern' or 'post-modern', 'Classical' or 'neo-Classical', 'high-tech' or even, in some circumstances, 'Georgian replica'; everything depends on the quality of the design, and on its surroundings. Well-informed judgements are not made on the basis of stylistic prejudices. Style, in the grand extensive sense, is not what causes trouble, nineteen times out of twenty, although equally it never ensures success. What has to be looked for, and what would be found in a recommendable design, is intelligent use of the site; good proportions; sympathetic relationship to the surroundings; suitable materials; variety in moderation; comprehensible relationship between the inside and the outside; and, of course, the promise of satisfactory use. These are what make a good building, although they may not be enough to make an outstanding one; that depends on the architect's gifts of imagination and controlled originality. As for public amenity and town design, they are not so much at the mercy of 'styles' as is architecture, and they too depend for good results on intelligent use of the site, proportion, materials and variety; to which must be added, a sense of space.

Suppose, then, that there is some body in existence which can recommend to the Government that the plans for a new development on an important site are good, but not so good that additional expenditure would not improve them; and that in the interests of the aesthetic quality of the buildings, or the amenity of the site, the additional outlay that is required in this instance should be provided by the Government. This implies that the scheme is far enough advanced to be submitted for planning approval, or that it is very close to that stage; public money cannot be committed to nebulous schemes or good intentions. It also implies that a very serious and skilful effort has been made by the architects and the developers to produce a good scheme, and that there are no defects or deficiencies in it which those behind the scheme could put right themselves at very little cost, if they were willing. In such a situation, how might assistance be given?

The most obvious method of subvention is to offer to pay a proportion of the costs. This arrangement is quite hopeless. It puts temptation in the way of the developer to propose a plausible but unnecessarily costly scheme in the hope that public money will be forthcoming to make it better. If the Government accepts the proposals and pays up, it pays more than it should have to and the developer profits at the public's expense. If the Government does not pay up, the developer then revises his proposals downwards to what they would have been if no subvention scheme had existed, and loses nothing. Cost-plus arrangements are never an efficient method of subsidization.

An alternative possibility, which at first sight appears attractive, is that when a scheme is put forward which seems to have excellent possibilities, but which bears signs of having been hurried in preparation and insufficiently thought out, planning approval (which in the absence of a subvention scheme would have been given) is withheld so as to provide time for more careful consideration and revision of plans, and compensation for the delay is paid to the developer. This seems an attractive idea, because it is often the case that an important scheme is put forward which is passable although not very good, which could be considerably improved, and for which the promoters 'urgently' want planning permission. Whether the urgency is always as great as is said is doubtful; but developers, as already remarked, are apt to be in a hurry, and local authorities are usually afraid that objections and delays might cause development to go elsewhere. To buy time and slow down the rush to build would thus be most advantageous. But it is not really practicable. Such an arrangement would soon founder on the central question of what time is worth. How much would the developer lose by each day's delay? Would it be £10 000 or £50 000 or £100 000? Arguments about this would be virtually endless, and the mere prospect of starting them would cause any developer to decline subvention and go ahead with the original plans.

There are, however, three possible ways in which assistance might be given, three ways which would not open the door to large hand-outs of public money, would not encourage waste, and would not cause serious delays in developers' building programmes. It should be noted that what is here proposed is not dissimilar in principle from the idea of 'matching money', which the present Government seems to approve as one means of supporting 'the arts'.

One of the principal reasons why so many present-day developments look drab and uninteresting is the poor quality of their external surfaces. Concrete is common, and the textural effect is almost always dismal; concrete may look all very well in 'the great grain elevators rising high above the plains of Nebraska . . . accepted almost as part of the landscape',[5] but in cities it is poor stuff. Yet the modern architect commands—at a price—a variety of materials that is greater than ever before. Besides stone, brick and concrete, he can use aluminium, stainless steel, solar glass and reflective glass in a wide variety of colours. And of course, he can use tiles, which add lustre to some of the world's most splendid buildings, from the Royal Mosque in Esfahan, completed about 1630, to the Sydney Opera House, completed in 1973. The choice is enormous, much wider than may appear, because of variations in the different materials; brick, for example, can be coarse clinker brick, or it can be fine and smooth with sharp edges; it can be red, grey, yellow or white, or it can incline to a brownish or a blueish tinge. The Victorians were connoisseurs of different kinds and colours of bricks.[6] But when Le Corbusier and his followers damned ornament in architecture, buildings became plainer, and this means that design and the skilful use of materials, almost necessarily materials of high quality, became more important than ever. Unfortunately, the severity and seeming simplicity of the International Style is very easy to do badly and very difficult to do well; and when poor design is combined with aesthetically second-rate materials, which abound in the twentieth century, the results can be grim. It is distressing to compare the dullness of concrete or the harsh and strident colour of most modern machine-made brick with the variety and subtle colouring of Georgian and Victorian buildings. It is the same with roof tiles, which seem in some cases to have been made by the manufacturers, selected by the architects, and approved by the planners as a deliberate insult to public taste. It must be conceded that many schemes would remain bad whatever materials were used. But it is not uncommon to see well-designed, well-thought-out schemes which would make a real contribution to the urban landscape if only they had a good facing material—or several good facing materials; Frank Lloyd Wright's Falling Water, for example, has walls of rustic limestone which contrast with blocks of smooth white concrete and shiny glass and steel. It is true, of course, that even the finest materials make no impression unless they are used with skill and understanding; it is the combination that counts. But architects who design good buildings nowadays are evidently seldom able to persuade their clients to spend money on good facing materials. That, it seems, would be a luxury, something 'just on the outside'. Surely this is exactly where Government help might be given. If, on prominent sites, first-class schemes had first-class finishes, what an improvement there would be! Even with existing structures, a welcome display of variety and liveliness would be added to the scene. The same would be true of pedestrian precincts, squares and other open spaces. If paving were of stone, or stone and brick, instead of coloured concrete (as it often is), and if seats were well-designed and did not look as cheap as possible (as they often do), and if more trouble were taken over the design and positioning of lights, these places would be made more attractive and given an aesthetic interest which they often do not possess.

A second possibility is that the Government might buy space. That is to say, when a site is to be used for a volume of building which is aesthetically undesirable, but to which the planning authority does not or cannot object, possibly for fear of the economic consequences, compensation could be offered for a reduction in the planned floor space. It often happens that proposals come forward for building to a height that damages the scale of a street or a neighbourhood, or blocks a view, or for building all over a site part of which, if left vacant, would add greatly to the amenity of the neighbourhood. Such proposals are often accepted, and it is easy enough to see why. The developer declares, perhaps correctly, that to reduce the floor space on the site would render his scheme unviable, and the planning authority accepts this argument, perhaps because it fears that the alternative to this development is no development at all, at least for some time. But a compensation plan would solve the problem. It would not be too difficult to determine the value to the developer of, say, two floors of a high building, or of half an acre or less on an extended site; and if this compensation were paid, the developer would not lose and the public would be the gainers. Deliberate planned over-development, in order to receive compensation, would not be profitable, because the value of the floor space to be eliminated would demonstrate that the planning authority itself could safely require the reduction, and no compensation would require to be paid.

The third possibility is that there might be subvention for landscaping. In many developments there is, of course, no room for landscaping, or so little room that the quality of the landscaping can make no real difference to the total effect. But this is not always the case. In particular, where a fairly large area is to be redeveloped, possibly with new streets and pedestrian ways, there may be a good deal of scope for imaginative planting, terracing, focal points and the like. In new 'leisure centres' or 'shopping complexes' steps might be taken to reduce the amount of ground given over to surface car-parks (either by providing underground parking or by putting the buildings over the car-parks) and then some of the space thus released could be used for playgrounds or parks. The amenity of open public areas, starting with the streets themselves, seem always to be no one's particular concern. They generate no revenue, whether they are publicly or privately owned, and so the most that is usually done for them is to keep them clean, lit and, as far as possible, safe. But streets and open spaces might be made attractive, in some cases even beautiful, at small cost. The idea of a beautiful city street in the centre of a large city may nowadays seem unrealistic, so far have our standards fallen. But such streets still exist, and an increase in the number of them would do an enormous amount of good.

It must be emphasized that subventions of the kinds indicated are only part of the answer. What might be done in the public sector is, as already argued, of prime importance, and that has nothing to do with subvention. Subvention is for private developments, and is suggested only for those plans which are of real aesthetic quality, or which promise to make a significant contribution to urban amenity, and which are to be on prominent sites. Subsidizing the second-rate is not the way forward, and the argument would fail for developments which would not be prominent in the public eye. Which of the three proposed forms subvention should take, or what combination of them—better facing materials, less building, landscaping—would depend upon the nature of the scheme, and no doubt the recommending body would give advice to the Government on this point.

Numerous objections may be made to these proposals, which is hardly surprising. There are always objections to doing anything that is novel and untried. The cost of implementation, some may say, would be enormous. But the cost would depend on the budget. Admittedly, if the budget were very small, the task of choosing one or two schemes to support would be invidious, and the whole plan would begin to look like another architectural competition. But, at the opposite extreme, the maximum amount of expenditure that could reasonably be incurred would not be so very great, provided that the schemes supported were truly first-rate and the sites truly prominent. The number that would satisfy these conditions, properly interpreted, might well amount to no more than a dozen a year. If the average scheme supported were to cost £20 million and if subvention averaged 10 per cent of the total cost, the budget would have to be £24 million, which is less than one fifth of the 1987/8 grant to the Arts Council. It would not be difficult to argue for a larger figure, but it would probably not be good sense to aim to spend over £50 million. Another objection might be that overdevelopment is not always the trouble; some schemes underutilize the site. This is true, but it would be much more difficult and troublesome to find additional uses or additional users in connection with a scheme than to cut out some of those already planned for. What might qualify for subsidy is to some extent a matter of convenience, and a subsidy scheme should start simple: simple to understand, and simple to administer. A more serious objection is, that if money, or additional money, were to be given for any of the three purposes proposed, the overall design of the project might require alteration, and this would cause delay. This might not happen in every case, but the difficulty might sometimes be unavoidable, and the delay might be costly. On the other hand, the developer would obtain a better development, and this would probably be to his advantage in the long run. Finally, it may be objected that what is proposed gives more power to central Government, and weakens control by the local planning authorities. That this change would take place is true, and it should be welcomed. In matters of aesthetic quality and public amenity experience shows that the local authorities are seldom to be relied upon. They enforce the rules. But they are basically in favour of development, because it adds to employment and raises civic income, and they know that they are in competition with one another. There is therefore in their eyes always a presumption in favour of accepting almost any scheme of development, and there is corresponding reluctance to insist on purely 'visual' or 'amenity' improvements to what is proposed. It is true that the local authorities have the powers to require better surface materials, less intensive development, better landscaping. But the use that they can sensibly make of these powers is limited by financial pressure and the mobility of developers. Only positive steps taken by the Government can secure exemplary improvements; and central government ought to accept the responsibility.

Is all this merely visionary? There seems to be no reason why it should be so. Not very long ago it seemed perfectly ridiculous to suggest that government might subsidize theatrical performances, or build flats and houses to be let at uneconomic rents. Yet these things have been done, and we have grown accustomed to them. It is far too easy to think that new departures are impossible, simply because they are new. All that is needed in the present instance is the will to begin. No revolution in architecture or in the accomplishments of planners is required, and as for money, twenty or thirty million pounds is a trifle to a modern British Government. If we really want to have cities that have more beauty and pleasantness in them—and beauty and pleasantness that we have created, which is not unimportant—we can have them. Single-mindedness in the pursuit of profit or commercial convenience would not always carry the day if there were strong leadership in the pursuit of urban quality. The trouble is, that as town dwellers we have grown accustomed to abysmally low aesthetic standards, and we simply accept them. We put enormous sums into roads and bridges in order to save fifteen minutes of travel time, and we electrify railway lines at a cost of a few thousand million pounds in order to travel to and from London, Manchester, Glasgow and other places at 150 miles per hour, but there is no money for civic beauty and amenity. They are seldom spoken for. They are so low on the list of priorities that they might as well not be there. But something has gone seriously wrong if we hope to better society by strict attention to the commercial, the comfortable and the convenient. In some parts of most cities basic living is in dire need of improvement, and improve it we must. But if that is all that we aim for we aim too low. We must also try to raise the quality of experience of urban living, to make the finer things of life accessible, as far as possible, to everyone. That is what the provision of architectural excellence and public amenity is about.

NOTES AND REFERENCES TO CHAPTER 5

  1. RFAC for England and Wales, *Seventh Report 1937–1945* (HMSO, 1946) p. 17.
  2. *Memorials of Alfred Marshall* (ed. A. C. Pigou, London, 1925) p. 345.
  3. The Royal Commission on the Ancient and Historical Monuments of Scotland had already been set up in 1908.
  4. Professor James Meade, in *The Stationary Economy* (1965).
  5. S. E. Rasmussen, *Experiencing Architecture* (London, 1964) p. 169.
  6. See, Stefan Muthesius, *The English Terraced House* (Yale, 1982) p. 206 ff.

Appendix

During the 1960s central Edinburgh was nearly wrecked by a combination of physical decay and proposed traffic engineering 'improvement'. The former, caused by the passage of time and the negligence of the inhabitants, was arrested and reversed by the New Town Conservation movement, led by Sir Robert Matthew. The proposals to speed the flow of traffic took the form of a plan, put forward by the Town Council, whereby the city was to solve its expected traffic problems—not the traffic problems it had, but the traffic problems that were confidently forecast.

According to the 1947 Development Plan for Edinburgh by Abercrombie and Plumstead, 'There is no doubt that a system of suitably designed dual carriageway roads is necessary and will become more so in the future . . . There will be a need for new bridges here and tunnels there'. More specifically, proposals were put forward for a new road from the top of Leith Walk which would begin with a tunnel under Calton Hill and then proceed southward under the High Street, over the Cowgate, and along a widened St Leonard's Street on the edge of Holyrood Park; for a new road immediately along the south side of Arthur's Seat connecting St Leonard's to Duddingston; for Melville Drive to become part of an inner ring road; for Ferry Road to become a 'sub-arterial dual-carriageway'; for a road running beneath Princes Street for its entire length ('a straightforward engineering job') with a roundabout beneath the Scottish Academy; and for numerous other allegedly essential transport improvements. Nothing happened for several years, except that these proposals were incorporated with little change into the City's Development Plan of 1957, which was approved by the Secretary of State for Scotland. Again nothing happened for some years, but in 1965 the City published a revision of its Plan. A few of the Abercrombie—Plumstead proposals were dropped, but there was still to be a road under Calton Hill and over the Cowgate, and a new one under the grounds of Donaldson's Hospital; Melville Drive was to become a six-lane highway; and a new sub-arterial road was to run beside the Water of Leith for a couple of miles. These proposals were to create an 'Inner Ring Road', besides which there was to be an 'Intermediate

Circular Route', an 'Outer Circular Route', a 'City By-pass Road', several 'radial roads' and numerous interchanges and 'gyratory traffic systems'. The Review moreover made it clear that the politicians and their advisers now intended to turn planning into reality. This alarmed the Secretary of State, who caused the proposals to be referred to Freeman Fox Wilbur Smith and Associates (transport consultants) and to Colin Buchanan and Partners (planning consultants). Their Final Report, published in 1972, endorsed the City's proposals with little alteration.[1]

Not more than a few scraps of all these roads have ever been built, although forty years ago they were declared to be absolutely necessary, and this claim was repeated over and over again for a quarter of a century. No new tunnels and no new bridges have been constructed. The plan to build them was defeated by the sturdy resistance of the citizens, aided by the economic recession which began in 1974. Had the scheme gone through, the damage to the amenity of the city would have been immense. The visual intrusion, noise and intimidation from fast-moving vehicles on several miles of wide highways in or near the centre of Edinburgh would have completely destroyed the picturesque and historic character of the city. The new road system would have dominated everything else, and the only amenity left would have been motoring amenity. It is now clear that what the planners pressed for was not needed. The changes to roads and parking that have actually been carried out have been little more than marginal: a few one-way systems, a few additional car parks, a hundred or so yards of pedestrian precinct, and that is about all. There seem to be traffic lights everywhere and parking is more difficult than it used to be; but Edinburgh continues to prosper. No doubt the system creaks a bit, and some hard decisions may only have been postponed. But the town has adjusted itself to the increasing volume of traffic, and the increasing volume of traffic has adjusted itself to the town far more easily, ingeniously and economically than anyone would have supposed possible twenty years ago. Not over-reacting to forecasts of transport doom has proved to be good policy.

NOTE TO THE APPENDIX

1. It is therefore all the more surprising to find that in *Traffic in Towns*, of which Colin Buchanan was the principal author, the great new American urban road systems are damned as having been designed 'with a brutal disregard for the appearance and the amenity of the cities they serve'. (p. 3)

Index